WEREWOLF

The True Story of an Extraordinary Police Dog

DAVID ALTON HEDGES

DAVID ALTON HEDGES

Printed in the United States of America
First Printing 2021
First Edition 2021

10 9 8 7 6 5 4 3 2 1
ISBN 978-1-7377818-0-6

Cover Design by Florfi
Cover photo by Rayshun Drayton

For Brag
and all the heroic working dogs
who fear no man

TABLE OF CONTENTS

INTRODUCTION

I don't know how this story ends. I'm not even sure what happens on the next page. There's a reason for this uncertainty: I'm a police canine handler and these are events that are happening right now. As a K-9 handler, it's my responsibility to respond to every in-progress car chase, man-with-a-gun, and hot mess where my partner might make a difference. Sometimes these calls do not end well. Usually, we prevail and no one gets hurt. But not always. The bad guys would prefer not to be caught and none of them give a damn about anything, certainly not about the lives of the cops trying to stop them. That is police work. Beat the odds for thirty years and you can retire. Most of us do not care to go that long, and many don't get the chance. But there is nothing else like it; being a K-9 handler is the best job in police work.

A dog's memory is far superior to a human's recollection but since dogs don't write, my notes and reports and memory will have to suffice. Some details are bound to be wrong; a night that I describe as moonlit may in fact have been moonless. I'll concede to these inaccuracies in advance, but know this: everything my partner does in this narrative is exactly as it happened. There is no need to exaggerate. The truth is enough.

Although every person I describe is real, I will change the names of suspects and other antagonists in order to prevent them from enjoying even the smallest measure of notoriety. Their real names should be forgotten and their misdeeds remembered only as cautionary tales.

So how does this madness end? I don't know. It's a living story, set down before the blood has dried. It could end suddenly in shock and agony, or long years down the road when these moments are faded memories. I hope it turns out okay, at least for my partner's sake. His name is Brag, by the way, and it is the name he came with when he trotted into my life. He is a German Shepherd dog, as pure a form of that animal as you can imagine. But my fellow police officers have chosen a more humorous – and sinister – term to describe him.

Allow me to introduce us properly. My name is David. I have a wife, a son, and a mortgage. I look like a regular guy, but I hunt down human beings for a living.

And my partner is a werewolf.

PART ONE

FATE

I move forward at a crouch, my left hand squeezing the smooth metal curve of a flashbang grenade. There is nothing else in the world at this moment but a suspect holding a handgun on the sidewalk in front of us.

When the shooting starts, I swear I can see the bullets. Danny McGrew crouches beside me and all of us move in slow-motion and when he pulls the trigger on his MP-5 submachine gun I spot the dark blink of three rapid-fire rounds as they streak toward the suspect. There's a lot of talk in law enforcement training about this altered state during high-stress situations, where perception mutates. It's unavoidable. Gunfire is muted; other sounds are oddly amplified. Time moves slower. This is familiar territory and my favorite place to be, where the adrenaline rush is so massive it stays with you for hours. Those bullets move at roughly fifteen-hundred feet per second. It's impossible – on paper – for a human to see an object that small moving that fast.

The six of us rush forward in tactical vests and gas masks. Someone kicks the suspect's gun away and the cuffs go on and then we're moving into the house where the tear gas is invisible but still concentrated. I search each room, shouting "Clear!" after I peer under beds and in closets. Our boots crunch on broken glass from the gas canisters we shot through the windows earlier. The CS – tear gas – forced the suspect outside, ending the stand-off. The bitter, chemical taste of the CS passes through my mask filter. I like the taste of it.

There's a communication breakdown as a paramedic rushes in behind us thinking he is supposed to make sure there is no one else injured in the house. He takes three steps past the entryway and gets a mouthful of tear gas and retreats, coughing violently. Danny and I make eye contact and burst out laughing, the sound tinny and constricted by our masks. Cops have a strange sense of humor.

A few minutes later we're pulling the sweaty masks off as the suspect is whisked away in an ambulance. Danny is somber, thinking about those rounds. The legality of the shoot will be determined after investigators pore over the evidence. Nothing is secret, and shouldn't be. It was the suspect's choice to use crystal meth, to shoot at passing cars, to point a gun at a SWAT team.

The ride back to the station is quiet as we all lean back and let the sweat cool us. The call-out is done, but the real damage is about to occur. During the incident de-brief at the station, my entire career is encapsulated by one word: no. The administrators come down from the third floor of the police department to share their insight into the call-out they weren't on. I can't stand these people. They were mostly mediocre street cops and now they're mostly mediocre leaders, men who fancy themselves to be police executives even though there is no such thing. They represent everything I abhor about bloated government bureaucracy.

As the team round-tables during our de-brief of the SWAT call-out, I catch myself staring at the administrators and wondering why they're even in the room. My turn for input comes up. Now is the moment I should probably thank the Third Floor for letting us make our tactical decisions, to make them feel like they helped resolve this event. But they didn't, so I don't.

"Do you have anything for the captain?" the SWAT Sergeant asks me.

"No," I answer flatly, and the captain hides his scowl by smoothing his silk tie.

I did it again. My contempt is palpable. The briefing room goes uncomfortably quiet. I guess I feel better, but my attitude is the most effective means to derail a street cop's career.

The de-brief ends and we spend the next hour breaking stuff down and readying for the next call-out. Could be next week, could be tomorrow. Every gun is cleaned, every battery replaced.

When we're done, I open my locker and am confronted by an old pic taped to the inside: me in the police academy, twenty-four years old and on the shooting range in my gray cadet sweats, kneeling beside a police dog. One of my Police Academy shooting instructors was a handler and brought his dog to the range. I couldn't take my eyes off the animal. Since that day I wanted to be a K-9 handler, but the timing was always wrong; I was doing another job every time there was an opening. But because the department only has two police dogs at a time and they usually work for five to seven years, it's hard to plan for it.

I close my locker as a cop strolls in announcing that the suspect we shot will survive. Good. I grab my gear bag. I don't know how I'm going to go home and sleep with all this adrenaline but I'm out the door, striding across the parking lot with purpose until I realize I forgot where I parked.

I don't even know which direction to look, since we all have to park on random streets nearby because our parking lot is tiny. So, I pick a direction and start walking, hoping it will come to me. I head one direction when I suddenly remember I'm three blocks the other way. As I turn around, a black and white patrol car cruises past me on the street. "Forget where you parked?" the cop says. I give him the finger but he's gone, laughing at me in his rearview mirror.

Santa Barbara is like many coastal Southern California cities, a troubled paradise. A hundred-thousand people live here, some very wealthy, most not at all. A sizeable Spanish-speaking population from the drug-cartel-afflicted Mexican regions of Oaxaca and Guerrero crowds into run-down apartments of the lower East side and the West Side. Most of these people are hardworking folks in the service industry that makes the city go. There's also large number of homeless, lured to the beach city by temperate weather and social services. The US 101 freeway runs up the middle of the map, cutting the city in half. A main street crowded with shops and restaurants – State Street – leads to the ocean, where a wide avenue runs in both directions past golden beaches punctuated with palm trees. The American Riviera, they call it. Santa Barbara feels frozen in time, with Spanish architecture that feels more Old Hollywood than new California.

But all of that is mostly invisible to me, an enchanting landscape painted on a see-through curtain in front of a stage where scenes of unspeakable horror play out. I can go for weeks without even seeing the beach, kept busy by emergency calls: fights, stabbings, shootings, burglaries, robberies, rapes, drunks, domestics, suicides. I spend more time in run-down housing projects and trailer parks than I do admiring sunsets. But they don't pay me to enjoy the view.

My lieutenant calls me into the police station, a decaying edifice squatting in the shadow of its magnificent neighbor, the county courthouse that looks like an enormous Spanish fortress.

When I walk into the Watch Commander's office, the lieutenant leans back in his chair. He's a pretty good guy with a big family so I suspect he promoted mainly to pay the bills.

"How's it going out there?" he asks. I sit in the chair facing him and shrug. He gets to the point: "I hear you're putting in for the K-9 spot." I tell him I am and he spends the next few minutes advising me on how best to prepare for the oral exam. But this is not really the issue. He knows I have fifteen years of experience, all of it on the street, as a SWAT Team Leader and Field Training Officer. On paper I'm a natural fit, but in reality I'm problematic.

"You need to play the game," he sighs. "Truth is, they don't like you much." By "they" he means the administrators on the third floor of the police station and by the way I am already well aware of this. I ask him what he recommends I do. "Write more tickets," he says cheerfully and eleven seconds later I'm out the door and back in my car wondering who in the hell gives a damn about how many traffic tickets

I'm writing. At this moment, nine cops patrol the whole city and we can't keep it contained.

The next day I write my memo to the captain, formalizing my interest in the K-9 handler position. The job would mean keeping a police dog at my house, being available for call outs 24/7, working nights, weekends, and holidays, for the next seven years or so. It's basically ordering up a divorce. It's also career suicide, because no former K-9 handler in that building has ever promoted above the rank of sergeant. That last part worries me the least.

A month later I'm sitting outside a conference room in my Class A's: navy blue patrol uniform with long sleeves, a black tie, and my lower left sleeve sporting three yellow chevrons, each representing five years of service. The door opens and my oral exam begins. I'm one of five applicants for the job. The exam goes well; I've worked with all of these people. We stick to a formal tone, mostly, but there are smiles and handshakes all around when it's over. One of the sergeants on the oral board calls me later and says, "You're our choice for the next K-9 handler." I drift to sleep that night more excited about my job than I have been in years.

A week passes. The patrol captain has the oral board results; all he needs to do is rubber stamp their decision and it's a done deal. Another week crawls by. On my day off my lieutenant calls me. "The captain denied your selection for the K-9 position," he says awkwardly. "He doesn't feel you'll be proactive and well-rounded." I hang up the phone, stunned into silence.

So, it was about the traffic tickets, after all. My career is officially derailed. Being a dog handler was the only thing left that I wanted to do in this business. The Third Floor has made an example out of me, for all the street cops to see: *defy us and you will pay.*

I declare war on them, on the stupidity of it all. I share few waking hours with my wife and my two-year-old son, who has just days ago been diagnosed as developmentally disabled. I am sick of the bullshit, of people who bully other people.

I don't like my job, I don't like my bosses, and I don't know what to do about it.

A few miles away in Montecito – a leafy, exclusive enclave south of Santa Barbara – a black-faced German Shepherd puppy enters the world ahead of his siblings. A dog trainer named Ted Bowman recently brought two dogs, a male and a female, from Europe with the intention of breeding high-quality watchdogs. The litter squirming around their mother is the result of that pairing of two fine working lines. Ted's specialty is *Schutzhund* (literally, "guard dog") training, and he can spot a good dog a mile away. He also happens to be the trainer for the Santa Barbara Police Department K-9 Unit.

As the pups grow and their eyes open, the firstborn asserts his dominance by being first at everything. Whether this is because he is stronger or merely more determined isn't clear, but this particular puppy has a fire burning in his belly from day one. When all of the puppies are brought outside into the daylight for the first time, it is this intrepid one that leads the way.

Ted matches the puppies with clients. The bold, black-masked pup goes to a surgeon in Santa Barbara with two young daughters. The surgeon's wife, Jill, takes one look at the pup's confident gait and names him "Brag." He's a handsome fellow with over-sized paws and a serious disposition. The official name for his coloring is sable, which means he has as much black on him as he does brown. Brag grows deeply attached to his new family, never straying far from the little girls and always with one eye on Jill, whom he adores.

Before Brag is a year old, Jill's husband – an amateur pilot – hops in his plane and flies to Bakersfield for business. On his way home later that night, with two friends seated behind him, he miscalculates his position and flies into a mountain north of Santa Barbara. The plane disintegrates on impact. No one survives.

Jill calls Ted in tears. She is exhausted with grief, alone with a toddler, an infant, and an active, adult-sized German Shepherd puppy. Ted promises Jill that he'll find Brag a new home.

Ted arrives to pick up the dog. Broken-hearted, Jill weeps as Brag is closed in a plastic dog crate and driven away to a new life. Confused, Brag arrives at Ted's house and is immediately schooled by Ted's older male German Shepherd, who bites the young upstart's muzzle, leaving a scar that Brag will wear for the rest of his life. Brag's world has changed; he is no longer certain where he belongs, or who he belongs with. He withdraws, no doubt worried sick about Jill and the two little girls. But there's no explaining things to him, and so he waits.

Right at about this time, I receive the call that I was not selected for canine handler. I am adrift, like Brag.

Ted brings Brag along to an afternoon *Schutzhund* club training, held weekly on a grassy field in Santa Barbara. From inside his crate, watching the other dogs train, Brag barks savagely at the "suspect" in a thick bite suit who stands menacingly on the training field. When Ted opens the crate, Brag explodes with a wild fury, straining at the leash, eager to engage with the intimidating suspect. Ted studies the enraged young animal, wondering if this dog could be a police K-9 someday.

If you took a hundred well-bred German Shepherd puppies and put them all through rigorous training and testing, you might get a dozen dogs worthy of police work. And out of that dozen, one puppy will be remarkable – a perfect storm of courage, intelligence, determination, and athleticism. Brag is strong-willed and fearless but he's also aloof, preferring to be alone in his kennel to being inside the house. This is a concern; police dogs must be able to safely interact with the handler's family, since the handler will be taking the dog home after every shift.

Having served as a police K-9 trainer for more than a decade, Ted knows the police dog must be matched to the handler. Ted made the mistake once of pairing a strong-willed dog with a tentative handler. The dog sensed the handler's lack of confidence and after a hard correction during training the dog decided he'd had enough and bit his handler. Ted was forced to replace a potentially-special police dog with a canine as mediocre as the handler. Their career was short and unexceptional. In a police K-9 team, the human is always the weak link. We are forgetful and our enthusiasm waxes and wanes. Dogs love to work and they forget nothing. Ted is aware of the potential problems with a strong dog, but he keeps these concerns to himself as he watches Brag mature. There is something special about this dog.

Meanwhile, I wage my one-man war on it all, racing to in-progress incidents, spending as little time in the police station as possible. I refuse to pull nice people over to write them tickets for meaningless violations like dark tint on their car windows. There is a common misconception that police officers sustain some sort of glee in traffic enforcement. The joy of writing a traffic ticket vanishes by the time you've written a dozen. The real danger is apathy. A cop gets paid the same if he drives fast or slow to a call of a suspect with a rifle. Administrators know this well; promotion not only pays better, it exposes you to far less risk. Or none at all.

One of the tactics in my one-man war against a screwed-up system becomes indifference. This condition has been years in the making for me, since the televised glamor of SWAT bears no resemblance to reality. SWAT is mostly about fatigue and discomfort, countless hours of crouching in heavy gear designed to stop bullets. For those who embrace the suffering, there is a bond with the other team members that remains forever.

During one SWAT call-out on a cold night, I sit on point looking down the barrel of my rifle at the front door of an armed suspect's house for about four hours before I am relieved. I shuffle to the back of the conga line of the Arrest/React Team and squeeze in behind Ed Olsen. He and I have spent years together on SWAT, and there are few secrets between us.

"I'm going to put my head down for a few," I say to him, and rest my helmet against his back, slipping my cold hands inside the back of his tactical vest at the shoulders. I doze in that position for thirty minutes, my hands warming, able to sleep less than a hundred feet from an armed maniac because I am leaning against a person I trust with my life. This is the standard by which cops should be measured: by their integrity and accountability, as if lives depended on it. Because they do.

Since few administrators were street cops for any noteworthy length of time, they rarely understand what it means to be a good police officer. The problem is how to judge whether a cop is a good cop. At some point someone on the third floor at the Police Department adopted a simple and pointless method of evaluating their cops: the stat summary.

At the end of every month, the watch lieutenant tallies the statistics of every officer on a patrol team: total calls for service, arrests, traffic tickets, parking citations, and reports. This is how cops are measured. "Well-rounded" means you wrote parking citations and traffic citations. Quotas are illegal, but the administration sidesteps that by calling it "self-initiated activity." You might be the most professional, caring police officer in the city but if your stats are not "well-rounded," you're dead in the water.

One of the categories in this stat summary is "field contacts", which suggests that the officer is stopping people on the street, writing down names. Some cops pad their stats by completing a field contact on people they arrest, a double entry of the same information that means nothing but looks better at the end of the month. I hate this practice, but I understand it.

One evening, while getting a coffee at the start of the shift, I decide the ridiculous pressure to pad statistics demands that I tweak the nose of an absurd system. I pull out a Field Contact card, click open my pen, and look around. I'm parked near a red zone and beside a pole. It's 7:14 p.m., and windy. I write down the name "Red Polaski" on the card. The fictional man's birthday becomes 7/14/77, and he lives on Windward Avenue. I log the information at the end of my shift.

Hereafter, several of my coworkers often meet me for coffee and help me create these characters extempore. The drudgery is eased for a few minutes as we invent new ways to transform meaningless details into meaningless statistics.

I understand that this subversive behavior is far from ideal in a paramilitary environment. But the chain of command system only works well when people up and down the chain have their heads screwed on straight, and in my experience most police administrators are abysmal leaders. As an example, a lieutenant shows up intoxicated for work one afternoon, then hops into a marked police car and drives around the city. Armed and in uniform, it's a miracle he doesn't kill someone. When the street cops demand someone intervene, the lieutenant is summoned back by another administrator and given an alcohol breathalyzer test. The test shows his blood alcohol content is above the legal limit and he is relieved of duty. After the internal investigation he somehow retains his rank and pay. Accountability failure.

The great wheel of law enforcement grinds on. I resign myself to being a cog. Meanwhile, Brag resigns himself to this life away from his family, no doubt still thinking of them every day. He is well cared for, but because he does not know where he belongs, he remains distant, reserved. Only when Ted brings him out to training is Brag animated with his now-characteristic savagery. The other handlers offer their own theories about this young dog's enthusiasm for confrontation. None of them guesses correctly.

The future seems uncertain, but Fate is hard at work, setting a collision course for dog and man.

WEREWOLF

Nine months later, I am sitting in briefing when my sergeant hands me a memo from the Chief of Police. It is a congratulatory letter, announcing that I lead the entire police force in Field Contacts. My stats have improved dramatically. It seems my public spanking the previous year had some effect on my attitude, after all.

"There's going to be another K-9 spot opening up," the sergeant says. "Now that you've seen the light, I assume you're putting in for the job again?"

I laugh, because I am going to do no such thing.

That night I'm getting ready for bed when my phone blows up: there's an active shooter at the postal sorting facility in Goleta, north of Santa Barbara. It's a SWAT call-out request for mutual aid from the Sheriff's Department, who has jurisdiction over the incident. I arrive at the command post with no details except that a former employee is inside the building shooting people. I yank on my vest and sling my rifle and jump onto the back of an armored vehicle that is rumbling toward the scene.

We have several SWAT team members inside the massive warehouse, creeping through the rafters and trying to locate the armed suspect. I'm in the arrest/react team, which means I'll be going inside with a dozen other SWAT team members to search for the shooter as soon as we get the green light. But for now, the place is quiet.

We move silently toward the main doors of the building, taking cover behind a low wall. Thirty feet behind us are people lying lifeless on the walkway: the first victims at the scene. We wait, crouching, listening to our radios for the word to move. I turn back toward the victims. One of them is a woman, facing away from me. On the ground beside her, among the scattered envelopes she dropped when she was senselessly murdered, is her phone.

The phone rings, creating a small pool of light in the darkness, illuminating her delicate hand. A minute passes and the phone rings again. Then again. Then again. We wait. I grit my teeth, eager to get inside, to confront the shooter. The phone keeps ringing and I can't ignore it, thinking about the people who are calling and calling and getting no answer and watching the news and hoping beyond hope that the unanswered phone doesn't mean what they think it might mean. We're still waiting and I look away but the phone keeps ringing and now I want it to stop. I want it all to stop.

I consider breaking cover and turning off that phone, which is not possible because it's a crime scene and besides it's just a phone ringing. But I can't stop watching it ring and wondering about the woman who was outlived by her phone battery. It isn't right. Anger boils inside of me because I couldn't save her.

Finally, we get the green light to go because a Sheriff's Department K-9 handler has arrived with his dog and we're going to search the warehouse for the shooter. The dog comes streaming past us on a fifteen-foot line, followed by his handler. We fall into place behind, moving away from the dead woman and her desperate phone, through the main doors and past splattered blood and items strewn across the lobby. I am so thankful to have that dog with us.

Deep within the eerily silent warehouse, we find the shooter dead by her own hand. Nearby are other victims, employees who were murdered while they sorted mail on the night shift. One of them was moonlighting to pay for his daughter's college tuition. All of them were killed in cold blood without a word of warning.

We search the rest of the building – a long, silent hour – but there's no one else to find. Everyone left inside is dead. Without the police dog it would have taken us six or eight hours to clear the building. The confidence the team felt with that dog in front of us was undeniable.

I pull off my soaked helmet and leave the building with the K-9 handler, McNeil. He's been a deputy for a long time and he's seen as much as I have so we both give the ringing phone on the ground a wide berth. He gets into his K-9 car with his dog and I walk alone back to the command post, avoiding the reporters and the bright lights.

I make a resolution: I'm going to put in for that K-9 spot and I'm going to get a police dog and we're going to make things better. Somehow.

When I get home the sun is up and my neighbor is mowing his lawn. He waves at me, unaware of the horrors of the previous night. I wave back and go inside and take a shower and climb into bed but all I can see when I close my eyes is that ringing phone and the delicate, pale hand beside it. Eventually my mind surrenders to exhaustion and I sleep. The dreams that follow are best forgotten.

I don't know it yet, but this is my last call-out as a SWAT team member because in a few weeks I'm going to ace the oral board and this time the captain will consider me cured of my attitude problem and will grant me the K-9 handler position on a "trial basis." It doesn't matter, because the captain wasn't there when that woman's phone was ringing. He doesn't know much more than what he reads on the monthly stat sheet in between hours of useless meetings he attends inside the safest building in the city. But what he has done is grudgingly stepped out of the way, a difficult feat for any obstructionist. The world has turned.

I have a problem: this police dog will not get back in the car.

I'm in my Class A uniform, sweating in my long sleeves and tie, in the back parking lot of the police station. I have an eighty-nine-pound police dog on a leather lead. I took him out of the car to brush him because we are on our way to City Hall to stand in front of the City Council so they can approve the acquisition of a new police dog.

The dog's name is Brag. He's a few days shy of his second birthday, and thoroughly intimidating. We met an hour ago when I stopped in my K-9 patrol car at the trainer's house to pick Brag up. He didn't wag his tail, lick my hand, hold still for pets, or do any of that traditional dog stuff. Brag had also never seen the inside of a police K-9 car before, but when I opened the back door he jumped inside, finding himself in a cage that fills the space formerly occupied by a back seat. Metal bars separate him from the front seat. The tinted rear windows are protected by a sturdy mesh. Once upon a time, police dogs rode in the back seat, which not only got incredibly filthy but allowed the dogs to release nervous energy by destroying upholstery.

I've tried to brush Brag, keeping him at arm's length and talking to him quietly to assure him I'm not an enemy. He endured a few minutes as best he could, but now his good will has been used up. He doesn't know me, doesn't know why I put a leash on him, doesn't know why I'm wearing a uniform, and doesn't like the idea of getting back in a car. It's a standoff.

I walk him away from the patrol unit and make a sudden U-turn, trying to get him moving faster toward the open rear door. "Come on, jump in!" I try. Brag skids to a stop and sits on his haunches. Sweat runs down my neck. We're late for the City Council Meeting. A few cops walk past us on their way into the police station, eyeing me bemusedly.

Bored with my ceaseless banter, Brag finally relents. Once he's safely in the car again, I lint-brush the dog hair off of my uniform, but I'm sweating so much it's sticking to my face now. The car doesn't smell like dog to me, it smells like a wild animal. We rush to City Hall, dash up the stairs toward the Council Chambers and in the hallway, we run directly into Brag's original owner, Jill. She shrieks with delight and Brag jumps up on her, his paws on her shoulders. Jill has demanded to donate the cost of the dog and our initial training. Police dogs can cost tens of thousands of dollars, depending on their age and training. Add to that the costs of paying the trainer to prepare the dog and new handler for the street, and the amount doubles. Jill is thrilled that her puppy is going to be a police dog, and I'm so taken aback by her generosity and graciousness at this first meeting that I can only stammer my thanks. My new K-9 sergeant is there as well, and he ushers us into the Council Chambers. There's a hush when Brag trots in with me, and I hear a few people gasp at the stunning dog by my side. The mayor says a few words about Jill and Brag and the council is all smiles as they approve the new police dog. I tell Brag to sit and to my utter surprise he does exactly that, looking up at me as if to say *who the hell are you, again?*

It's over: I'm now a K-9 handler with a police dog. Jill and Brag and I go downstairs and out the main doors to chat for a moment before a few official pics are taken. A shaggy transient man ambling across the plaza outside City Hall spies me in my uniform and makes an obscene gesture, hollering unintelligible insults at me. Brag takes one look at the man and barks loudly – he's been a police dog for nine minutes and he's already decided he doesn't like the cut of that man's jib. The man moves on, shouted down by the dog. Jill and I look at each other and laugh. This is the official beginning, but of what I'm not sure. With a bittersweet farewell to Brag, Jill heads the opposite direction. Brag watches after her with great intensity until she's out of sight, but he does not utter a single whimper of protest. It is my first taste of his incredible stoicism.

Back at the K-9 car, Brag jumps into the back this time without hesitation. I climb into the driver's seat, unclip the itchy tie at my neck, and look in the rearview mirror at the pair of amber eyes studying me from the cage.

"It's you and me now," I say to him. "We're going to be friends, right?"

Brag sighs through his nose and looks out the window.

He's not exactly warm and fuzzy. I wouldn't say I'm disappointed by my new partner, but I did expect that when I met him, he would lick my hand and look me in the eye and I would say "we're partners now" and our life as crime-fighting buddies would commence.

That's not happening. Instead, I have this enormous dog who doesn't seem interested in looking me in the eye and wondering what plans I have for our future. He's aloof. He brightens up when I produce a brand-new red Kong ball, but nearly takes off a couple of my fingers with his business-like fangs when I offer it. From now on, I'll toss it to him.

I've driven home with my new K-9 patrol car. It's not a new car, just new to me. The previous K-9 retired months earlier and the car has been waiting for the next K-9 team. I've squeezed the car into my garage and discovered that the Ford Interceptor is longer than I realized: over seventeen feet. By policy I have to park it in a garage. The reasons for this will be made clear later, when I have $30,000 worth of narcotics and an AR-15 semi-automatic rifle locked in the trunk. I have to squeeze out the driver's door and let this massive dog out of the rear cage. He pushes past me and out into the back yard, where his chain-link kennel awaits.

I'm not going to introduce Brag to my wife and my three-year-old son yet. Frankly, I don't trust him. He's big, he doesn't seem to care for people much, and I'm not sure how he'll react to a small child. My elation at getting my new dog has become tainted with apprehension. What if he bites someone he's not supposed to bite? What if goes right over that six-foot fence? How am I supposed to control this animal, much less do police work with him?

Brag runs the perimeter of the back yard, inspecting the fence line, marking his new territory. He's got an enormous, blocky head to match his massive paws, and he struts around like he wants to knock somebody out. I put him in the kennel and close the gate just to make sure he'll go in there willingly, and call two of my buddies to come over and check him out.

Chad Hunt shows up first. He and I have been on SWAT for years and worked the streets together on patrol for at least a decade. We know each other so well that when we used to carpool to work at zero-four-thirty in the morning we often wouldn't speak a word during the entire commute.

Chad nods his head with silent approval when I let Brag back out of the kennel. The dog hardly takes any notice of him.

"Is he trained?" Chad asks.

"Sort of." I look around for the Kong, the only object that captures the dog's attention.

"I guess you're off of SWAT," Chad says.

I don't want to leave the team, but my new responsibility is to provide full-time patrol support with the dog. It's wrong to throw away thirteen years of tactical experience, but Chad and I both know how little that experience is valued by the people who run the department.

Another cop named Craig Rullman joins us in the back yard. A former Marine and real-life cowboy from the California/Nevada border, Rullman possesses not only the most extensive vocabulary I've ever run across, but the most incisive observations on human behavior. He and Chad and I stand with our thumbs hooked in our pockets, watching Brag trot around. I locate the Kong ball and call him. He rushes at me like a wild animal, skidding to a stop a few feet in front of me, eyes fixed with alarming intensity on the ball I'm holding up. I take a picture of him, the first picture of my K-9 partner. He's not looking at me, he's looking at the ball. But when I don't give it up right away, his eyes slide over to meet mine, and I glimpse a deep intelligence there that is unsettling.

"Look at the *cabeza* on that dog," Rullman observes. He's right. Brag's head is enormous.

I toss the Kong to Brag and he explodes off of the ground, jaws snapping shut around the ball like a great white shark ending the life of a sea lion. He ambles away with the prize in his mouth, biting down on it with the sound of grinding rubber.

"That is not a dog," Chad says, "that is a werewolf."

Chad nailed it. There is something monstrous about this animal. He is a werewolf.

Later, I bring my three-year-old son, Strieker, out to meet Brag. Brag stands at the wrought-iron gate, staring at Strieker with those feral eyes as the boy approaches. Strieker is used to dogs – we have three other dogs already – and doesn't seem to notice how large this animal is. I hover over my son as he pushes the gate open.

"This is Brag," I tell Strieker. "He's going to help me catch bad guys."

Strieker walks past Brag, disinterested. Brag sniffs the air as the child goes by, then turns back to his Kong ball. Introduction over. It may not be a heartwarming moment, but at least it isn't a medical emergency moment.

That night, Brag sleeps in his new dog house with his new dog bed for the first time. My wife comes out to meet him before bedtime, and he displays the same indifference. She doesn't seem to mind, and drapes a couple of old horse blankets on top of his dog house, making a flap that he can push past to go in and be cozy. She demonstrates it for him by pushing it open. He goes inside.

Brag doesn't make a sound all night. But in the morning when my neighbor comes outside to sweep her walkway, Brag comes unglued, barking so fiercely that my neighbor calls me.

"It's my new police dog," I tell her. "Say his name and he'll probably stop barking."

The next ten minutes are filled with the sound of my neighbor repeating Brag's name, which only incenses him further. I notice that his bark is twice as loud and ten times as threatening as an average dog's bark. I put Brag in his kennel again and call my neighbor back to apologize, promising we'll find a solution.

"That's a scary dog," she says. "I'm glad he's on our side."

As I hang up, I realize I'm not so sure about that.

TRAINING WRECKS

Ted Bowman looks more like a surfer than a dog trainer. He's tan, always smiling, and always pushing his blond hair out of his eyes. You'd never expect him to suddenly bellow out dog commands in German – the language of *Schutzhund* training. Taller than most, Ted has a sturdiness that I soon learn is necessary to train police K-9's. He's also fearless around big dogs, which is not to be confused with foolhardiness, because he's been bitten enough times to understand what it means to get the business end of the animal.

Our training begins today. It's just me and Ted and Brag, and we meet on the wide grass at the Earl Warren Showgrounds. I wonder aloud about the absence of any fencing to contain the dog. Ted smiles broadly, "He's not going anywhere." He knows Brag far better than I do. Ted glances at the gear in the trunk of my car and to my surprise tells me to grab my brand-new, four-foot leather lead and leave the dog in the car.

I join Ted on the grass. He shows me how to hold the lead in my right hand and attach it to my invisible dog, who will presumably be sitting on the outside of my left knee. It's time to learn how to do obedience, which means to walk around a field with your dog on lead. The dog must pay attention to what you're doing or you'll trip over him or get your arm stretched an extra few inches when he decides he'd rather bolt after that cat.

But for now, it's me holding a leash. Ted shouts "forward" and I march forward. I feel utterly foolish. "Left," he shouts and I turn left sharply like I learned at the academy, eyes focused on some distant object in front of me. "Right," he shouts and I turn right. "About face," he shouts and I realize that if my dog doesn't turn with me, I'll have the lead wrapped around me. I'm bored after five minutes, but Ted is still yelling commands. When I turn left instead of right, he asks if I need to take a break to review my notes on right and left. I scowl at him and keep going. He joins me, holding onto the dog end of the leash and walking beside me like a movie set stand-in for Brag. Now I realize how important it is that the dog knows what I'm doing. Every first step from a stop must be made with the left foot so the dog can see it. Coming to a halt must also be exaggerated. As we march, Ted explains one of the most important principles of dog training that is also the most violated: you must be fair. Training a police dog is physical and the dog must be corrected to understand he's done something you didn't want him to do. But often the problem is not that the dog is ignoring the handler, it's that the handler is not being clear with the dog. If you begin an obedience session with your dog and take a small step with your right foot, how the hell is the dog supposed to know you're moving? Yet because he's on a short lead with a pinch collar he'll get automatically corrected by not being at your left knee while you're walking away. That's not fair, and dogs have a good understanding of fairness. They'll try to cooperate to avoid getting corrected, but to build real trust the dog must know that you're doing your best to communicate with him.

We march around like this for half-an-hour. People passing by slow down to stare at the police officer leading the lanky surfer around with a leather leash.

The other K-9 handler for our department, Mike Claytor, shows up in his K-9 car. I can hear him chuckling at the sight of us. Claytor and I are partners but not equal ones because he's far past all this beginner stuff. His dog is trained and they are a certified working team. I envy him, especially when he lets his dog out to run.

Ignaz is a beautiful, three-year-old German Shepherd. He's lighter in color than Brag, almost golden, and his eyes are brilliant hazel which gives him a strangely human expression. When he lopes across the grass I can't take my eyes off of him – he has the most graceful gait I've ever seen, like a race horse. His obedience is solid, too; he makes an abrupt U-turn when Claytor recalls him, sprinting back to his partner and coming to a stop directly in front. Claytor tells Ignaz to heel and the dog whips around to sit at his handler's left side and Claytor attaches the leather lead and they go back to the car. I want to be able to do that.

"It's going to take a little longer for you two," Ted says to me. "Ignaz already had a lot of obedience before he arrived. Brag hasn't had any."

I guess we'll learn it together. Ted says that in the end it might even make us a better team. I feel encouraged until he adds: "It also might make you enemies." He laughs and I'm not sure if he is serious but before I can determine that his smile vanishes and he says, "Get your dog."

Brag has been watching all this marching around from the back of our K-9 car. I pop the trunk and get out the pinch collar, with metal prongs that face inward toward the dog's neck. The idea of it is to simulate a correction from a higher-ranking dog – a nip on the neck to communicate disapproval. I don't like this collar much; it looks like a medieval torture device. Ted doesn't care what I think and shows me how to put it on Brag, tight and just below the ears.

Brag walks beside me, shaking his head to try to loosen the collar. I go to the middle of the grass and tell him to sit.

Brag ignores me, looking at something far more interesting a half-mile away. Ted yells "forward" and for some reason I start on the wrong foot. We continue and it gets worse. Brag thinks I'm turning right and cuts in front of me and I stumble over him and he side-hops away, bewildered by my clumsiness. We march on. It's a disaster: my corrections are too late, I'm sweating and my face is burning with embarrassment because nothing is worse than looking like an idiot in a police uniform. Brag is clearly miserable. We're the worst dog and handler team in the history of humans and working dogs.

Ted finally tells me to put Brag away and the dog pulls me to the car, eager for our time together to be over. I go to take off his collar as I open the rear door and Brag jumps in with my fingers caught beneath the prongs. I finally extract my hand and when I slam the door and turn around, Ted stands behind me.

"Harder than it looks, isn't it?" he says cheerfully. I frown, examining my throbbing fingers. "You'll get better," Ted promises. We can't get any worse.

It's been a long time since I've been so lousy at something. I honestly don't know how I intend to do police work with this dog when I can't walk in a square around a field with him.

The next day we're at it again. This time I'm determined to be a good leader but that lasts about fifteen seconds before I confuse Brag and trip over him again. Now he's done with me, and tries to turn away while I'm walking straight. I correct him, and Ted shouts out "sissy correction!" We march on, Brag turns away from me again, and I give a tug on the lead to bring Brag back. Ted shouts out "sissy correction!" again. This goes on for ten minutes. I stop and ask Ted how hard I'm supposed to correct. He says "you don't have enough strength in your right arm to correct that dog too hard." I look down at Brag, who is looking anywhere but at me. I try again, and this time when I correct Brag he yelps and walks where he is supposed to walk.

"Now he understands what you want," Ted says, and for the next few minutes my dog and I are actually walking together. When I stop, Brag sits at my left leg. Ted claps his hands dramatically as I put the dog away.

Over coffee later Ted tries to make me understand: "All those little corrections don't work. You're just pissing him off. One good, clear correction is better than a hundred tiny ones."

There's only so much training you can do in a day, so I finish out by doing patrol calls for the remainder of the shifts with Brag in the back of the car. It gives him a chance to get used to the car and the protocol of police work. He's mostly quiet in the cage, watching. He barks at people he doesn't like, but never at me. I take that as a good sign.

That night I pull into the garage and let Brag into the back yard, which I've split in half with a fence. Brag gets the run of the rear half when he's not in his kennel, and delicate things like flowers and miniature lemon trees get the area closest to the house. Before I open the metal gate to the rear yard, I make Brag sit.

"You did a good job today, Brag," I tell him, patting his neck. He doesn't look at me and the instant I open the gate he is through it and trotting around the yard, marking his posts and ignoring me entirely. I go into the house to get off of my feet for a couple of minutes, but I'm so tired from training that I fall asleep in my clothes.

In 1899 a former cavalry officer named Captain Max Von Stephanitz spied an unnamed type of herding dog at a dog show in Germany. Stephanitz, who had served with the Veterinary College in Berlin, immediately purchased what he believed was the perfect working dog, one that possessed intelligence, durability, and determination. This animal would become the foundation of one of the most beloved working breeds in the world: the German Shepherd Dog. Since herding was disappearing, Stephanitz promoted competitive activities as a replacement: obedience, tracking, and protection. Decades later, the breed would find popularity all over the world, especially in military and police work. As visionary as he was, Stephanitz likely never imagined the value of a well-trained German Shepherd dog to cops facing the dangers of patrol a century later.

In police and protection training, traditional German commands are still commonly used:

- *Sitz* (sit)

- *Platz* (down)

- *Fuss* (heel)

- *Hopp* (jump)

- *Such* (track)

- *Voran* (search)

- *Packen* (bite)

- *Aus* (out)

Not all are direct translations; *packen* means "grip." I guess dogs don't have thumbs so they grip with their teeth. The recall command ("here") is pronounced the same in German and English. Some posit that since suspects won't know German commands, they are less likely to take verbal control of the K-9. I can barely get Brag to listen to me. I doubt a German-speaking suspect locked in mortal combat with Brag could convince the dog to stop. I'm much more worried about making this police K-9 work with only a handful of rudimentary commands. Taking action on dangerous, in-progress police calls is dynamic and final.

Brag and I train every day. When I think we're improving, Ted adds a new wrinkle: off-leash obedience. That means there's no leash to keep the dog near as you march around but the dog's desire to stay. To complicate matters, we do this as a group. Handlers from neighboring agencies – all of them more experienced – join us once a week to train their dogs with Ted. This means there's at least six dogs loose on the field all at once.

Brag hates other dogs. He doesn't like them looking at him, coming near his K-9 car, or breathing his air. In the canine world, "alpha" means top dog. The alpha puppy in a litter often makes the worst family pet, since that dog usually believes that he or she must assert their dominance over other dogs, and sometimes people as well. Brag, an intact alpha, seems ready to fight at any moment. A few of the other police dogs recognize this and want no trouble with him; some are less deferential. Since dogs communicate mostly in their silent language of posture and eye contact, by the time I've gotten Brag on the training field, the communication between these animals devolves from menacing stares into growling and barking.

Dog trainers weigh in on this topic readily, but training a Labrador Retriever to walk pretty on a leash has little in common with training a police dog. These working dogs are extremely strong-willed for a reason: they must do police work. Therein lies the problem.

Brag has no interest in pleasing me. He'll only listen if he gets a reward for doing what I ask or a correction for failing to do it. I must be clear, faster at corrections, quicker at verbal affirmation even when it seems like Brag couldn't care less about it. I'm also aware that he has no qualms about biting anyone, including other handlers. They're pretty good-natured about the way Brag barks loudly if any of them get too close to his K-9 car; they usually shake their heads and call him the Werewolf. But I'm nervous when he's out of the car. I try to keep a safety bubble around us, since any dog can move faster than his handler can react. It's nerve-wracking.

Ted is always there, good-naturedly prodding me to improve. Once, when six of us handlers put our off-leash dogs on a down from across the field, I'm determined that Brag will not be the one to break his down. I lean forward like a man facing into a gale, body stiffened, holding my dog in position by my glare. Ted sees my posture and nudges Claytor. They enjoy my exaggerated pose for a moment before I realize they're laughing at me but it's too late; I am awarded the nickname "Mad Dog" for my steely, cartoonish stare.

Not surprisingly, Brag excels at protection. This is confrontation, chasing a man and biting him. The hunt and the fight. One of the worst mistakes you can make in training is to injure a green dog when he is biting a "suspect." In protection training, the "decoy" (or "agitator") wears a bite suit or a protective sleeve on their left arm. It's a taxing role that requires expertise because to build confidence the dog must always win. Retreat or evasion cannot be an option for the dog. Ted usually does the decoy work himself; he can look in a dog's eyes and know where the dog is in terms of drive and defensiveness. He can dial down the confrontation if the dog is wavering. Most dogs are intimidated by Ted so he is careful about being too hard on them. With Brag, he is constantly dialing it up. The more Ted fights, the harder Brag bites.

"This dog wants to work!" Ted shouts, grinning as he engages in an epic struggle with Brag. Yes, he does. Brag fights like he'd prefer to take a body part with him than let go.

One day during training, the K-9 supervisor joins us to act as a decoy. As a former dog handler, Sergeant Fryslie knows what we need from him. Outfitted with a bite sleeve, Fryslie "flees" into a wooded area and climbs into an oak tree. Brag tracks his suspect by scent to the base of the tree and spies the man up in the branches. Not content with barking from the ground, Brag surprises all of us by scrambling ten feet up the trunk to latch onto Fryslie's shoe, which promptly comes off the man's foot. I rush in to try to catch Brag but all I can do is break his fall as he topples backward with a shoe in his mouth. We land in a heap and I have to hold onto the dog to keep him from going up again. Fryslie drops the bite sleeve as a reward and Brag snatches it up, parading around in a victory lap. Everyone laughs, and I see a glow in Brag's eyes: pleasure. I let him carry the sleeve to the car and he hops inside like an animal returning to its den to feast on captured prey. When I open the opposite door to get the sleeve, Brag makes no objection. I take the sleeve and praise him again and he looks at me. His tail doesn't wag, nor does he lick my hand, but he seems to appreciate it. For as much difficulty as it has caused me, I admire his will. He may be oppositional but he reminds me of the dog version of me. The better version.

Brag goes to work with me every shift. He can't get involved, but he can watch. I find myself talking to him a lot, explaining what I'm doing. He also gets to hear my colorful running commentary on people's behavior. I'm still taken aback when someone yells out "Brag!" when I'm driving past them in my patrol car until I remember that Brag's name is written on the outside of the car. He stays in it unless we're on a break, because he's not certified for patrol yet.

Claytor and I share tacos at a stand and discuss the K-9 program. I'm excited about the future but worried about my ability to be a good handler. Our equipment account is dangerously low; the city only pays our salaries and cost of the K-9 cars. We need money for equipment, and it must come from private donors. Also, the K-9 Unit has no codified training standards, and no training uniform. Some handlers have taken to showing up in flip-flops and shorts. Those days are over now. We can't demand respect from cops, but we can at least look like we might be able to earn it.

After weeks of intense training, Brag has had enough of me. During obedience I can feel him growling against my left knee while we march around the training field. In my ignorance I assume he's growling at the other police dogs, but when I correct him he rolls his head sideways at me and lets out a snarl worthy of a monster in a horror movie.

"I heard that," Ted announces from the sidelines. I stop abruptly. Brag sits, glaring straight ahead. He looks so pissed that I don't reach down and praise him; I don't need stitches today.

It's a critical moment. Ted strolls over to us, examining me to see how I'm reacting. I wouldn't say I'm afraid of my own dog but I'm not exactly comfortable with the animal. We're not a team like the other handlers and dogs: there's no connection. My dog doesn't like me and I'm certain everyone knows it.

"If you back down now, it's over," Ted says. I don't want it to be over, but I feel like this dog wants nothing more to do with me. I'm not sure I want anything to do with him.

"What am I supposed to do?" I ask Ted, doing a bad job of hiding my frustration.

"Correct him like it's time for him to come to Jesus," Ted answers cheerfully.

We keep going, and I dial up my focus. I try to be crisp, consistent and fair. We finish the obedience session and I offer Brag the sturdy tug toy that has been in my thigh pocket the entire time. He bites down on the tug, crushing it and shaking his head so violently that he nearly dislocates my shoulder. I'm nowhere close to being outweighed by this dog, but his strength is astonishing. The other handlers avoid us as they take their own dogs back to their patrol cars.

"Let's do some recall!" Ted announces. "Brag first!"

After that hideous obedience session, he wants to start with Brag? What is this man thinking? Recall is sending your loose police dog across an open space after a human decoy and then calling him back to you when the dog has run about half the distance. It's hard to teach, hard to enforce, and it goes against the dog's instincts. Because Brag's drives are so strong it's especially difficult. He wants to bite that suspect and when I call him back it means he doesn't get to do it. Nine times out of ten he doesn't call off. It's a source of great amusement for the other handlers, because I have to march down the field and attach my leash to Brag's pinch collar and tell him to out. Most of the time Brag outs on his own the instant I attach the leash, preventing any correction. It's incredibly frustrating. I can't explain to this dog that according to State law – not to mention the United States Constitution and some noteworthy Amendments to it – he cannot bite a suspect who suddenly decides to surrender after I've sent a police dog to bite him. I'm the one who will lose his job and get sued, and prosecuted. More importantly, that behavior is the opposite of what we're supposed to be doing out there. We're supposed to find bad guys, convince them to give up, use the dog to bite them if they are violent, and restore peace. We are not in the business of doling out punishment, as satisfying as that might be in some instances.

Ted slips into the bite suit and all the dogs blow up in their cars, barking their heads off. With a big grin, Ted strides away across the field like some enormous Pillsbury doughboy.

He spins around and cracks the whip. "Send him!" he shouts at me.

I tell Brag "*packen*" and release him. Brag launches away from me and makes a beeline for Ted. Some of the police dogs put a little bend in their attack, coming in at an angle away from the whip Ted brandishes. Not Brag; he goes straight in.

He's halfway there. I yell "*AUS!*" as loud as I can. Brag slows, almost imperceptibly. "*AUS!*" The dog veers a few degrees off and blows past Ted, turning hard.

"Here!" I bellow and Brag circles Ted and runs back. I'm flabbergasted. Brag runs right at me and I throw my arms wide in welcome, but instead of stopping he runs past me to our patrol car and jumps in the open back door. He's sick of this nonsense.

"Go get him!" Ted hollers at me. "Let's give him a bite!"

I collect Brag again and this time when I send him, I don't call him off and he hits Ted like a locomotive, his massive body airborne in a circle as his jaws clamp down on Ted's upper arm. It's a beautiful sight.

Brag outs clean and I quickly attach his leash so he cannot change his mind. I put him away, swelling with pride as the other handlers golf clap.

"That's called avoidance," Ted tells me later as he peels off the sweat-soaked bite suit. "Brag ran to the car because he didn't want a confrontation with you." This is good news; Brag would rather avoid me than confront me, a shuffling half-step in the right direction.

We focus on detection work for the rest of the day, which is a game of hide and seek. Brag knows I've hidden a baggie of cocaine or heroin or crystal methamphetamine somewhere in the search area and when he finds it, he plants his butt on the ground and looks at me. If he's right, I toss him the red Kong ball, his favorite ball in the world. It's deceptively simple, and not stressful. It also allows me to act like a fool when Brag alerts correctly: I praise him in a high-pitched voice and celebrate like he's the best dog in the world. If you sound ridiculous when you're praising your dog during detection work, you're doing it right.

After a few weeks of detection training, I have noticed something about Brag. He's good at it, and more focused than dogs who have been doing it a lot longer. I am changing my opinion of this dog. He's not trying to be difficult; he just performs every task as intensely as he can.

Certification day approaches, and I'm nervous. You cannot deploy a police service dog until it has been certified according to the California Peace Officer Standards and Training guidelines by a recognized certifier who is in no way attached to your department or training group. This is how it must be. But here's the problem: if the dog doesn't perform perfectly during certification, he won't pass. For example, when you send your dog for a bite during the test and then tell him to out, the dog must out. If the dog so much as touches the decoy again, he fails. Period. You can try to schedule another test a week or two later and hopefully get it right that time, but you can never erase the fact that you failed a certification. It's on your record forever. I wish I could explain this to Brag, to let him know that if he does not do exactly what I tell him to do during the certification, his career might be over before it begins.

The day before certification arrives too quickly. Our last training session doesn't go well; Brag won't recall and won't out. Ted doesn't seem concerned. If he looked worried, I would consider re-scheduling the certification.

At the end of training, Ted grows suddenly serious: "Don't feed Brag dinner tonight."

I'm astonished. "Why not?"

"It'll make him more focused," he replies.

I don't try to conceal my reluctance to follow this advice. I feed Brag once a day, at the end of our shift. This is common practice among handlers, since a working dog presumably has hours to digest a meal before going back on duty. It's dangerous to work them after they've eaten, given the exertion and stress of a patrol shift. A lot of trainers believe feeding at the wrong time can cause bloat, a sudden and catastrophic medical condition that claims the lives of many dogs. When a dog bloats it essentially means the stomach has been pinched off so no food can pass through it. The pinch causes gasses to build up in the stomach and enlarge it, which constricts blood flow to not only the stomach but surrounding organs. By the time the dog is showing signs of distress it is often too late to save them. No one is certain why this event occurs but German Shepherds are particularly susceptible. If you pair bloat with a related condition called torsion – where the stomach flips – the odds of survival are even lower.

"Are you worried he might bloat?" I ask.

"No," Ted says. "Skipping a meal the night before a certification is common practice. Imagine a wolf pack that hasn't eaten for days; if they don't hunt down some prey soon, they'll die. They need to work as a team, and pay close attention to the alpha." He smiles. "That's you."

Ted is an experienced trainer who has forgotten more about dogs than I know about dogs. But I'm not happy about this skipping a meal directive. I realize that dogs evolved to hunt in packs and use their noses and endurance to survive, but this is going to be difficult.

By the time I get home, I'm so worked up I'm sick to my stomach. I let Brag out of the car and he trots into the back yard and I close the gate. He marks the trees, eyes on me expectantly. When I don't go back to the garage to get his dinner he comes to the gate again, studying me.

I know what I'm going to do.

"We're not eating dinner tonight," I tell him, expecting him to whimper for his food. That's not what happens. He watches me for a moment, then goes back to marking his favorite spots in the yard, like he understood me perfectly and doesn't give a damn.

He is tough as galvanized nails, this dog. I suddenly realize that's the problem: he's tougher than I am. All those years on patrol, on SWAT, sweating in that tactical gear, all of it is nowhere near the level of discomfort this animal can and will endure to do what he wants to do. Brag isn't the one who needs to toughen up, it's me.

I go inside to get ready for bed because we're up at zero-five-thirty to certify. I'm not sick to my stomach anymore. I'm hungry, but that's acceptable. Brag will do it, so I will do it.

I sleep like crap, dreaming of loose dogs and bystanders screaming as they are attacked, but every time I wake up it is dead silent. I wonder if Brag is sleeping.

Morning arrives, gray and misty. When I go outside, dressed in my training gear and carrying Brag's flat collar, he comes pouring out of his dog house. He's ready to go, even at this unexpected hour, and hurries to the car and hops into the back. His breath is hot on my neck as I back the K-9 car out into the street.

Certification is a blur; trainers and handlers from agencies all over fill the parking lot with K-9 cars and I shake hands and forget everyone's names immediately. Dogs bark, trunks open and shut, cops sip from steaming coffee cups.

I'm not interested in conversation until about ten in the morning on a good day, so on this day I hardly crack a smile. My stomach is in knots.

Brag nails it. He finds the hiding suspect and barks. He leaps from the car when I am "attacked" and bites the decoy. His off-leash obedience isn't pretty but he passes. Then, to my utter surprise, he calls off and he outs – the two tests that are saved until the end of the certification and are the most likely to completely cancel out the day if you fail.

I can't believe it's over as I put him away. We did it. I'm giddy and I pat his shoulder before I close the car door. "Good job, Brag," I tell him. He glances at me sideways, looking satisfied, like he knows this was important.

I hold my hand out for him to lick. He doesn't, but it doesn't matter. I'm so proud of him, I would hug him if I didn't know he disliked me so much.

As the handlers stream out of the lot in their cars, one of the certifiers – an LAPD sergeant who has supervised that agency's Narcotic Dog Unit for a decade – pulls me aside.

"There are good dogs and there are special dogs," he says, inclining his head toward my car. "That is a special dog."

I thank the sergeant and he walks off, to leave me pondering his observations. What does he see that I can't see? Brag watches me from the back of our car with his typically emotionless gaze. For some reason, I give him a thumbs up. Ted strides toward us.

"I'm so proud of you two!" he says, pulling me into a dramatic hug so his sweat soaks into my shirt. I laugh for the first time in at least a week.

Brag and I are a team. We're going to do what we're supposed to do, what Brag was born to do: catch bad guys. But first we are going to go home and eat breakfast.

It's all ahead of us now. The Werewolf is certified. A team of two distinct species will work as a single entity, hopefully combining the best of both. Our call sign will be K9-1.

ROOKIES

After my first week as a cop, I realized I had no idea what I was doing. Freshly graduated from the police academy, I thought I had all the training I needed to be a good cop. Wrong.

To describe field training as challenging is an understatement. My training officers had no time to hold my hand. It was real, and a complete shock. Suspects fled, fought, crashed, lied to us, tried to hurt us and tried to hurt themselves. The nights were long and unpredictable. Boredom becomes the enemy working graveyard shifts in winter; swing shift in the summer is a sweaty, chaotic blur. Calls for service never stop.

As I stumbled my way through field training, I discovered I needed to change if I was going to survive this job. I needed to think differently. I even needed to figure out when not to use my flashlight. Every rookie arrives with the latest flashlight with a million-candlepower bulb and uses it as often as possible. Turns out too much light gives your position away, ruins your night vision, and blinds other cops. Experienced cops know the darkness is their friend.

Those first days as a cop are sixteen years gone, but I'm a rookie again. Brag and I are hitting the street like absolute beginners. I'm learning a lot about police dogs from Ted and other handlers, but I'm getting the best information from Brag. He teaches me every night how his senses are sharper than mine.

A dog's eyesight in daytime is not better than human eyesight, but a dog's ability to see movement in darkness is superior. Their depth-perception is surprisingly bad, which is why police dogs on searches sometimes blithely walk off of the roof of buildings and fall to their deaths. It is obvious to the humans present that there are ten stories of nothingness beyond that ledge, but the dog doesn't perceive it.

On the other hand, a dog's hearing is remarkable – behold those moveable, radar-dish ears. Brag spends a good portion of our work shifts cocking his head at sounds I never hear. I can only imagine all the noise he hears and must sort through.

By far the greatest enhancement a canine brings to law enforcement is his nose. Some experts maintain it's a hundred times better than ours, other say a thousand or more. Their ability to detect odor is so far beyond the capacity of available technology that it seems like magic. This is what I want to tap into, the murky depths of this animal's primordial abilities. I want to use the Werewolf to catch monsters, which means I'll have to learn to use his nose.

By now I know the nomenclature of my dog the way I know my patrol rifle. But where the separate elements of a rifle add up to a defined performance, the police dog is a mysterious sum of his parts. On paper, Brag is a piece of city equipment. I am mandated by policy to store this equipment at home, maintain it, and return it when I am ordered to do so. If Brag had a military-style identification tag it would read: Police Dog, One, Large, Sable, Patrol and Detection. Although he is technically a piece of equipment, Brag has a will of his own. He is my partner, not a machine, and we're heading into undiscovered country to see how far his extraordinary senses can take us. I don't know where that is, but I am certain that it is a place enveloped by darkness and chaos. The kind of stuff I signed up for. But what about Brag? Does he have any idea what he's getting into?

It's our last training day before we hit the streets. Among other things, we work on hand signals: down, sit, here. For some reason, dogs don't like to sit from a down. I'm stunned when Brag performs this, again and again. We seemed to have reached a stalemate agreement – I bring him to training and he does mostly what I ask him to do. It makes him happy to work and to bite humans, so he endures my oversight. When Claytor hugs Ignaz and the dog licks Claytor's face I feel a twinge of jealousy for their deep friendship. But there's a dangerous side to that, one I've observed over many years of law enforcement. Most handlers come to view their dog partner as their best friend. As a result, they must filter the decision to deploy the dog through their love of the animal. This is a problem, because the city has not gifted the handler with a pet dog to cherish. It is a police dog, a highly-specialized tool, and the animal must face danger daily. How many times has a dog handler refused to use his dog because he loves the animal?

I put Brag in the car at the end of training. He looks past me at the training field where the other handlers gather up equipment. He's ignoring me, as usual.

"Here's the deal," I tell him. "You don't seem to like me much. But without me you don't work, and without you I can't do what I want to do. So, let's just agree to do this together. I promise to get you in as many scrapes as you can handle."

He doesn't look at me but he's listening. I've worked with plenty of cops I wasn't crazy about and we conducted ourselves professionally because we both understood what we were supposed to do. I respect Brag's fearsomeness and drive, and that will have to be enough.

In our modern world – especially in this country – we have the luxury of feelings. This is not allowed in law enforcement. You can't violate someone's civil rights and explain later that you were out of sorts that evening. Even if you perform your duties within the law and department policy, sharing certain emotions off-duty could get you into big trouble. This doesn't mean cops don't recognize feelings, it's just that our own have no legal relevance. They don't matter.

What does matter to street cops is action. If you arrive alone at the scene of an active shooter at an elementary school, how scared you are at that moment is irrelevant. You must act. Any time wasted on your emotions might cost another life. Including your own. It sounds robotic, but it's what this culture demands.

I've made a career out of doing, so why would I change now that I have a police K-9 with me? I'll be doing the same job, with a fearsome new tool. The streets are waiting. I'm not crazy about this dog, but in the end, I hope that will make us a better team. We've got some dangerous work to do.

Patrol shifts begin with briefing, a meeting where all the cops working that watch receive their patrol car and beat assignments for the day as well as any pertinent information. Sometimes briefings include uniform inspections or short training. This briefing is different because I walk in with an enormous police canine.

"He looks cuddly," one cop quips from the other side of the room as I march in. I head for the far corner and put Brag on a down, then sit near him to keep an eye on him. He's supposed to stay there until I release him. The room fills up and a cop named Hove rushes in as briefing starts and lands in a chair near the dog.

After the sergeant goes through the briefing book – a binder updated daily with Be-on-the-Lookout flyers and other time-sensitive bulletins – he goes round the room asking if anyone has useful information from the previous day. He saves me for last and says, "Hedges, introduce us to your new partner." All heads turn toward Brag.

Realizing he's blocking half of the room's view of the new police dog, Hove scoots his chair back and pinches the hair at the end of Brag's tail.

Brag springs up, teeth bared, barking viciously at a hundred decibels a foot from Hove's nose as I grab the dog by the collar. Brag's eyes never leave Hove's face as he allows himself to be steered away. Poor Hove goes stock still and beet red.

"Ho-ly shit," someone says.

"This is Brag," I offer, trying to sound light-hearted. "You can also call him the Werewolf, for obvious reasons."

Hove laughs with everyone else but keeps his hands folded in his lap.

"Good to know," the sergeant says, closing the briefing book. As the room clears out, I hold onto Brag. Not a great introduction.

Worried about running into any more unwitting humans in the hallway, I hurry Brag out to the car. He hops into the back the instant I open the door.

A few officers from other shifts come around, curious about the new K-9. Brag barks like mad and claws at the inside of the cage because they're all standing too close.

"I hear your partner almost bit Hove's face off," one of them says cheerfully, as if biting someone's face off might be a good way to start a shift.

I roll my eyes. "Maybe briefing wasn't such a good idea."

"If he'd really wanted to bite Hove's face off, he would have done it," another cop offers. "Wouldn't you, Brag?"

More maniacal barking. A wall of noise coupled with a violent rocking of the patrol car as the dog throws his weight around inside. The officers move on. No one asks to meet for coffee.

It will take time for all of the cops to feel comfortable with Brag. I'll win over all one-hundred-and-fifty of them, even if it I have to do it one at a time.

I climb into the car. Brag looks at me through the metal grate with one amber eye. A feral gaze from a creature that seems hardly tame. Trained, yes, but as savage as any predator that lurks in the dark.

I keep my eye on his as I turn on the radio, grab the mic, and utter these words for the first time: "K9-1 in service."

The Ford Crown Victoria Police Interceptor is an eight-cylinder, 250 Horse-Power workhorse designed to survive the rigors of modern police patrol. It is also surprisingly agile. The K-9 patrol cars are no different than regular patrol cars, except that they are outfitted with indestructible cages to contain the dogs. A narrow sliding door separates the front and rear seat. Many handlers leave this door open, allowing the dog to move freely between the two spaces. This is not an option for me. I don't like the idea of Brag's sharp parts having access to my face parts. Also, Brag will simply not fit up there with me.

I rig a string of carabiners on the underside of the trunk lid so the leather leashes, chains, harness, long lines, muzzle, and collars hang within easy reach. It looks like a collection of naughty bindings but every item in there is part of our daily K-9 routine. Because of the cage door between the front and back seat there is no room for my patrol rifle, so the locked rack is in the trunk as well. Beside that sits a metal lockbox containing my narcotics training aids, real drugs for real training. Next to that are bite sleeves and the rest of my gear. I'm not sure how much this car weighs with me and Brag and all the war gear, but the rear tires sure stay glued to the road when I crush the accelerator.

The K-9 car also has an ignition override switch, a button I can push so that I can remove the key and leave the engine running. If someone were to get into the front seat and put the car into drive, the engine cuts out. This ignition override is a critical feature of the K-9 car, not to prevent theft but because the air-conditioning is running all the time to keep the dog cool. German Shepherds do not get cold, but they are far less equipped to deal with the heat than humans. Unable to sweat, they must pant. If the air isn't cool enough, they overheat. I have seen news reports where police dogs died of heat exhaustion inside their K-9 cars. The headlines alone fill me with anxiety; the stories that follow rarely provide sufficient explanation. What a shameful failure, to be responsible for the death of your partner. I won't pass judgment on these handlers without knowing the individual circumstances, but I make a silent vow that I will never be responsible for such a preventable tragedy. Working in coastal Southern California makes it easier than other parts of the country where the temperatures soar to punishing levels for months.

Brag is my partner, despite his indifference to me, and I will do whatever I can to keep him alive and working.

I cruise down the driveway running the length of the police department, passing rows of parked patrol cars where the cops are going through their pre-shift checklists like pilots ticking off flight preparations. Brag barks at all of them as we go by.

Within a few weeks, Brag gets his sea legs. He leans into turns, shifting his weight back when I brake. I drive differently now; every maneuver is deliberate. Whenever I slip up and take a corner too sharply or accelerate too suddenly, his body bangs against the metal interior and I wince and apologize. I don't know if he cares, but he's my partner so I owe him that much.

Our first official shift as a K-9 handler team is unremarkable. I show up too late on a few calls to even get Brag out. I bring him out on an alarm call at a business with an open window late in the shift, but before we can even look inside, the owner of the business suddenly comes out of the building; he forgot to turn off the alarm when he stopped by to pick up some paperwork. We roll on a few fights and Brag barks viciously at combatants and cops and bystanders alike. When the shift ends, I realize I could have done all those calls without Brag. There would have been far less noise.

Brag and I make the drive home over the hill, a thirty-minute commute that allows me to decompress. It's 3 a.m., so there's little traffic on the road. After I pull into the garage

I walk outside into the backyard with Brag, where he busies himself by marking all of his spots. It's dark and I figure no one could possibly see me, so I relieve myself beneath a shrub. As I'm zipping back up, Brag trots over and marks the same shrub, then flips around and burns out in place with his back feet, spraying me with debris as he does so. Annoyed, I kick dirt back at him. He glances over his shoulder at me and kicks harder. This has to be the most absurd interaction since we were paired up: kicking dirt and twigs at each other in the middle of the night, witnessed by no one but the moon. After this brief skirmish, we go our separate ways for the night.

It's our second shift, and cops are pursuing a stolen car through the city.

I grab the mic: "Five-five, K9-1 is enroute Code Three."

"Copy K9-1 enroute Code Three. Code Thirty-Three on channel one."

I punch it and hit the lights. The siren wails and Brag is peering through the cage at the road ahead, not exactly sure what is happening. He lets out a low howl to match the siren.

I'm trying to picture where the suspect is and where they might be headed. Catching up to a vehicle pursuit is a lot harder than it sounds; the suspect is driving as fast as he can, so just keeping up requires all of your concentration. Also, they are far less concerned about the safety of innocent people driving around than the cops are. The last thing a cop wants to do is run a red light and plow into some innocent person. You cannot count on the police car emergency lights and siren to warn people in time.

We're speeding closer when the suspect crashes and bails out on foot. The concise radio traffic of a moment earlier now becomes muffled and urgent as the officers chase the suspect across parking lots and behind darkened warehouses. He's caught after a mad sprint. I'm disappointed because I would have loved to use Brag. But he's unproven; I'm not sure if he gets it yet.

I cruise slowly past the arrest location where half-a-dozen cops are standing over the handcuffed suspect, who is only thirty feet from the street but hidden from view by a low wall.

Brag stares out the window as we roll by. He knows something interesting is happening. I hear him sniffing the air deeply. The arresting officers stand the suspect up and Brag explodes into barking. The cops wave at me as I drive on.

So, Brag knows, after all.

Three days under our belt. Brag still thrashes around in the car whenever someone gets too close, whether they're wearing a badge or not. I'm beginning to think it's more about context: if there's a potential bad guy around, he's focused on that person. If there's no one but cops around, Brag's barking is a declaration of his seriousness. When I open the door he doesn't charge out and go after a cop, he looks at me for direction. He's not vicious. But I want him to be friends with his co-workers, so I discover the key to his relationship with cops: the tug.

The tug is a stuffed reward toy made of durable canvas-like material with a heavy-duty nylon tape loop at one end. It looks like a long burrito with a handle. If you hold onto the handle and dangle the toy out in front of you, Brag will hurl himself at the tug and clamp down on it, shaking it violently to break your grip. Then he lowers himself and tugs as hard as he can. If you're not ready, you'll lose the prize and he'll leap back into the K-9 car with it.

Whenever a cop asks to play with Brag, I get the tug out and demonstrate how to hold it so they won't lose any digits. Then I open the door and Brag fires out of the back and hits the tug hard and the game begins. Brag growls and rolls his eyes like a wild beast but he does it because he's into tug-of-war, not because he's about to disembowel anyone.

The game also releases tension and allows Brag to get to know his cops one at a time, their individual odor and voice. This will be critical later when Brag is searching in near-total-darkness with cops all around him. The truth is, at this point I'm not certain Brag cares who he bites.

One cop in particular, Corina Terrence, asks if she can give Brag treats. I keep him at fighting weight so I don't usually allow treats but since she's the only one who's asked, I tell her she can offer him one as long as the treat is small. I warn her that the fate of her fingers is her own responsibility, then I let Brag out and Corina says – very sweetly – to my dangerous dog, "Want a cookie?" Brag immediately plants his butt on the ground, cocking his head at Corina. She hands him a small dog treat and he takes it ever-so-gently with his front teeth. I'm stunned; I've never seen him do that. She pats his head and goes back to her police car.

A burglary-in-progress call goes out and I'm blocks away. Sometimes you can be too close to a call and be arriving before critical information comes in, such as "the suspect has now exited the house with a rifle." More than one cop has been killed at close range while they pulled up on a call before these details are broadcast. This is the reason cops park down the street or around the corner from any in-progress call. Pretty much every law enforcement tactic is a lesson learned from a dead cop. Sometimes it takes a few fatal repeats for a new tactic to become common practice.

In this case, we're definitely too close because when I turn the corner onto the street where the burglary just occurred, the suspect walks casually away from the scene and is suddenly right next to my car. He has, as they used to say in the Old West, the drop on me. In that instant that all cops know well, the suspect makes a split-second decision to run, shoot, dump evidence, or play it cool. But this suspect is thrown off by the deafening bark that blasts out of the back of my car. He's so close that if I hit the door-pop button (which forces open the right-rear door with pneumatic piston), Brag would be able to leap out and bite him without touching the ground.

Brag's ear-shattering cacophony is so loud that the suspect freezes mid-step and throws his hands into the air. I jump out and cuff the suspect before he's recovered. Brag claws at the cage, incensed; I can feel the heat of his breath.

I move the suspect away from the danger zone and sit him on the curb. It's at that moment that I realize he has peed his pants. Three minutes ago, he was a terrifying phantom climbing into a woman's apartment. Now he's in custody and soaked with his own urine.

It's Brag's first official apprehension and he never got out of the car.

THE HUNTING OF MAN

One of the most difficult elements of police work is the actual catching of bad guys. I use the term "guys" because most suspects are male. I'm certain there are experts who could explain why men commit more crimes. Frankly, I don't need to know why. If a call goes out of a robbery with the suspect fleeing the scene on foot, I'm looking for a man every time.

Suspects run. The moment a crime occurs, a stopwatch starts ticking. Each minute that passes puts the suspect further from the scene. They shed clothes, change directions, climb fences, get into waiting cars, run to their friends' houses, and generally do whatever they can to evade capture. Sometimes they commit more crimes in their effort to escape, such as carjacking. The longer a cop spends getting to the area where a suspect has fled, the greater the likelihood that the suspect will get away. Some argue that if you know who the suspect is it's better to let him go and get him later, when he's calmed down and hopefully less likely to fight. I disagree.

There's no better time to catch him – with the evidence, wearing the same clothes – than within minutes of the crime. Identifications by victims and witnesses are problematic enough, and in my experience, they are slightly more reliable when they're immediate. Also, you can reduce the number of victims by getting the suspect now.

I've always loved the chase. It's a weird competition where you can't see your opponent but you know he's working against you. The instant a call of a crime goes out over the police radio, I activate something I call the Extrapolometer. This is a device that does not exist, except in my head. It extrapolates where the suspect is going. All the info is fed into it: crime, suspect description, time of day, neighborhood, weather, where the other cops are and if they're going in with lights and sirens. No sound makes a wanted person run faster than the wail of an approaching police siren.

What you cannot do if you want to catch someone is go directly to the scene of the crime after the suspect has left. A cop does need to go there immediately, but this is usually not the cop who will catch the bad guy. The cop that goes to the crime scene gets critical information from the victim and broadcasts it quickly so I can adjust the Extrapolometer.

In this particular case, the suspect is fleeing, last seen leaping a fence. The fact that he jumped a fence suggests that he's feeling under pressure. If he keeps jumping fences he'll tire quickly. He will take the path of least resistance. He will unwittingly turn downhill, and will usually make right turns unless he's on the left side of a street, in which case he will make left turns because he wants to be out of view as quickly as possible. He will shed outer clothing if he can. He will run toward the familiar, preferring darker areas to more well-lit areas. He will run until he tires, then hide or continue at a much slower pace.

It's an old joke: someone asks a cheetah, "If you're so fast, why does the gazelle get away so often?" The cheetah replies, "He's running for his life. I'm running for my breakfast." Suspects are highly motivated to escape, which makes them dangerous to follow. I used to think that the greatest danger to cops were bullets. Yes, bullets are deadly. But fences hurt more cops than bullets. Few cops can scale fences with the reckless abandon of a fleeing suspect. The twenty-plus pounds of gear isn't helping. Once I was trying to catch up to a foot pursuit where a cop was chasing a felony battery suspect through darkened backyards. The suspect went over a fence and the cop went over the same fence, landing heavily onto a six-inch-long length of rebar sticking straight up out of a concrete slab. The rebar punched through the officer's boot sole, impaled his foot, and emerged between the boot laces on the top. Firefighters had to saw off the rebar before they could take the cop to the hospital. The suspect escaped both injury and arrest. Fences are dangerous. This is why I prefer to activate the Extrapolometer; it's much better to meet the suspect at the end of the chase than join him on his mad dash.

Best case scenario is that I predict where the suspect will emerge into view. If I can be there before he pops out of that creek bed, I can surprise him. The shock of a cop suddenly appearing in front of him is sometimes enough to bring about an immediate surrender.

Now I have Brag. He's ready to chase and fight a combative suspect. But popping the rear door of the K-9 car so Brag can run across a fenced training field and bite a decoy wearing a bite suit is worlds away from the darkness and chaos of an actual incident. To describe an active police pursuit as a "fluid situation" is an understatement. Parking lots have innocent bystanders. Streets have speeding cars. Suspects sometimes jump off of bridges and cliffs to their deaths while fleeing the police. They also sprint across busy freeways. In one case a fleeing felon we were chasing ran across four lanes of the US 101 highway on a busy night without a scratch, then turned around and started back across again. On the return trip he took three steps before he was killed by a passing truck. If a police dog were chasing the suspect in this case, he would have been killed, too. This is a problem for dog handlers; no deployment is as safe as it is in training.

Now the trick is to get the suspect to hide. That is where the power of the perimeter comes in.

A perimeter can be established by two cops or twenty. The goal is to get a cop out in front of the fleeing suspect and create a line that the suspect will not cross. This line is not physical – we don't roll out hurricane fencing – but it can be effective if the suspect believes that crossing that visual barrier will get him caught. Perimeters should be noisy and bright, with flashing lights and spotlights aimed down streets so the suspect knows the cops are watching. If you set up a perimeter quickly enough, you can make the suspect go to ground. Now you must go into the search area to find him in a high stakes game of hide-and-seek, usually in dark and unfriendly territory. The suspect always knows you're getting close before you see him. Sometimes he is waiting for that moment to attack you. This is where the police dog comes in.

Dogs love to play hide-and-seek. It's a natural behavior. Brag loves this more than anything. For police dogs, hunting for a suspect can be very stressful because of the impending physical confrontation. People are bigger than dogs. Not every K-9 loves going toe-to-toe with an adult human, and you don't always know this about a police dog until he's on the street. Brag fears no man; he can't wait to find them.

On this call the armed suspect has robbed a pizza delivery driver of $30, the value of a human life to a criminal.

When I arrive, it's been three minutes since the call was dispatched which means the suspect is at least five minutes ahead of us.

There's a lousy perimeter, mainly because the terrain is hilly and none of the streets are straight and we don't have enough cops available to set one up properly.

I pop the trunk and grab the harness and the long-line, two items that are already emerging as the most important pieces of equipment in my short K-9 handler career. Brag struggles with me as I put the harness on him and I attach the 15-foot flat nylon long line to it. I coil up most of that line and step out of the way so Brag can come out. He's on the harness which means it's comfortable for him to pull me, but less comfortable for me to hold onto him. I'm always impressed by the power of this animal when I have him on harness, and it feels turned up a notch now that we're on a real call in the dark.

We begin our search, hoping to pick up some scent that might lead us to the suspect. Problem is, we're in the parking lot of an apartment complex and there is human odor all over the place. A few people lean over balconies and offer a running commentary on what I'm doing. This is a constant irritant to cops; people count police cars out loud as if engaged in some pre-school lesson, then exposit on why that number of cars might not be necessary. Brag pays them no attention as he pulls me through an opening in the fence into another parking lot. Two cops follow us, guns drawn. Brag ranges back and forth on the long line. I coil up the line again as we approach another building and when I see the side is clear of people, I drop most of the coils and Brag bounds away from me. The nylon line *zzzips* unchecked through my hand, burning my palm, and Brag comes to a jerking halt as the line runs out. We reach a busy street where there is no perimeter and I realize we're done.

We suck at this. More accurately, I suck at this, but because as a team we're only as good as the worst member. Brag is doing what he does as well as he can do it. This is where some handlers go wrong; they blame their dog. When you fail on the street it's never your dog's fault, it's your fault. The cops with me don't mind the fruitless hunt; they're glad to work with such an impressive-looking police dog. But I can't help thinking Brag and I are just for show at this point, strutting around in our gear but not helping much. It would have been better to have a few cops drive aimlessly through the neighborhood hoping to spot the suspect. That's how cops usually do it. It's the least reliable way to ensnare suspects but it does work sometimes. This failed search was a waste of time. I want to get better, but I'm not exactly sure how to do that.

When we go home that night, I research books online about police dog tracking. There are countless experts, and many of them contradict each other. There is a saying in the police K-9 world that the only thing two dog trainers agree on is how screwed up a third trainer is.

The next day I'm discussing the topic of tracking with another experienced cop named Mike Lazarus outside the jail loading door. Lazarus is an ex-Army sergeant and an avid hunter and has the best straight-face game in police work. He's also well-read.

"Have you read Jim Corbett?" he asks me. "He hunted man-eating tigers."

It's a brilliant suggestion. Humans are animals, as dangerous and unpredictable as any. Within days I'm devouring Corbett's stories.

Corbett grew up in India. In the 1920's, he tracked and killed dozens of rogue tigers, some responsible for killing hundreds of people. There is no animal more terrifying than a tiger who has come to appreciate the taste of human flesh. Corbett's accounts of his hunts are honest and gripping. Many were resolved through Corbett's highly-developed sixth sense. One detail that struck me was how intently he concentrated on the movement of odor on the wind; a mistake in walking the wrong direction and sending his scent toward a tiger behind would have been instantly fatal. Corbett may have been unremarkable in appearance, but inside he had transformed into something that hunted frightful predators many times his size.

Humans are one of the few animals who can will themselves to evolve. A hawk cannot re-design her wings or study ground squirrel tunnel models to improve her hunting odds. But I can. I am not the same person I was when I started this job, so I've already changed. I can continue to evolve and become less man and more canine.

Man-eating tigers are arguably the most dangerous game, but men can't be far behind on the list. And no tiger ever waited in a dark place to shoot you in the face.

We begin training more realistically. Tracks are never repeated in training now, so the second and third dogs cannot follow the odor of the preceding dogs. Ted is open to this evolution and listens when I tell him what doesn't seem to work on the street.

Finding places to train is always a challenge, and it's harder now that we're laying a new trail for each dog. We start some from cars with no idea which way the decoy ran, so the dog learns to figure out which direction to go. We also try to have the decoy run with the prevailing wind so the dog will keep his nose closer to the ground and not wind-scent the suspect. Vectoring in with the nose up is the most efficient way for a dog to hunt, but you can't count on the suspect always being upwind of you. Think of a wasp honing in on your burger at a picnic: they approach from downwind and zig-zag in the "scent plume" of your plate. Dogs run that same pattern. Once that dog is zig-zagging back and forth across your scent-plume, he's got you.

Ted sets up a track and I attach the long-line to Brag's harness, letting my partner guide me across an empty medical building atrium. Brag freezes, and I look up and see Ted – stripped down to his skivvies – dancing behind a pane of glass in an office lobby. When Ted shouts unintelligible challenges at us Brag goes nuts, barking at this madman in his underwear. I push the door open as Ted slips on the bite sleeve, giving Brag a bite as a reward for the long track. The other handlers laugh at the sight of a mostly-naked Ted writhing while a dog bites him, but I see the wisdom of it. I've been a cop for a long time: a bad guy in his underpants is realistic training.

"Fifty-five to all units: man with a gun at Fresh Supermarket, 100 West Carrillo Street."

I grab the mic and whip a sudden turn in heavy afternoon traffic. "K9-1 enroute."

Brag keeps his feet and leans forward against the acceleration. He knows we're going somewhere important. The first cop arrives and says the suspect is out front with a handgun.

I'm here. I slam on the brakes outside the parking lot, grab the long-line, and open the back door. Brag's head emerges and this time he's not fighting me so much as I put the harness on. He's trembling with excitement at being out of the car and actually doing something.

Ducking down, I lead Brag between parked cars in the lot to where I can see the suspect standing outside of the supermarket, facing us and holding a black automatic handgun. He's mid-forties, short beard, left-handed. He can see us, but we're a too far for him to shoot at us with any accuracy. Shoppers still try to pull into the lot but the cops are waving them off.

Sergeant Danny McGrew comes creeping up between parked cars, followed by Greg Hons: two super-experienced SWAT guys. Our odds of winning this without loss of life just got better.

The suspect is shouting demands at us, holding the gun straight up in the air. I don't see anyone in the store behind him, so I'm not sure if people are hiding or if anyone is shot or if they've locked the doors. I'm not counting on that last part, which means the suspect could turn around and go inside and have hostages.

A gigantic cop named Burleigh arrives. He's a hostage negotiator and one of the nicest people of any size, one of those men who uses his size to calm people. The four of us have a bizarre meeting, crouched down behind a parked car, and decide that Burleigh should try to get a dialogue going with the suspect.

Burleigh hollers a greeting, asking the suspect if he is okay. Funny thing is, Burleigh isn't following some script. He actually cares. To be honest, I don't. I want this suspect separated from his handgun and wearing handcuffs.

Brag whines, wanting to move. He studies all the cops crouched around us, trying to figure out what's going on. It would be like being on a hot police call in a foreign country where you don't speak the language and have no idea what the call is or what anyone is saying.

"Fifty-five, 21X on-scene and deploying rifle from the north-east, one-four corner."

That's Rullman, the SWAT sniper. We have a long gun now: a cop with a rifle and scope and the sense to know when to use it.

Burleigh keeps at it, tireless. The suspect will not put the gun down; he's holding his ground. Twenty minutes pass without any improvement.

Rullman has been examining the suspect through his scope this whole time.

"21X to units on-scene: the suspect's handgun might be a replica."

I make eye contact with McGrew as he keys his mic: "21X, give me a percentage."

A long silence, then Rullman answers: "Ninety-percent."

I trust Rullman with my life, but that ten percent is worrisome. The handgun replica has always been a problem for cops. People commit robberies with them. They look plenty real, especially when they're aimed at you. From where I am, peeking over the hood of a parked car, the gun looks like a nine-millimeter. But Rullman's glassing the gun hard, and he's meticulous.

The suspect is getting agitated and I realize his arm is getting tired. If he lowers the gun toward us, Rullman might have to take the shot. We have to act, now.

McGrew puts his hand on my shoulder. "You willing to use Brag?"

I nod, but I'm not at all sure. It's twenty-five yards to the suspect across open parking lot. If that gun is real, the suspect will shoot my partner. If it's not real, Brag might be able to close the distance before the suspect can dart back into the store and shut the door behind him. But there's a big problem: Brag hasn't seen the suspect yet. He doesn't know what a gun can do and he doesn't know why we're hiding or what's about to happen. There's no way to explain this to him. I have to trust him, trust our training.

McGrew and Hons and I come up with a plan: Hons will roll out from behind the parked car with the beanbag shotgun and fire two rounds at the suspect, which will hopefully stun him and buy us a second or two. Simultaneously, I'll send Brag directly at the suspect for a bite. McGrew will hold a ballistic shield and lead the rush at the suspect.

Hons readies the beanbag gun. He's an expert in less-lethal weapons so no one has a better chance of hitting his target twice in under two seconds.

My hands are sweating as I unclip the long-line from Brag and grip his leather collar, my palm pressed against one of the two small metal SBPD badges embedded on either side of it. Sensing a fight, Brag is surging forward, ready to do go. I put a hand on his flank and I can feel his muscles trembling. This is his moment.

McGrew counts down: "Three, two, one –"

Hons rolls out as I side-step into the open and in that instant Brag gets his first glimpse of the suspect, a man standing sixty feet away holding one hand in the air. Two beanbag rounds go off and the suspect flinches as I aim Brag's nose at the suspect and send him.

"*Packen, packen, packen!*" I yell as Brag explodes into a sprint at the suspect. It feels like slow-motion as the suspect turns toward the doors. He never makes it. Brag hits him in the left arm and the handgun goes flying and I realize I'm almost there though I can't remember running.

Brag twists, throwing the suspect off-balance, and they go down in a heap. In that moment I know Brag has won – you might stand a chance against him on your feet but once you're down in his world it's over. It's like trying to outswim a gator that's clamped onto your leg; you're not going anywhere except underwater.

"GOOD BOY!" I shout, reassuring Brag that he's doing what he's supposed to be doing.

We reach the suspect and I grab onto Brag as the other cops grab the suspect. Brag comes off the bite and it's over. Handcuffs click. The handgun is recovered – a replica, just as Rullman suspected – and cops stream into the store to make sure the people hiding inside are okay.

I back away, straddling Brag and gripping his collar with both hands. He barks savagely, wanting to bite the suspect again. I praise Brag over and over, my heart pumping with adrenaline. We go back across the parking lot as the news crews rush in to get better footage. Brag barks enthusiastically at a cameraman. I plop into the driver's seat, trying to contain myself. My dog took down an armed bad guy. Brag's enormous face is directly behind me and he's panting a mile a minute.

"You are a police dog," I tell him. "Good job, Brag." I'm pretty sure he smiles.

Later, I see the pictures of the suspect's injuries. Hons hit him with beanbag rounds once in the ribs and once in the hand that was holding the gun, preventing the suspect from pulling the trigger. I have no idea how Hons made that shot from that distance. He would say it was lucky, but I know better. Brag bit the guy's arm and held fast like he's supposed to. The puncture wounds from Brag's enormous canines are ugly but require no stitches. The suspect is booked and psychologically evaluated. I call Ted.

"I saw a standoff on the news," he says. "Is it over?"

"Brag took that guy down. He was perfect."

"Can't wait to hear the details. I'm proud of you two."

"Let's re-create this call for the other K-9's to train on next week."

Ted agrees that would be a good idea.

"Hey, thanks for this dog," I add. "He may be an asshole but he's an ass-kicker, too."

Ted laughs. "You two are more alike than you think."

The Werewolf has friends; the cops who were on-scene yell out his name as we roll past the rows of police cars at the station. The fastest way to a street cop's heart is to catch a bad guy.

Brag's popularity grows. He sniffs out a hidden compartment in a drug dealer's car, exposing a trove of crystal meth. He shows up on fight calls, throwing himself against the cage to get at anyone not wearing a uniform. The patrol officers ask for the K-9 on the radio now as they're rolling to an in-progress incident.

I've developed a new policy: Never Say No. That old problem with K-9 handlers getting close to their dogs will constantly be in conflict with our role in law enforcement. There is always a reason to say no, to not put the dog in danger. But those calls are often the very reason the police dog exists, to reduce the danger to the human police officers. He's not cannon fodder; I've seen plenty of videos of handlers sending their dogs against suspects brandishing firearms. Most of these incidents ended tragically for the dog. I know a local handler whose dog was stabbed to death by a suspect, so I understand the reluctance. But to keep it from seeping into my work process I need to go whenever a cop asks for the K-9 or I hear a call where the K-9 might be useful. When I arrive I can decide whether or not to use him. Another bad habit is to roll into the scene late, knowing full well it's over and just driving through the area with the dog barking in the back of the car. It's not fair to the dog, who wants to work. Brag and I go to as many calls as we can, reassuring the cops that Brag is here to help. I'm building Brag's reputation on the street, where it matters.

When a call goes out of a gang member shooting into a passing SUV, the gang units charge into the location on the lower Westside. In many gang-related shootings like these there are often no witnesses willing to talk to us but since this occurred in broad daylight with children playing outside, there's no shortage of people pointing at the open front door of a residence across the street from the shooting. Nine-millimeter shell casings and glittering bits of shattered car window glass litter the street, but no one's arrived at the hospital with a gunshot wound yet. So, we may or may not have a wounded victim. Gang members don't call us when they get shot, so we rely on the emergency room staff to alert us when someone walks in with bullet holes.

The gang unit surrounds the dilapidated house and waits for Brag and I to arrive. We have little information: the Hispanic male suspect has a gun and fled into this house. Since none of the cops wants to get shot through a closet door, I'm going to try to use Brag to make the odds more favorable. One of the gang officers, Oscar Gonzales, turns the search over to me.

"How do you want to run it?" he asks.

"Brag goes first in each room, then I'll pull him out so you can search by hand."

He draws his gun and places his other hand on my shoulder-blade, SWAT sign language for "I'm your cover and ready to move when you are."

I put Brag into each cluttered room after announcing our presence and waiting for any reply. The suspect is gone; he fled out the back before cops arrived. But as I'm searching with Brag, I notice that all of the cops on the interior search – three from the gang unit, two from patrol, and one from the downtown bike unit – are also on the SWAT team. We're doing a SWAT-style search with the police dog, who is NOT a SWAT dog. But the only difference between this search and a SWAT search is that the guys with me at this moment are wearing different uniforms instead of the matching uniforms they'd be wearing if it were a SWAT call-out. Afterwards, the cops remark how much better that search was than poking into closets not knowing if the suspect was waiting to ambush them.

It's an epiphany for me; good patrol searches are the same as tactical SWAT searches.

I'm plotting. The K-9 handlers train on Wednesdays and the SWAT team trains every other Wednesday. What if, by pure happenstance, we were to find ourselves at the same training location? We would have to be polite and share, maybe even do a little training together.

FEAR

I wake up suddenly, my heart crashing like broken dishes in my chest. Dread grips me as a half-waking nightmare of a figure moving across the bedroom toward me to deliver a message I don't want to hear. Before I can focus on this shadowy form, it fades away like smoke.

It's not real, I tell myself. Fully awake now, I can see there's no one there. There never is. But my heart still bangs against my ribs. This is where fear manifests itself.

I sit up and look at the clock though I already know it's 3:37 a.m. because I awaken at this time every night. It is my hour of the wolf, my own personal curse. It's PTSD, no doubt, and it defies rationalization. I know there's no emergency, no reason to feel this dread, but when I wake up I'm ready for a fight. It usually takes me thirty minutes to fall back asleep using an assortment of mental games to calm down. That's not going to work tonight. I'll need to walk through the house and see for myself that every door is locked, every window shut tight.

Fear. Humans are born with this instinct. It is inextricably tied to survival. We spent millennia being afraid of the dark, for good reason: apex predators roamed the night. These animals were faster, stronger, and after nightfall their superior senses made them especially dangerous. Over time we all but eliminated the threat of carnivores lurking near us in the dark. The most dangerous predators were no longer four-legged beasts, they were people.

We responded to this problem by creating a night watch whose sole purpose was to prowl on equal terms with these human predators. The modern police officer was born. But to do the job properly these men and women needed to do one thing first: divest themselves of fear.

I've seen cops scared on calls. I've been afraid on many occasions. But fear is an emotion, and therefore must be rejected as the enemy of reason. The only standard for action is reasonableness and the rule of law. Brag does not act out of fear. The human predators should fear us, not the other way around. Foolhardiness is equally unwelcome in police work and must never replace sound tactics.

The FBI has spent considerable effort interviewing convicted cop killers in the hope that these interviews will result in fewer line-of-duty deaths. Invariably, when asked about the cop they murdered, the convicted killers always say that they didn't believe the cop was prepared to use deadly force to protect their own life. On an animal level the killers knew their opponent would hesitate; in all instances they were correct. Another commonality among these interviewees is the absence of remorse. The murderers place most or all of the blame on the police officers who were not prepared to do what was necessary. When they saw fear in the cops' eyes, they saw weakness and inaction.

A police dog, similarly, must feel no fear. In training, we try to teach the dogs that they will win every fight. The stronger and more experienced the dog, the more difficult the physical fight should be. At the end of these training confrontations, the agitator submits. He never wins.

Ted is a master at this. He understands Brag and as a result fights him harder than any other dog in our training group. Each dog is worked according to individual personality and life experience. The newer dogs especially must be treated with care; if too much pressure is put on them they may learn to fear confrontation. This is disastrous on the street. Sending a police dog to bite a suspect only to have the dog spit out the bite and back off, or – worse yet – avoid contact with the suspect entirely, is every handler's nightmare. Yet it happens, and it is never the dog's fault. They do not intellectualize confrontation. Handlers must also exude calm confidence at all times; the dogs rely on their human partners to be strong pack leaders. A police dog will know if his handler is afraid, and fear is contagious.

Brag has been with me long enough to know which human emotion drives me.

If you start in the middle of downtown Los Angeles and drive east for a dozen miles, you'll pass through Baldwin Park and West Covina. The line between these unremarkable municipalities is the neighborhood where I grew up, underpasses and concrete flood channels and chain-link fences dividing up a failed suburban sprawl. The world, at least as I understood it as a child, was run-down and smelled like old cigarettes. This was the place where I decided to become a cop, I just didn't realize it at the time because I was eleven years old.

I lived like every other "latch-key" kid with working parents and no supervision after school. Our only restriction was to be home when the street lights came on. We may have had the run of the neighborhood, but we also felt a responsibility to watch over it.

One day a group of four of us – me, my older brother, a boy named Clinton, and my best friend Rich – approached our house after school and saw the front door standing open with one of the glass panels broken out; a burglary. My parents weren't due home for hours. Here was a crucial moment, because we should have tried to locate an adult, or gone to another house to call the police. But that's not what we did.

I was furious—my family didn't own much, and someone was stealing it right now. We decided to go inside. Rich and I entered first; he brandished an aluminum baseball bat. In the front room I snatched up an iron poker from the fireplace, gripping it like some medieval weapon. We crept through the house, three eleven-year-olds and a twelve-year-old, ready to confront the burglars. The house felt menacing, different from the one I'd left that morning.

We found no one. The burglars were long gone, along with our television, stereo, and my mother's costume jewelry. My father scolded us for going into the house but didn't punish us. Life continued on and we never spoke much about it.

Years later, I wonder what was it that possessed an eleven-year-old boy to grip a fire poker and search his house for criminals. The answer is anger: at the intrusion, the defiling of my home, the feeling of powerlessness. I scrubbed the thieves' dirty footprints from the carpet in my bedroom, gritting my teeth. I wanted to erase their presence, but the house was no longer the sanctuary it was before. In my mind it had become less comforting, the way most magical things we believe in as children are eventually exposed as fraudulent. In truth, that neighborhood was far from a place of innocence: a man murdered his wife with a rifle around the corner, and my friend Clinton suffered constant physical abuse by his foster parents. Although we never dwelled on these dark events—this was just life, after all—something grew inside of me, a determination to hammer the dents of an imperfect world back into shape. I may have looked like every other skinny kid wearing his brother's hand-me-down shirt, but deep inside there was a smoldering ember that had all the fuel it would ever need.

Fear was paralysis. Anger was action.

I will banish fear from my mind. Brag must be certain there is nothing that we ever need fear. We are the apex predators moving in shadow beyond the firelight. Our prey must fear us more than anything else in the night.

My pulse is no longer pounding as I walk through my darkened house. I stand beside my son's bed for a moment, listening to his rhythmic breathing before moving on. I check the doors and the windows and go barefoot into the backyard. I want to call out to Brag, who is sleeping in his dog house in his kennel, but I don't want him to think we're going to work. It would make me feel better to have someone sit with me for a few minutes but I won't wake him. The cool darkness at least is comforting, as is the silence.

I'm about to go back inside when I hear Brag's hurried trot across the woodchips toward me. I made no sound so I probably woke him up with my scent. His head is high, ears erect, and I can see he's wondering what the hell I'm doing outside at this hour.

I push through the gate and crouch down beside him. He sniffs my neck with his huge muzzle and almost knocks me over when he whips around to disappear into the darkness again. A moment later he returns with his Kong ball in his mouth and he drops it on my foot and sits, looking at me with his eyebrows raised. I'm not going to play a game with him in the dark – that's ridiculous. But I pick the Kong up and toss it at him anyway. He catches it with far too much enthusiasm for this time of night and trots around, marking his spots and watching me. The ghosts of a few minutes earlier vanish entirely.

He comes to the gate as I go back through it.

"Goodnight, partner."

Brag watches me go inside. When I get up again hours later, I look out the kitchen window and see Brag sleeping beside the gate in the exact spot I last saw him. He didn't go back to his dog house.

Training days are an opportunity for Claytor and me to de-brief the K-9 calls that didn't go well during our work weeks and decide how to fix them. The only way this will be possible is for us to adopt another policy: It's Always the Handler's Fault. This prevents us from ever blaming the dog if a call doesn't go as planned. If you assume that when things go awry that it's your fault as the handler, you're much more likely to find a solution. Clarity is the main problem. Before a call the police dogs aren't briefed on the details, don't study the suspect's photo, and don't know the plan. They're doing it live. This is why the handler must be clear; the suspect won't wait around for you two to figure it out.

I don't glare at Brag anymore during training, trying to control him with my mind. That doesn't work and it was weird. He's more relaxed during obedience because of it.

We train with the handlers and dogs at Vandenberg Air Force Base, with the K-9 units from Santa Maria PD, and California Highway Patrol. We try to bring honesty to our training, to confront our individual weaknesses. It's uncomfortable sometimes but since my dog has the hardest head of any dog in our group, I'm the handler who often has trouble with our scenarios. But the training has gotten real. The cigars and flip-flops are long gone. We have a training uniform and a training schedule and a core skills list to make sure we cover them on a regular basis, from obedience to complicated searches. During one training, Claytor and I bring out the plastic, paint-marking rounds for our handguns. We practice drawing under fire while trying to control the dog. Claytor does better with that last part than I do because Ignaz is more obedient. We trade roles as the bad guy, shooting each other repeatedly with the painful plastic rounds. When it's over, we're both sporting a collection of bleeding welts. We're also faced with the grim reality that winning an armed confrontation while you're attached to a police dog is damned difficult.

And we train with SWAT, the same team I was ordered to *not* train with. Under the guise of an "annual familiarization training" I share with them what I've learned about the police dogs and how we might be able to use them for searches in a patrol capacity. But I'm really talking about the dogs as an integral part of the team. The SWAT team members are enthusiastic about incorporating the K-9 as a tool. I'll let them bug their bosses until someone finally caves in and agrees to let us train together regularly.

It's early August and Old Spanish Days arrives – a boozy week of parties and parades and packed bars. The population of Santa Barbara doubles and there's a sharp uptick in arrests, fights, and stabbings during this fiesta. I avoid downtown, mainly because I don't believe it's my duty as a dog handler to babysit drunk people, but Claytor takes Ignaz downtown to help monitor the unruly crowds. Ignaz is less confrontational and doesn't lose his mind when someone comes near his car, so it's no big deal for him to be on State Street around all those revelers.

Around eleven on Saturday night, Claytor and several other officers see two men suddenly come to blows outside a nightclub. Ignaz sits in the K-9 car a dozen feet away. As Claytor steps in to break up the fight, one of the combatants pulls out a handgun and aims it at his opponent. Claytor quick-draws and shoots the suspect dead, saving the other man's life. When I come screaming into the scene, it is chaos. Brag goes nuts in the back – he smells fear. I smell gunfire.

I find Claytor standing on the sidewalk near the suspect. Blood droplets freckle his boots.

"Are you shot?" I ask him.

"I don't know," he says, turning sideways so I can examine him. No bullet holes.

He grips my arm. "It was exactly like training," he says. "When you and I were shooting at each other point blank with those sim rounds."

There's a saying in law enforcement tactical circles: When the time to perform has arrived, the time to prepare has elapsed. Statistically speaking, K-9 handlers are involved in more shootings than other patrol officers.

Back at the station, the concern for his life has changed into concern for his liability. Claytor surrenders his service gun and magazines for evidence processing and then the reality of his having just taken a human life hits him. The fear he had no time to feel during the shooting pours out of him now. I call his wife and tell her that he's fine and then print out the use of force policy from our department manual and give it to him to read. It states that any use of force must be objectively reasonable, given the facts available to the officer at that moment. Reasonableness is the legal standard of the United States Supreme Court. But no legal reassurance can erase the emotional aftershocks of shooting a man to death.

Claytor is sequestered in the station awaiting his attorney so I go outside to give Ignaz a pee break. Ignaz is obviously worried about what is going on with his partner. He relieves himself on one of the spindly bushes in the rear parking lot, his intelligent, hazel eyes on me the whole time. He wants an explanation. I kneel down beside him.

"Mike is okay," I tell Ignaz, and he listens intently. "He's going to take you home in a few hours, all right?"

Ignaz jumps back into Claytor's K-9 car, looking relieved.

I can see Brag's silhouette watching us from the back of our car. Usually, he would be barking his head off, but he hasn't made a peep since I got Ignaz out. *Does he know?* I wonder.

Claytor is placed on administrative leave until the investigation is complete. Until then, I'm the only dog handler working.

I take Brag to Oxnard to train with their K-9 teams. The Oxnard Police Department handlers and I do the same job, with some subtle differences, but the training in Oxnard is well-planned and realistic. They work mostly Belgian Malinois dogs: smaller, high-energy cousins of the German Shepherd. They're hard-working dogs and absolutely ferocious.

I don't know the Oxnard handlers and they're stand-off-ish at first, but once they see Brag leap a six-foot wooden fence to nab a decoy in a bite suit, all is well. We exchange ideas and I'm grateful that they welcomed us to their training, an act of professional courtesy.

Brag is visibly spent from the demanding day and it's over an hour back home. I was so proud of him when he cleared that fence to bite the decoy. Our relationship feels different now, less like an ongoing disagreement and more like a partnership. Brag even looks like a different dog to me; his implacable expression has subtleties I never saw before. I can tell when he's frustrated or irritated by the look in his eye, the way he moves his head.

We arrive home and I go out into the backyard first to make sure the gate is open. When I come back into the garage, my son, Strieker, has climbed into the back of the car with Brag. There's a second of mortal terror until I see Brag's face; the dog looks mildly amused by this child invading the metal cage that Brag is eager to defend to the death when we're working. This particular four-year-old boy can, apparently, violate this sacred dog space at will. I take a picture of them in the back of the car. Brag's face is relaxed. Strieker looks equally at ease.

When I let Brag into the backyard, it dawns on me that my property is enclosed by a six-foot wooden fence. The same type of fence he hurdled with ease a few hours ago. What keeps him here in my yard? Not me, surely.

After a couple of weeks, Claytor is cleared in the shooting. He returns to full duty, but this does not mean he is fine. Nothing is ever going to be fine; a man lost his life and another man had to take it. Claytor must carry this with him forever.

OTHER DUTIES AS ASSIGNED

The K-9 demonstration is an event where the public watches the police K-9 run, bite, and bark. Sounds like fun? Not for me. No event creates dread in a police dog handler like a K-9 demo. On the surface, it sounds easy. But behind all the smiling and applause lurks the bane of all handlers: the accidental bite.

It is not natural for a dog to bite a human the way we want our police dogs to bite people. Most dog bites are a shallow bite that means "stay away from me." That's not what we want. We want a deep, full-mouth, "you're not going anywhere" bite that only ends when we say it ends. Many dogs can be taught to bite but most of them will not bite correctly. Brag's first bite, like a lot of police dogs, was a bite and spit out and re-bite. That's okay for the first time. To the dog that first bite clearly feels different from the bite sleeve and the bite suits; muscles moving underneath skin and bones beneath that. Once a good dog figures it out, they bite like they mean it. The problem is that a dog will not necessarily check in with the handler before biting someone if they feel that either of us is in danger.

My sergeant informs me that I will be conducting a K-9 demonstration on Saturday afternoon at a park where they are having a special Dog Day event. It's a double threat - children and dogs all over the place. I try to weasel out of it but Fryslie is having none of that. He reminds me that at the bottom of the list of my K-9 handler duties in the policy manual is the line: "other duties as assigned." I am hereby assigned to conduct this K-9 demonstration. I can't refuse, but maybe that afternoon there will be an urgent police call somewhere in the city and I'll be so busy doing real police work I'll have to no-show to the event.

No such luck. Saturday afternoon finds me cruising into the parking lot of the park while Brag barks his head off at every mammal he sees. I contact the woman who runs the event and she's so pleased that I've arrived that I feel a bit guilty for all the cursing I did when I saw the crowd. She guides me to an area half the size of a soccer field with yellow caution tape along one side to prevent people from entering.

I ask her to make an announcement that all dogs MUST be on leash. Watching myself on the internet trying to break up a dogfight while children shriek in terror is not how I want to spend my evening later.

"You and Brag are the headliners. Everyone is excited to meet him."

"Unfortunately, I can't have people get too close to him."

She looks less thrilled. "Is he dangerous?"

"He's… not friendly. He's a working dog."

The truth is a lot of police dogs have no problem with interacting with all kinds of folk. But the Werewolf does. The woman nods understandingly but I think she pictured a police dog petting zoo as part of the demo.

I pace nervously until the woman makes the safety announcement and I get Brag out on a pinch collar for obedience, stuffing his tug into my thigh pocket. The crowd OOHS over Brag when he struts out onto the field beside me and I can't help smiling with pride. He is one impressive animal and he seems to stand taller when he's in front of a group of people. A few dogs in the audience bark at Brag but he's focused on his obedience while I tell the audience about him. As long as he is occupied and physically unable to get to anyone there is much less chance of him deciding that lanky kid swinging a stick is about to ambush us.

Sergeant Fryslie – dressed in regular clothes – comes onto the field to take a bite, and the moment of truth arrives when I cut Brag loose and send him tearing across the grass. Fryslie catches him perfectly and the crowd cheers when Brag hits the sleeve like a guided missile. I hook Brag up on leash again and we're done.

The woman organizer ducks underneath the yellow safety tape to walk over and thank me and I'm feeling pretty good about it now because there were no incidents and Brag is calmer because he got to bite the sleeve. Even so, I stand between Brag and the woman and answer a couple of her questions before turning back around.

My heart stops cold. Six kids, aged five to eleven, surround Brag. A couple of them pat his sides, one strokes his tail, another one crawls underneath him and the sixth one examines Brag's open mouth like an explorer peering into a cave.

Brag looks up at me as if to say *they're kids – what can you do?*

"Okay, everyone" I stammer, my mouth dry. "It's time for Brag to go to work now."

Brag leaves his entourage and we trot back to the parking lot. I lean into the car once he's inside, pressing one hand on his thick coat. He is perfectly calm.

"You gave me a heart attack, Brag."

I am certain he's smiling when I close the door. The rest of the shift is nowhere near as harrowing.

As much as Brag enjoys showing off for children, he also loves a good game of find-the-drugs. It's very different from hunting men, and despite how official it may sound, searching for narcotics *is* a game – one that Brag plays every day now. Sometimes the calls for searches stack up and we rush from one to the next. Brag keeps getting better at it; he sniffs out heroin hidden in engine compartments, methamphetamine stashed in cereal boxes, and finds $60,000 of drug-scented money rolled up in a drug dealer's underwear drawer. The bad guys stash firearms, too. We seize these when we find drugs or if the owner is a convicted felon, but we often have no legal right to do so and must leave them behind. I'm never comfortable with this, but the rules are the rules.

I assist the narcotics detectives on a drug search in the city of Santa Maria, and Rullman – his cowboy past on full display because he has grown a rusty beard thick as chaparral – tells me their informant suggested that the goodies might be buried outside.

Brag does not alert anywhere in the yard which makes the narcs scratch their heads. There's no indication of drug dealing at all in this normal-looking tract home, in contrast to the narcs' information that a lot of cocaine and meth move out of the place. I bring Brag into the living room, kicking out all of the narcs except Rullman and a task-force agent from the Department of Justice. Too many cops milling around distracts Brag. Cops are also famously impatient; they'll search ahead of us if they're left waiting in the house too long.

When we go into the master bedroom Rullman exclaims "That one is mine!" and points at a closet shelf where a life-sized plaster bust of a Mexican man with garishly-painted eyes and thick eyebrows stares back at us. It is Jesus Malverde, patron saint of drug dealers.

Most Mexican cartel dealers have an image of this venerated person somewhere in their residence. Jesus Malverde is said to grant protection to those who sell narcotics. He's not officially a saint but he is revered among the traffickers. Supposedly he was a real person who was – depending on who you ask – martyred in a drug shootout or hanged by the Mexican police and left to rot; in the afterlife he allegedly intercedes on behalf of those dealers who pay him homage. The representations of Senor Malverde are simultaneously comical and chilling: he looks like a male mannequin with an ill-fitting wig and a fake moustache, usually sporting a bolo tie that reminds me of Colonel Sanders. But instead of fried chicken by the bucket you've got cocaine by the kilos. Whenever we serve a search warrant and run across his likeness, I know we're in the right place. I've seen his face on thumb-drives, candles, and in gold-framed lithographs. I always imagine him giving the dealer a wink and thumbs up when we come up empty on a search. Police K-9 teams need their own patron saint.

We can't find any dope on this search, which is making the cops testy, including Brag who acts like he smells it but can't get close enough to alert. Then it suddenly occurs to me that something is amiss about the house. I go back outside and pace off the walls. The cops watch me like I've lost my mind except Rullman, who knows exactly what I'm doing. The room dimensions don't match the exterior measurements. There's a secret room. Rullman locates a hidden and locked door in a closet and after a few good kicks they're inside and laughing at the suitcases full of cocaine in the chamber. There's even a kilo press. I can't let Brag into the room because there's a fine dusting of cocaine powder on all surfaces. But I make the narcs shut the door and let Brag into the closet – now cleared of baby clothes and childcare items – and he alerts on the door and I toss him the Kong ball. He carries it happily out to the car but I suspect he knows that last part of the search was staged for his own personal satisfaction.

It's my fault: I kept Brag out of that closet and off of the baby stuff because I didn't want him to ruin anything belonging to a child. Turns out the drug dealing parents were less concerned about their children. I won't make that mistake again.

Whenever Brag and I arrive on a call to assist a cop with a narcotics search I have to be careful about each step because dogs are masters of pattern. Just like a dog knows you're going out for a run the minute you head to the closet to get your running shoes, Brag knows we're on a narcotics search long before I tell him.

When I arrive, I ask the primary officer about her probable cause, and discuss any other legal considerations. If it's a car, the first step is to remove the occupants. They can't stand near to the search because if they do something Brag perceives as a threat he will switch from narcotics sniffer to suspect eater in one-tenth of a second. Once the occupants are out of the way, I go to my trunk and open the narcotics safe, rummaging around in it as if I'm pulling out narcotics training aids to hide in the car. If I don't do this, Brag will begin to realize that – unlike training days when I go into the safe and hide narcotics – these real-life searches often yield no results. This could make him less enthusiastic about searches and he's such a hard worker I don't want him to ever search thinking *I already know there's nothing there.*

I walk to the suspect vehicle, pretending to carry something in my hand. Brag watches me closely. I also make sure the engine is off and the keys are out of the ignition. One handler in a nearby beach town forgot to do this and when his K-9 went into the car that was parked facing an overlook with a lovely view of the ocean far below, the dog bumped the car into gear and it drove slowly away with the dog inside. Luckily, the cliff was overgrown and the car lodged in the brush below the lip. I can only imagine the handler's expression as the car rolled away with the dog peering out the back window in confusion. The dog wasn't hurt in that incident, but I still wouldn't want to have to write that report.

I'm looking in the car for hazards: broken glass, poison, loose narcotics in plain view, guns. Brag will happily munch on a desiccated French fry he finds on the floorboards and continue his search, but I am in charge of his potty breaks and he doesn't have the constitution for these human snacks. German Shepherds are not known for their iron-clad stomachs, so I will pay dearly for the mistake if I miss spotting that elderly chicken nugget.

I go back to Brag and open the door, attaching the four-foot leather lead to his flat collar. He knows I am holding the Kong ball and that he will win both the Kong ball and lavish praise if he finds the narcotics I have just pretended to hide in the suspect car.

"Ready to find it?" I ask him, acting as if we're about to play the most exciting game of hide-and-seek that was ever played. He's so pumped up that he barks, a high-pitched puppy bark that means *let's do it!*

He pulls me to the suspect car and goes in, following his nose. My job is to watch from outside and make sure he runs his nose over any surface that could lead to narcotics: the roof upholstery, the AC vents, and the pile of dirty underwear in the back. He always goes to the center console first because people are so unimaginative that they actually store contraband there. I don't need him to check the glove box – I can do that – what I need him to do is alert on the good hiding places, the custom-made compartments invisible to the naked eye.

When Brag alerts, he usually takes a deep confirmation sniff of that spot and plants his butt, staring at me with a hilarious intensity and rocking his eyebrows back and forth. Since he's so enormous he rarely has the room to sit so he drops his back end as low as it will go and freezes, his eyes on my hand as I reach slowly into my pocket and withdraw the Kong ball.

"GOOD BOY!" I yodel, tossing the ball into his mouth. He grinds on it with satisfaction as I re-attach the leash and trot with him back to our car. He hops inside with his prize. Brag is what they call an "honest dog," meaning he doesn't false alert to get the prize. Any dog could develop that bad habit, so it's vitally important to train properly and reward consistently. Some handlers never reward their dogs without confirming that there is dope hidden there, but I always do. There have been times where Brag alerted and I found nothing, but he's alerting on odor and I'm searching for product. So, the kilo of cocaine that was hidden inside the spare in the trunk left plenty of odor behind, even if it was taken out three hours before the cops arrived. Brag isn't wrong, we're too late.

As much as Brag loves a good dope search, he prefers hunting people. It's rare to find a dog so good at both, a star MLB pitcher who also leads the team in home runs. That kind of dog doesn't come along often, which is what that LAPD sergeant meant all those months ago on Brag's first certification day.

Later that night I park in our spot behind the police department and a voice yells out "BRAG!" Brag perks up as Officer Shamordola comes over to say hello; she adores Brag and, in her eyes, he can do no wrong. I open the door and hold up the tug. He snags the tug from me, and gallops over to his friend. Sham plays tug with Brag, reminding him how handsome he is. He growls and thrashes his head but it's all an act; he responds to her praise. Sham and I chat for a few minutes and the entire time Brag fights for her undivided attention.

I keep reminding myself that Brag is not a pet. I'm his handler, and the minute I make a deployment decision based on how I feel about him and not about how he should be used properly, I've lost perspective. He's made it clear to me that he wants to work and understands what we're doing. We have a job to do, to keep good cops like Sham safe.

I've adopted another mandate to add to my list: Complete the Mission, a term from the SWAT and military community. These three words will help carry us through fatigue and adversity, and serve to remind me that we have a mission to catch suspects. I don't want my partner to get hurt. Brag never signed up for police work but now that he's doing it he clearly loves it. It's hard to tell if he's an extension of my will or if I'm the enabler of his.

I'm thumbing through the SBPD Policy Manual when I spy some fine print at the end of the police canine section. It specifies that on any call, the handler shall have final say on whether or not to deploy the K-9. It's a surprisingly reasonable solution to the problem of a supervisor having no clue if a given situation might require the use of the police dog. Simply put, I am in charge on any K-9 call, rank be damned.

Now I understand some of the administrative reluctance to grant me the handler position. Too late now; this genie ain't going back in the bottle. Not with those teeth.

LOSS

"**D**oes Brag feel like biting someone today?" It's Kushner – a gravel-voiced and wickedly-sarcastic gang unit officer – calling me while Brag and I are prowling through afternoon traffic. I look on my MDT screen and see the gang guys are on the lower East Side. Where else.

"You know the answer to that question," I reply.

"Good," he says. "A wanted gangster ran into a house on Liberty. We got it locked down."

I turn onto Liberty Street, an ironically-named road deep in Eastside gang member territory, sandwiched between trailer parks and a partially-paved creek bed. There are no friendlies on this street, and several houses you'd never approach without four or five cops.

Eastsiders and Westsiders. These criminal street gangs hate each other for the simple reason that one lives on the east side of town and the other lives on the west. The hostilities go back for generations. Many of the gang members' homes have been in their families for generations. Most of them are dilapidated domiciles where humans crowd into all available space, including sheds and windowless basements. Extension cords snake down into these dark undercrofts to provide electricity. Separate "rooms" are created by hanging a sheet over a length of twine stretched from one wall to another. This is the Santa Barbara that tourists never see.

The first code in the gang world is loyalty to the gang. The quickest way to earn respect is to hurt a rival gangster or a police officer. Murder is not an abomination; it is a declaration.

Mexican immigrants living in these neighborhoods are most vulnerable to gangs. With an inherent distrust of police officers – corruption in Mexican law enforcement may be among the worst in the world – these innocents are reluctant to report crimes. They are stuck between the old ways of their native country and the puzzling labyrinth of a new one. Their children desperately seek an identity and safety; a gang provides this. But it is a lie. To belong in that world, you must prove yourself through senseless violence. Some of the most cold-blooded crimes I've seen were perpetuated by gang members under the age of eighteen.

When I pull up there are already half-a-dozen Eastsiders with shaved heads standing on the sidewalk, staring me down. I'm able to detect they are Eastside gang members because one of them has "ES" tattooed in four-inch letters on his face. Brag barks at them but they don't budge.

Danny McGrew and Kushner meet me at my trunk as I pull out the harness and long-line. The wanted guy is Francisco Graznido, a gang member who's been on the run for two years, dodging child abuse and sexual assault charges. I've never dealt with the man but he sounds charming. Kushner says they try to drive by the house about once a week to see if he's there but he's been laying low. That is, until today when they surprised Graznido in the front yard and he ducked into the house. But in this case the gang guys were rolling four deep in their plain car and when Graznido fled Officer Gonzalez ran around and got to the back door before Graznido could have escaped. They're certain he's inside. Another gang cop named Cruz was the first SWAT team member through every door for a decade and now he's crouched by the front looking like he's the one who wants to bite somebody.

Graznido isn't going anywhere. His adult sister stands her ground in the front yard, loudly proclaiming that her brother was never there. She threatens to sue each of us and the police department. Since there is no time to explain the Supreme Court-tested doctrine of "hot pursuit," McGrew tells her to get out of the way or go to jail. She chooses the get out of the way option.

I open the rear door of the K-9 car and Brag lifts a front leg so I can slip the harness on and I clip the long line onto it and wrap the nylon flat and smooth one time around my right hand, gripping it about a foot from the harness so Brag is close as we move toward the house. The gang members are tossing obscenities at us and I'm eyeballing them to make sure no one gets close enough to provoke Brag when suddenly a big Chow dog with a dirty orange mane and a head as big as Brag's comes charging out of a neighbor's yard.

The Chow slows to a menacing stalk when he gets close, his eyes locked on Brag, who is glued to my left thigh. Six months ago this would have been a dogfight, but Brag has learned two things since then: he's not here to fight dogs, and if we're in a dogfight we're not hunting people. So Brag stays tight against me doing his best high-speed-reverse obedience as I circle counter-clockwise away from the Chow as it lunges at Brag.

I kick out with my right boot trying to catch the Chow off-guard but he dodges like a boxer slipping a punch. I circle away again and throw another snap kick, harder this time, but the dog slips again. Brag – who has not barked once since this ballet began – stays glued against my left leg as the unfriendly crowd watches us in silence, enjoying the show.

I'm still spinning and kicking and missing. This is absurd. I can feel my face getting hot with embarrassment and I wind up, kicking as hard as I can but this time when I miss the dog I kick the bumper of a parked car and the alarm goes off. This startles the Chow long enough for me to move away and then McGrew is there, dousing the Chow with pepper spray, who finally decides he's had enough and retreats between parked cars. Brag and I hustle through the ubiquitous chain-link gate into Graznido's yard.

Kushner communicates a hundred sarcastic observations of that ridiculous dance to me with a smirk as I collect myself by the front door. It's time to make my announcement.

"Santa Barbara Police Department K-9! You are under arrest! Answer or I will send the dog and you WILL be injured!" Brag barks into the open doorway. There is no response.

"This is your last warning! Come out now or I will send the dog and you WILL BE INJURED!" Brag barks again, translating my message into dog.

No sound. No movement. We wait for ten seconds.

"*Voran,*" I whisper to Brag, which means "go on," his cue to search. He gives a sharp whistle of anticipation as he surges into the front room, straining at the end of the fifteen-foot-line as he sucks in the odors of the residence, sorting them out. Brag and I go from room to room, covered by Cruz and McGrew and Kushner, until we run out of rooms. No Graznido.

I turn to Kushner. "He's not in here."

Kushner doesn't look convinced. "You can search it again," I tell him. They search, poking under beds, but I know there's no way Brag would have missed him. Still no suspect. The gang cops are baffled. It's a duplex; there's an uninvolved neighboring residence that shares a wall and a different entrance, so there are only three exterior walls and only two ways he could have gotten out, through the back door or one of the number four side windows.

"Are you sure he didn't make it over the back fence?" I ask and Gonzalez frowns, offended by the suggestion. I didn't mean to imply he was wrong about how fast he got to the back but suspects don't magically disappear from houses. At least none I've run across. Also, Brag didn't pull me into the backyard, which he would have done if Graznido fled that direction.

The cops debate possible options when Brag suddenly stops panting and cocks his head, looking up at the ceiling. He hears what none of us can: a man crawling above us.

I snap my fingers at the arguing gang cops and point up at the ceiling. Kushner smiles. Cruz goes back to one of the bedroom closets and spies a dark opening up into the attic.

Leaving one cop behind, we knock on the door of the neighboring duplex (with a shared attic space) and when they answer I can see in their eyes that they are afraid to tell us something.

"Pull them out," I tell McGrew. He ushers them out into the street, returning a moment later to tell me they said there should be no one else in the house.

Brag is straining at the harness, barking savagely. He can smell Graznido. I make another announcement and this time Brag pulls me directly to the bathroom door. Locked.

I knock. "Graznido, open the door."

McGrew raises his size-13 boot to kick it in.

"I'm opening it," someone croaks from the bathroom, and I back away as Graznido opens the door with his hands up. He looks exactly like his mugshot, except with spider webs and dust clinging to his head. His body language is so defeated that Brag looks past Graznido as if to say *was there supposed to be someone else more interesting?* Kushner cuffs Graznido and it's over. Gonzalez points up at the bathroom ceiling vent that has been yanked open to expose the shared attic space.

On my way out the gate I pass Graznido's sister, who pouts in the front yard. "Thanks for the help," I offer cheerfully. "Have a nice day."

She glares but has no witty retort.

I put Brag in the K-9 car and praise him lavishly, making sure the gang members standing nearby can hear me: "You got that bad guy, Brag. Good boy." Brag seems disappointed. He doesn't realize that without his dog hearing we would have left without our suspect.

We pull away from the curb and the Eastsiders flash gang signs at me in defiance.

I extend one arm out in a flat wave at them. As I roll away down Liberty Street my waving hand flips over and one middle finger points straight up at the sky. It is a satisfying gesture but it is also a policy violation which could result in disciplinary action. It's worth it.

In law enforcement there are two dueling documents to be found in your watch file. One is a letter of reprimand when you get written up for some transgression of policy or procedure. My letters include several instances of "unauthorized footwear" for wearing ankle-high boots back in the early days of my career when – inexplicably – dress shoes were mandatory patrol footwear. I keep every one of these; they are time capsules of bureaucratic absurdity.

The other document found in a cop's watch file – hopefully, more plentiful – are letters of commendation. These can come from supervisors, other agencies, private citizens, or the Chief of Police. Since Brag and I hit the streets together my commendations have multiplied. Brag and I essentially share one watch file and his presence in that folder has greatly improved it. His enthusiasm for police work is contagious; I no longer dread the beginning of my shift and I feel a renewed sense of pride in catching bad guys because it's mixed with admiration for my partner. Every afternoon as the time grows closer to our leaving the house for work, Brag plants himself at the gate, his backside pressed against it so that the brown and black fur pokes through. I've spied on him from the kitchen as I eat lunch, gazing up at the sky to pass the time. I can tell he's daydreaming of work and I wonder *when did I lose my enthusiasm for the job?* I have it back now because Brag has plenty to spare. When I come out of the garage to get him, he sees me in my black t-shirt and boots and whines with happiness, pawing at the gate until I open it. He sprints to the garage, waiting at the K-9 car for me to let him in. Once we back out of the driveway he flops down onto his elbows contentedly, enjoying the thirty-mile commute to his favorite place: the city he patrols. Over the years I had fallen out of love for that city – too many bad experiences and enemies – but Brag has made me feel differently about it. I see it more the way he does, as a place where we can do what we love to do.

No government agency is tasked with keeping records of police K-9 on-duty deaths. It's unfortunate, because police tactics are improved by examining what went wrong. If Brag were killed because of a mistake I made, I would want other handlers to learn from it. The dedicated people running the Officer Down Memorial Page have taken important steps in compiling and storing data on K-9's. Although the numbers are incomplete – due primarily to the absence of reporting requirements – they are at least helpful. They are also sobering.

In the ten-year period of 2004 to 2014, at least 101 police K-9's died in the line of duty. Two were killed by other animals, two were killed by assault, two were drowned, one died of exposure to toxins, seven died in falls, six in auto accidents, five died due to duty-related illness or injury, fourteen were struck and killed accidentally by vehicles, sixteen died from heat exhaustion, three were stabbed to death, six were killed by intentional vehicular assaults, three died in training accidents, and thirty-four were killed by gunfire.

Each one of these incidents ended tragically. How many could have been prevented with better tactics? Police dogs may be courageous, but they are undeniably mortal.

We celebrate my birthday with a dinner get-together with a dozen friends at a Cajun restaurant in Santa Barbara. Ted is there but Claytor is conspicuously absent, even though he has been back at work for months. Ted pulls me aside and shares bad news: Ignaz died a few hours earlier. Claytor came home and found his partner struggling to stand and rushed him to the emergency vet but it was too late. Intestinal torsion: rare, deadly, and no one's fault. There was no way to save him.

When I see Claytor at his house the next day we throw our arms tightly around each other. No one else understands what it means to work with these determined animals. I keep repeating "I'm so sorry" and it is Claytor who finally steps away and grips my shoulders.

"I'm lucky to have had him as a partner," he says. "I thought he'd retire someday and we'd hang out in the backyard together doing nothing."

We end up talking and laughing about Ignaz, how much he didn't like Ted and how gracefully he moved through training scenarios while Brag lumbered like an ogre. After a while Claytor and I are talked out and smiling with the memories and it's time for me to go. But as I pass the K-9 car in the garage with the name "Ignaz" written on the side, the emptiness of it feels overwhelming.

In police culture, the K-9's are loved and respected. But dogs are not people, so they do not get the same treatment as a fallen officer. I'm determined to not let Ignaz be remembered as a piece of equipment that needs to be replaced.

We hold a K-9 memorial service at the training field and dozens of handlers come with their dogs to show our respect as Claytor and his family say goodbye to Ignaz. Our K-9 unit supervisor invited the Third Floor to join us in honoring this brave police officer, but not one of them takes an hour out of their day to make an appearance.

Claytor drifts in professional limbo for a few weeks, not sure if they intend to let him have another partner. He worked Ignaz for three years. At the SBPD, when you complete your K-9 tour of duty – the working lifetime of the police dog – you rotate out of the unit and back into patrol. This is called "career development" and it is designed to keep cops from stagnating. It also has the effect of keeping any cop from being a true expert in any discipline.

Claytor hunts me down in the station one day and I can tell by his expression that he's rotating out of the K-9 unit. But what he says takes me by surprise.

"I told them I don't want another dog," he says, apologetically.

I'm baffled. "Why?"

"There will never be another Ignaz," Claytor says. He is grieving for his friend. I was selfishly worried more about losing Claytor as a unit partner. It's us against the world most of the time and I didn't want him to go. I'm wrong to feel this way. I feel even worse when he asks me if I'll be okay.

Claytor's heart is broken but he has a career ahead of him. The effort of starting a new dog and training and bonding and certifying and learning each other is an exhausting, years-long process. And Claytor knows by now that being a K-9 handler is bad for your career in that building. Brag and I are on our own again.

I'm reminded today that I don't know the ending to this story Brag and I are living. When I get home later, I stay in the backyard and sit with Brag for a while. I tell him we're the only K-9 team now so we're going to push even harder. He lets me scratch the thick mane on his neck and listens while I talk. When I go quiet, he walks away to mark and sniff.

I sit there, listening to his paws crunch on the ground in the darkness and when I stand up he appears suddenly at my side and escorts me to the gate. He knows we're not going to work and he has no interest in coming into the house; he just wanted to see me out. I can feel him watching me as I go into the house.

A few weeks later I receive a package from Jill, the woman who owned Brag as a puppy and donated him to the police department. It's a book. A note inside says she realized that I never knew Brag as a puppy and she wanted me to have baby pictures of him. I open the book filled with images of Brag and Jill and the little girls hanging out. Barbecuing. At the beach. Brag is a puppy in most of the pics, with big rabbit ears that bump into each other. But I notice young Brag is never captured lounging on his back or being silly. In every picture he guards his family, looking out at the world. Even as a puppy he assumed responsibility for his people, kept himself ready to protect them. Then one day, without explanation, he was taken away.

Now I understand. He had a family he loved. He was wounded by the separation, and he was angry. No one could explain it to him, to make him understand he'd done nothing wrong. It was nobody's fault, and perhaps it was Fate, because he has found purpose as a gifted police dog. This new complexity lets me see the Werewolf through a different lens.

I want to go outside and tell him I understand and I'm glad he's with me now. But I don't.

Brag as a puppy. Already so serious!

(photo courtesy of Jill Vaccaro)

Brag's first day at his new home, wondering where we go from here.

Brag and Officer Terrence, one of his favorite cops.

(photo courtesy of Corina Terrence)

Brag being very serious about his kiddie pool.

PART TWO

THE LIMIT

Sometimes you win in police work by pure luck. Every street cop knows this. There's a liquor store on Haley Street called Howie's Market, a crumbling shack built sometime in the early part of the last century that remains in business to this day because it supplies the neighborhood with booze and cigarettes and lottery scratchers. Also, the occasional box of diapers and jumbo bag of corn chips. It also contains something bad guys want: cash. Most customers pay with cash and because it's a "Mom and Pop" establishment the safe drop protocol tends to be a bit looser so it remains a popular target for armed robbers.

On a cool evening one of those robbers walks into the store and waits for the other customers to leave before leaping the counter and bashing the clerk with the butt of a large knife and demanding all the cash in the drawer.

The stunned clerk complies but takes a bit of a beating for good measure and in less than a minute the suspect is running out the door with the money. The clerk calls 9-1-1 and two of my favorite young cops arrive: Merrett and Epstein. Sounds like a law firm, but these two cops did not miss their calling. Both of them have less than five years on and they are hard-workers who catch a lot of bad guys.

Merrett takes the report while Epstein prowls the area in the patrol car. The suspect description is unique in that the male is older – in his 40's – so Epstein knows he's not looking for a gang member. Merrett has to wait while the shaken clerk calls the owner who walks the clerk through the steps of creating a video file for Merrett, who wants to get a look at the suspect. Merrett knows that important description details are lost when the victim is getting his ass kicked, so getting this video file now would be helpful. This takes far longer than expected, especially since the clerk is also still ringing up potato chips and malt liquor for regular customers so by the time the video file is uploaded onto a thumb drive it's well past the hunting phase of the call. The suspect is long gone. I've been busy on another call this entire time as well, so there was no opportunity to try to track the suspect properly.

Merrett is preparing to leave when the clerk suddenly goes wide-eyed and points at the doorway of the liquor store, where the suspect is standing. Since there have been no cop cars in the area for at least an hour, the suspect has returned for either any cash he missed or to harm the clerk for calling the police in the first place.

There's a split-second of stunned disbelief before the suspect turns tail and sprints down the sidewalk and Merrett hurdles the counter to go out the door after him.

After a brief foot pursuit through darkened yards, Merrett loses the suspect. He wisely goes to the nearest street and puts out his location. I can hear the frustration in his voice that the suspect escaped a second time.

When Brag and I show up, a perimeter is already being established around the block. Merrett paces.

"We're going to catch this guy," I tell him as I harness up Brag and uncoil the long line. Merrett is too busy grinding his teeth to pay much attention to my assurances.

Epstein joins us and he's practically sparking with energy, ready to hunt. He's half-again my size and strength and I've seen him pick adult male suspects up like they weighed nothing.

Brag hops out, his nose in the air already and pulling me as hard as he can through the gate into the tiny yard where Merrett emerged. Brag is ready to hunt right now but he's becoming accustomed to these delays while we humans jabber at each other.

I get on the radio and advise dispatch that we're beginning our search at 311 Cottage Street. My plan is to search yard-to-yard with these two young cops while the perimeter hopefully holds our suspect in place. I want him to hide and sweat.

I turn to Epstein. "Ready?"

A cop shouts in an alleyway nearby; the suspect has popped out of hiding and is running.

With our ears cocked toward our shoulder mics we freeze, trying to get our bearings on which way the suspect is running when suddenly a 40-year-old Hispanic man comes charging around the corner of the house and crashes directly into me, nearly knocking me flat.

The suspect bounces off of me, limbs flailing, and there is a split-second of stunned silence as Merrett draws his gun and Epstein springs forward to make the tackle. But Brag is faster than all of us; he lunges and hits the suspect's upper arm and they both go tumbling into a tangle of shrubbery. Fumbling with the knotted long-line, I straddle Brag and pull him off of the bite as Epstein and Merrett cuff the suspect.

The suspect doesn't make a sound. Brag barks like he's been supercharged, snapping his jaws together like a monster. I pull him back but he breaches in the air, twisting wildly, and then it dawns on me that he is furious about the suspect surprising us and crashing into me. In Brag's mind, it was a sneaky, direct attack on the pack. Never mind that the suspect knew we were there the same time I did: when our heads knocked together.

The suspect goes to the hospital in an ambulance. The cash from the robbery was in his pocket. He hadn't had the time to spend a dollar of it.

I open the back door of the K-9 car and ruffle Brag's mane, thanking him for looking out for me. After we stop by the hospital, we're going to go decompress with a game of Kong ball at the showgrounds – our new after-bite protocol. I'm starting up my engine out in front of the house where the tussle went down when Merrett calls me.

"Guess where the suspect lives," he laughs. "311 Cottage Street. We were standing in his front yard."

Epstein and I knock on the door to 311 Cottage Street and the suspect's wife opens it. She knew he'd been involved in some illegality when he came home with a wad of money. He'd refused to tell her where he'd gotten the cash, so she kicked him out of the house. That was when he left and walked past the scene of the crime again.

Shortest manhunt ever. Sometimes you get lucky.

With Claytor and Ignaz gone, Brag and I are alone and likely to remain so for some time. There is no money for a new K-9 and no money for equipment. As a result, I become a first-class scrounger. Our bite suit is trashed, so I contact a generous lady who offered to buy training supplies for the K-9 unit. I don't ask for permission to put this equipment into service because if I'm told no, it will be returned to a very confused donor who has no use for it.

There is also a hidden danger to being the only police K-9 team: the expectation that Brag and I can handle every call by ourselves. I discover this the hard way, during a SWAT call-out.

Two probation officers park inside a labyrinthine trailer park on the lower Eastside and knock on the flimsy door of a young woman in violation of her probation terms.

But her boyfriend is there. He's a gang member and when he realizes these two officers are about to cart his girlfriend off to jail, he pulls a gun suddenly and sticks it in their faces. The suspect – Johnny Malo – says he's going to shoot both peace officers. The probation officers try their best to calm Malo down but they're both wearing guns which brings an ominous finality to this situation. Luckily, after long minutes of desperate, sweating terror, Malo's girlfriend manages to convince him not to kill the two officers. She and Malo both flee the trailer and the ensuing breathless radio call of a probation officer announcing that he and his partner were just held hostage by an armed man creates a moment of stunned radio silence. SWAT is activated immediately.

I'm at home and not officially on SWAT so it is an hour later before the watch commander calls me in to search for the armed suspect. I'm getting ready to barbecue burgers with my son when I get the call; I abandon the uncooked patties on the grill and rush into the garage with Brag and a ten-word explanation to my wife, Rachel. I've already made a critical tactical error: I parked my K-9 car at the city yards for its scheduled maintenance the day before and left most of my gear inside it. In exchange I have a beat-up, high-mileage, loaner Ford Explorer patrol vehicle with no K-9 equipment in it. I didn't even take the harness or long-line because I was planning on bringing the Explorer back in the morning to get my K-9 car back.

I barrel down Highway 154 toward Santa Barbara, siren wailing. The SUV is such a worn-out piece of junk that I'm barely able to maintain the speed limit anyway. By the time I crawl over the top of the pass and descend into the city, my siren has burned out and now produces a muffled bleating about as loud as a kazoo. It's so embarrassing that I turn it off a mile before I reach the incident scene.

Now I have arrived but I have no equipment, just a gun belt and my vest and flashlight. Luckily, a Santa Barbara Sheriff's Deputy K-9 handler is on-scene at the trailer park, helping hold down the enormous perimeter.

"Do you have a long-line I could borrow?" I ask him.

He pulls an extra one out of his trunk and tosses it to me. "Happy hunting."

I hook the long-line up to Brag's flat collar, which must be terribly confusing to him since we're about to hunt and he's not in his harness. It's also going to be uncomfortable because instead of pulling me with his shoulders he has to pull me with his neck. I'll have to adjust how I work him because if he hits the end of the line hard it's going to feel a lot like a correction.

Rullman has been in a hidden position on the far side of the trailer park, backed into some shrubbery with his rifle. A male matching the description of the suspect approaches in the dark and when Rullman challenges him the man turns around and flees into the darkness.

Brag surges forward, wheezing as he pulls on the long-line and I'm on the radio trying to keep cops from trampling all over the scent and making my job harder. When we finally pinpoint where the suspect was last seen, a half-dozen cops have stomped all over the area. Since Brag does not seem to pick up on one particular odor, we'll have to search trailer-to-trailer. We don't try to go inside them; there are too many. Also, it's not the friendliest of places: drug dealers, drug addicts, gang members and doomsday preppers all live in disharmony here.

We search, a dozen SWAT team members clustered around us as Brag and I work through each tiny yard, sniffing beneath trailers, moving along a seemingly-endless line of the things in darkness. It's a wet, gray night, the kind of weather where you can be hot and sweating and cold at the same time. Danny McGrew is with me, and as SWAT sergeant he coordinates the search with a map to make sure we're checking every mobile home. But there's no way to know if the suspect is sheltered by someone or if he has taken another hostage. Human odor is all over. Brag is confused about having to constantly dismiss the scent of people, but I'm banking on the likelihood that he'll recognize the smell of fear if the suspect is hiding under someone's trailer.

As the hours pass, the search transforms into a blurry half-dream where every trailer and yard looks the same and it seems like there's no end to them. I'm only vaguely aware of time passing. How many have we searched? Fifty? Two hundred? I can't tell. There's no more quiet banter among us. We get a fraction sloppier and less safe with each trailer we search; it's hard to perform the same task perfectly each time. The long-line slides through my palm, then I coil it, then go to another yard and whisper the address to whoever is behind me so they can broadcast it on the radio in case we get in a shooting in a few seconds. Brag waits while I open the gate then goes first past me, his nails clicking on concrete. The long-line slides through my palm, then goes slack as he comes back. I coil it again.

In one cramped yard Brag runs his nose along the fence and doubles back and the long-line tangles up in some weird lawn sculptures. Before I can untangle it, he hits the end of the line and circles back again, getting more entangled and tightening the line. Strangely panicked, he lets out a yelp as I work to free him.

"That was weird," Chad Hunt says. He's spent enough time around Brag to know that yelp was unusual.

"*Voran*," I tell Brag, putting him back in search mode. We continue, but he looks disoriented and uneasy.

In the end, we run out of trailers. No suspect. Over five hours of searching with only one short ten-minute break in the middle to switch out radio and flashlight batteries. It's after 3 a.m. now. Brag hasn't been pulling me at all on the long-line for at least an hour, and when he walks he bobs his head wearily like a horse trudging across a desert in punishing heat. We're done. When we reach our loaner patrol Explorer, I have to coax him to jump up into it.

A police administrator in charge of the incident who has been hanging out at the warm and dry command post drinking coffee and eating orange-ginger muffins comes over to question me about the search. I mumble about how the suspect probably has a friendly in the area who is harboring him. It reminds me of the post-game interviews where some irritating reporter asks the player on the losing team, "What happened tonight?" We lost. The suspect got away.

While I'm talking, I look in at Brag, who is standing in the back of the Explorer with his eyes half-closed and falling over in extreme slow-motion. He catches himself with a start and forces his eyes open again and I realize that he is exhausted. During that entire search he was concentrating at his highest level because he didn't know how big the trailer park was and how long we were going to be searching. There was no way for him to know. He expected it to end with a fight any second. It would be like asking a friend to join you for a short run and then making them finish a marathon.

I end the pointless conversation and shut the door, feeling horrible. Now I understand why Brag yelped: he was so fatigued that when he got tangled up he thought he was being corrected and didn't know what to do to avoid it. Five hours of searching – that's far too long. Once we're alone in the Explorer I turn around and put my hand on Brag, who has collapsed onto his side behind me.

"I'm sorry, Brag" I tell him. "I wanted us to catch that guy."

I don't know what else to say. Brag closes his eyes while I leave my hand against his powerful shoulder, feeling his muscles underneath, his ribs rising and falling.

"Will you forgive me?"

He lets out the biggest sigh I've ever heard.

A gut punch of guilt hits me. I'm a horrible handler because I worked my dog too hard. I should have had the Sheriff's Department K-9 replace us halfway through but I wanted Brag and I to be the team that caught the suspect. I wanted to force the Third Floor to recognize Brag's value. I wanted the win at any cost. I'm so upset with myself that I don't try to find the SWAT team leaders and ask about a debrief. For the first time in my career, I avoid it. I'm ashamed of the way I ran my partner into the ground like that.

As I'm driving home McGrew calls and I let the phone go to voicemail. I listen to the message and he thanks us for coming in and working so hard to keep the SWAT Team safe. McGrew's such a good cop and leader and he means every word and I just feel worse.

At home I feed Brag a special dinner in his kennel and sit down on the wood chips outside the open door while he eats. He's famished, but he pauses halfway through his meal and looks at me as if to say *is there something wrong?*

Yes, there is something wrong. This dog will never complain. I have to remember this. He has more drive than I've ever seen in a police dog but he is not immortal. He is flesh and bone and fur and he will never quit, so it's up to me to look out for him. At the end of that search Brag was in no condition to fight with a suspect. I won't fail him like that again.

When Brag's done eating, he staggers out into the darkness and comes back with his Kong ball. He won't go into his dog house as long as I'm sitting out here; he doesn't want to miss anything.

I'm so spent I could easily curl up in the kennel beside him and fall asleep, cold and filthy in my boots, and a part of me wants to do just that. But I don't. I put my hand on his massive head before trudging toward the house. Brag lets me walk alone to the gate.

As I pass the barbecue, I can feel the warmth of the coals. I realize that I don't even know if my son got to eat a burger that night. He's asleep now and I'll be back working my shifts for the next four nights so I won't see him until next week.

Feeling morose, I go into Strieker's room and stand there for a long time watching him sleep. He's six years old. He doesn't understand guns or evil or how people can fail those closest to them without ever meaning to.

When I go to bed, I'm relieved that it's after 3:37 a.m. so I won't wake up again until well after the sun is up. When I do get up, I'll eat breakfast alone with pictures of my family hanging on the walls. Brag will be awake, too, waiting outside at the gate to go back to work.

WET DOG

There is a saying in the K-9 business: a man believes nothing until he sees it, a dog believes nothing until he smells it. Until a police dog experiences something, he does not know what it is. You cannot explain to a dog how an escalator operates, then take him into a department store and point and say, "See, exactly as I described it." That doesn't work. You must show the dog. This is how police dogs fail in real-life scenarios; there is some element that they've never experienced and it completely screws with their process. If we train a dog to chase down and bite running suspects but never train that dog to bite a suspect who is lying perfectly still, there is a good chance the dog will not bite in that latter instance. We would have failed as trainers and handlers. Remember the first rule: It's Always Your Fault.

Many people ask me, "Why would you want a police dog to bite someone who is holding perfectly still?" The answer is simple: if that person is armed he is equally dangerous if he is moving or not moving.

Imagine a suspect is hiding in a dark warehouse, partially hidden. He is perfectly still and only his lower legs are visible and accessible. If Brag has not trained on passive suspects, especially partially-concealed ones, there is a strong chance he will dismiss this person as non-threatening and move on. That is the last thing I want Brag to do. The suspect is armed and dangerous. I want my dog to bite him, to hold onto him, to alert us, to diminish the suspect's ability to escape or harm a police officer or anyone else.

This is why we must train in passive suspects. This is also why we must train on escalators, in crawlspaces, buses, airplanes, outhouses, attics, warehouses, grocery stores, machine shops, and chicken coops. Dogs are not intellectual, they are experiential. Every potential setting for a police dog deployment must be experienced by the dog before you ask him to do his job in that environment. This is the challenge of police dog training.

Ted puts on the bite suit and crawls beneath a car. We cover his ankle and foot with sandbags, leaving only his lower leg in the bite suit exposed. The dogs go one at a time, and each one bites his lower leg savagely. Ted comes to life, screaming and thrashing and the handler rushes in, praising the dog. These are rewards for the dog: bite the passive suspect and he will shriek and struggle and your handler will be proud of you and you will win the fight. This matters to police dogs. They want to win.

Brag hits Ted like a truck, dragging the man out from beneath the car. Ted is an accomplished amateur actor; his screams are so realistic that we've had people near to our training sites call 9-1-1 to report someone screaming in the area.

With training scenarios where dogs are hunting and biting, even with the best safety equipment and careful observation of safety protocol, there is always the likelihood of a decoy getting bitten where there is no protection. The more realistic the training, the greater the possibility that this will occur. The problem with a real bite is that it will always be painful, sometimes to the point where the agitator can hardly speak. Screaming isn't helpful; the handler will assume the decoy is an excellent role-player. The code phrase to end this scenario-gone-bad is "real bite." Saying it as calmly as possible is best; trying to pull free from the bite is not recommended. As much as I hate to admit it, it's often a humorous moment when the decoy suddenly blurts out, "REAL BITE!" and the handler rushes in and the dog's eyes roll around as he realizes the bite feels different. The best dogs won't let go until they're told to by their handlers.

On this particular training day, we are shooting a short video clip for a local news station doing feel-good piece about the police dogs. Ted sits in the full bite suit behind the wheel of a car and I send Brag who leaps up and bites Ted high – a little close to the neck for my comfort – but Ted is dragged out of the car and I stroll up and take Brag off of the bite. Ted gets up stiffly. The cameraman and reporter smile and thank us for that last video clip and as they're packing up, I see that Ted has a strange look on his face.

"You okay?" I ask him.

"Real bite," he says, about five minutes too late.

He twists in the bite suit to reveal that Brag went in partially between the torso and the arm padding, leaving some hideous punctures where the teeth dug in to his shoulder. Ted kept quiet because he didn't want to ruin the video. He's done working dogs for the day. At coffee later I buy him a muffin as an apology and he holds it against his shoulder as if it would ease the pain. A sense of humor is required to train police dogs for a living.

It doesn't rain here, unless it's pouring. Sometimes the wet season at this edge of California never arrives, sometimes we get a year's worth of the stuff in a matter of days. Does crime slow down because of the nasty weather? No, it does not.

It's dumping rain. A man stabs his ex-girlfriend downtown and flees from the police back toward his house. Brag and I take up a position on the rear corner of the house. We're standing in the rain because you don't choose a position based on good dryness, you choose a position based on good tactics. We wait. More cops arrive. Someone asks for a negotiator. They want to try to talk the suspect out. It's a good idea, but it's going to take a while.

Brag and I stand in the downpour. It doesn't matter how good your rain gear is; after a few hours in such weather, you are soaked. Brag, who at all times behaves with complete indifference to all weather, stands at my left knee. He's soaked, too. We're both watching the darkened windows, listening to the rain clattering on the roof, the gurgle of the waterfalls running off of corners.

An hour passes. The negotiator has been trying to get through to the suspect. The rain keeps falling. Water is streaming off of the barrel of Venable's handgun. He's our cover, and he and I stopped whispering sarcastic observations to each other at least thirty minutes ago. Now it's just a silent festival of discomfort.

Brag knows we're waiting to go in and search a house. He might have already caught the suspect's odor from the foot chase earlier. When we're stuck somewhere for this long I let him sit, stand, or lie down if he wants. But he isn't going to lie down anytime soon because we're all standing in two inches of muddy water.

I would never have waited this long if it was my call but Danny McGrew is on scene and I trust him to make the best tactical decision.

Another hour crawls by. Finally, Brag has had enough. He steps away and looks up at me with the most exasperated expression that a dog's face can generate. It communicates one thought, loud and clear: *what the hell are we doing?*

I try not to laugh as I reach down and pat him, sending a cascade of water out of his soaked double coat. He sighs and plops his backside down in the standing water.

McGrew calls us to the front door and we search the house, leaving the muddiest paw prints all over the place. The suspect is gone. He ran out the back door before cops could lock the place down. Another miss.

I put Brag in our car and it's end of watch so we're done for the night. The entire commute is occupied with me blasting the defroster to keep the windows from fogging into total opacity as two large, sopping wet mammals breathe and steam in the car. To say it smells like wet dog in the car is an understatement. The air *tastes* like wet dog.

At home I rub Brag down with a pair of beach towels, which he endures for the sake of our professional relationship.

By the time I'm done he looks like he's been blow-dried and I'm laughing at him which he finds irritating. He just wants his dinner. I mix hot water into it to warm him up. I like to imagine that he appreciates this, but I can't say for sure that he cares.

The next day, it is still raining just as hard. Crime continues, despite the downpour. Two cops are sent on a burglary in progress and I roll on that call as well and before I can arrive the cops are in foot pursuit, splashing down alleyways and jumping wet fences. They lose the burglar and stop, which I love because that means I might be able to trail the suspect.

There is a lot of discussion in police dog circles about tracking versus trailing. The majority of experts in this field agree that what most people call "tracking" is actually "trailing." In other words, when I bring Brag to the scene of a crime and he follows a particular person's odor that has been left behind or eddying about, that is trailing. If I show up on a call without Brag and I follow the suspect's footprints across a muddy field, that is tracking. Dogs don't seem to rely on tracking much, especially the visual cues. They certainly smell the crushed grass, the broken twigs, but I'd be pretty surprised if they ever noticed a footprint and thought *that's the human I'm looking for.* Dogs work in a visual fog when they're hunting, which is why it's imperative for the handler to keep his eyes open.

Human odor is a complicated casserole of scent. Skin is the largest organ in the human body, averaging about twenty-five square feet. We shed two million skin cells per hour. Each of these skin cells carries glandular secretions, bacteria, dietary and environment odors, and tertiary odors such as soap and lotion. These are just a few of the ways a dog can separate one human scent from another, and dogs are still better at scent discrimination than any machine. This may change as technology improves, but I doubt the machine someday beats a dog at odor discrimination will also be hurling itself over fences to chase bad guys. Until then, dogs rule this world of man hunting.

I used to laugh off the idea that dogs can smell fear. Not anymore. Whether it's adrenaline or some other stress secretion, dogs can smell it. That doesn't mean that if you're uneasy about a dog approaching you must think happy thoughts or you'll get bitten. Their world is entirely constructed of odor, so one scent is not necessarily going to elicit a response. I think it much more likely that Brag would find the tuna sandwich you ate for lunch more interesting than any fear scent emanating from you. Unless you're a suspect.

But now it's pouring and I've got the windshield wipers slapping back and forth on the highest setting and Brag and I are driving to the corner where the cops lost the burglary suspect they were chasing.

One of the officers waves me down at an intersection and I get out of the car.

"Can Brag hunt in the rain?" she asks, looking down at the water sheeting across the street.

"Not sure," I admit. "But we'll give it a try."

It's more of a downpour than a rain, but Rule Number Two is Never Say No.

The long-line and harness are still wet from the night before. Brag is so eager to hunt that he practically puts the harness on himself.

I have Mike Little with me as cover officer. He's perfect for this moment because he is indifferent to getting soaked in the rain if it means doing a good job.

I let the long-line slide through my hand until Brag is straining at the end of it, ranging back and forth about sixty degrees in either direction. Perfect. All I know is the suspect was last seen running into this intersection and no one saw which way he went from there.

Brag's nose is down, then up, then down again and he snorts water out of it and pulls hard, like a big fish hitting a lure.

We're off. He's definitely following a trail. He pulls me into a back yard and his head comes up as he runs a high wooden fence. His movement is jerky, faster, which means he's getting a lot of odor which means we're getting close. I hear movement on the other side of the fence and the suspect is up and running. Brag tries to mirror him but we've reached a pile of junk we can't go over and I put out that the suspect is running.

Another foot chase ensues as the suspect pops out and comes face to face with the perimeter units. I don't put Brag over the fence because we're going around instead. He's incensed; he's had a few misses lately and I can tell he does not want to let this one get away.

The suspect has vanished again. We move the perimeter to contain him. Little is patient, and asks me no questions when we go to where the suspect was last seen and restart our search.

Brag leads us in and out of yards, sometimes losing the scent then picking it up again. I let him work, keeping an eye out for random people to pop out in front of us; the specter of the accidental bite is always along for the hunt. We reach an alleyway and come face to face with a perimeter unit. The cop, Gary Gaston, has set his car up with the ambers flashing and the spotlights shining two different directions to try to keep the suspect in hiding. It's raining hard and I wouldn't blame Gaston for sitting in his car while this search drags on but he is out in the weather, standing in a puddle and doing his job even though it is dark and no one would know the difference. It's one of those moments where I realize what kind of people I get to work with.

Brag suddenly makes a hard turn down a driveway and we're headed back to where we were five minutes ago, but he's moving faster again, nose up and his eyes burning with determination and when we get stuck in a narrow, dead-end walkway we have to double back and Brag snaps his jaws at the air in front of Little, as if he were telling Mike to get the hell out of the way.

We push through a gate into a backyard and Brag is wheezing as he drives forward like a sled dog. Suddenly he plunges underneath a deck toward a blue tarp covering some old toys.

Brag bites the tarp as if it were his mortal enemy and though I can't discern any reason why he should be biting a tarp I pull back on the long-line and as Brag pulls the tarp out with his teeth it suddenly takes on the shape of a man. A muffled shrieking emanates from inside the tarp and I straddle Brag and take him off the bite while Little takes the suspect into custody. It's our suspect, exhausted from running, bleeding from the bite, and finished fighting. Brag stands erect, his tail stiff and wagging as he barks at the suspect who lies prostrate in the mud before him.

I let Brag bark for a minute before taking him out of the yard – it feels like he is telling off the suspect in dog speech and I think both of them deserve this moment.

I don't hate the suspect. I don't dislike him. I'm not sure why he's doing burglaries and it doesn't matter. That's the weird thing about police work in general and my job in particular; I rarely learn the suspect's story. My job was to catch him. That's it. There's always another call waiting.

The officers that started the foot pursuit thank Brag as we pass them on their way in to collect their burglar. Brag looks relaxed as the windows fog up on our way to the showgrounds. It's time for a wet game of Kong ball.

Now I know. The next time a cop asks me if we can trail a suspect in a downpour, I will say "yes." Brag already knew this. I'm still catching up.

We get to the showgrounds and I open the back door and Brag sticks his head out, scanning the dark grass. Instead of letting him out, I rough up his soaked mane. He doesn't smile, but he doesn't seem to mind it, either. We're partners, and it feels like he's happy with that. I am, too.

A MAN RUNS

There's a crow staring at me. He's on the telephone wire across the street, watching as I sweep my walkway. He's all black but I can see the glitter of his eyes. I meet his gaze and he shifts uncomfortably, ready to fly off; he knows people are unpredictable. For reasons lost to history, crows are maligned.

"I know how you feel," I say to him, and he swivels his head to one side to study the human being that has addressed him, likely for the first time in his life. To me, he looks more curious than ominous.

The longer I work with Brag, the less I see him the way I used to see a dog. He doesn't feel like a dog at all, more like some creature that possesses entirely unique behaviors and motivations; a werewolf, I suppose. I trust him, some of the time. When I release him to do his job and I've done my job to try to limit the number of possible outcomes (biting another police officer, biting an innocent civilian, biting anyone he's not supposed to bite, whether they are innocent or not), I'm confident he won't fail. His courage and work ethic are never in question. He excels on the street, on the training field, and during re-certifications. He may not wag his tail and lick my face like the other police dogs, but I'd still take him over all of them.

When I park my K-9 car somewhere public during our shift, I get uneasy if I'm more than a block away from him. Especially if I know there are idiots in the area, like on the lower Eastside, the Westside, or downtown. It's like I can sense he's too far away and it feels wrong. Since the back windows are always open during darkness to give Brag fresh air, he is exposed to whatever is out there. There's a metal cage to contain and protect him from hard objects (not bullets), but I've returned from calls to find liquid splashed all over the back of the K-9 car – usually a soft drink since booze is precious to these people – and many times I've come back to my car parked downtown to find the rear cage glistening with spittle from someone spitting on Brag. This doesn't discourage him from barking and only serves to incense him further, but it always makes my heart sink to picture someone standing there spitting on a dog. This is why I don't like to let Brag out of my sight. I have to keep the doors locked all the time as well, or at some point I'm sure someone would walk up and try the rear door, releasing the K-9. Little do they know that one of two things would happen: Brag would either run right past to find me or he would bite the crap out of that person. Either scenario is unacceptable. Also, I would likely be found at fault for that occurrence, no matter how foolish it is to approach a police K-9 car and open the door while the dog is barking furiously inside it.

Any time I let Brag go off-leash to do his job it is unnerving. Many police dogs are killed by cars, the most common danger found on the street. Even if Brag manages to avoid this, there is the suspect himself, a large, unpredictable animal that may be armed. Dogs don't understand the danger of guns. If I send my partner to bite someone and that person suddenly draws a gun, Brag will not abandon the bite and run in a serpentine pattern back to me to avoid getting shot. He will charge into the gunfire. There are videos on the internet of police dogs being shot to death by suspects. Some of these moments are a complete surprise and sometimes you see what's about to happen before it happens. Every one of them is gut-wrenchingly awful.

Since there is no way to deploy a police dog in perfect safety (except to not use him at all) I try to stack the deck in Brag's favor. Timing the release to send him when the suspect is facing away, sending Brag under cover of darkness, or otherwise disabling or distracting the suspect are the small advantages I'm always looking for. Brag is action; he does not hesitate. He won't bark when he's supposed to bite, a delay that could be deadly for him. And once he gets his teeth on somebody, he bites with all he's got. This alone is a surprisingly difficult thing to counter. I know; I've been bitten on a couple of occasions by other dogs during training and it is always shockingly painful. Brag's head is about half again as large as most other police dogs so I know the compression he generates must be remarkable.

When my face is near to Brag's face I look past those enormous canines into his maw and feel lucky that I'm the least likely person to be bitten by him. I think.

"Fifty-five to all units: a man with a gun on Islay Street. Numerous 9-1-1 calls. Woman screaming in the background. Black handgun."

The details trickle in because the dispatchers put out the incident immediately – common procedure for calls of a man with a gun. "Suspect is Ben Reck, twenty-three-year-old male, six-two, one-ninety." I take the next off-ramp too fast and my tires squeal.

"Suspect is wearing shorts and a basketball jersey. He has fled the scene with the gun."

I slow down, letting the Extrapolometer work in my head as dispatch adds a critical detail: "The suspect lives at nineteen-hundred Chapala Street."

I turn north away from the call. The suspect is on foot. He might go to a friend's house or he might go home. I'm banking on home. The Extrapolometer tells me that he has three options to get to his house on the other side of the freeway: two under crossings and a footbridge. I pick the northernmost undercrossing, at Mission Street. Brag leans into the turn and we go that way, passing two other police cars heading with their sirens on toward the incident location on Islay Street. There's no reason for me to go there. I want to be where the suspect is.

It's after midnight so there's not a lot of people on the street. I'm looking for movement, for silhouettes on dark sidewalks. Brag is looking, too, and he doesn't know who he's looking for. As I turn onto Mission and head toward the undercrossing, I descend under the freeway and see a man in a basketball jersey running on the sidewalk away from me.

I gun it and hit him with the spotlight. The running man hears my engine and glances once back toward me and kicks it into high gear. It's him. I'm on the P.A., telling Reck to stop, to get on the ground. He keeps running and before I pull alongside him he suddenly turns and runs up through the shrubbery on the slope on the far side of the freeway, disappearing into shadow. I don't see a gun.

Without looking behind me, I know Brag has eyes on him. I brake hard to a stop right next to where he disappeared and hit the door pop button.

"*Packen, packen!*" I tell Brag as the door flies open and he fires out of the car and vanishes up the dirt trail into the darkness. I just sent my dog after a man with a gun who is running toward the freeway. If Reck turns right he will be on the US 101 highway, a very busy thoroughfare at all hours of the night. If he goes straight he's got a mile of homeless trails winding through thick vegetation between the creek and the freeway.

I'm out of the car and onto the sidewalk, suddenly alone. It's that moment, that quiet separation. I don't know where Brag is. I don't know if he's about to be shot. I don't know if he's going to get hit by a car.

As I start up the steep hillside, I hear a man screaming. It's Reck, shrieking in the darkness somewhere. Brag has him.

"GOOD BOY!" I shout, scrambling up the dusty trail on all fours. But there's no need to go any farther, because Brag is bringing Reck to me.

They appear in a surreal cloud of flashlight-beam-illuminated dust. Brag is dragging the man by the lower leg, thrashing his head like a shark, digging his paws into the dusty earth. I retreat backwards toward the sidewalk below me, one hand grasping at the shrubbery as I try to aim my handgun past Brag at Reck and order him to show me his hands.

Reck doesn't hear me. He's in his own world of pain, eyes bulging with fear and fixed on the furious creature that drags him down the loose earth to the sidewalk.

Once there, Reck suddenly recognizes that there is another human present and his screams become pleas for help. I can see he has lost the gun and I holster my own firearm as a solitary car stops at the red light on Mission Street directly behind me, the driver gawking at the spectacle of a cop standing over a screaming man while a huge dog savages the man's leg.

I straddle Brag and take him off of the bite and once Brag has let go, he unleashes the paralyzing wall of sound into Reck's face. I warn Reck to keep his hands where I can see them but again there is no need; he wants no part of this dog anymore. The light turns green behind me and the solitary driver pulls away as a police unit zooms up and skids to a stop.

My cover officer jumps out and cuffs Reck, who is dusted in a fine powder that clings to his sweaty body like sugar on a cookie. Blood from the deep punctures in Reck's calf mixes thickly with the dirt.

I put Brag away. In minutes the ambulance arrives to take Reck to the hospital. The man is subdued, a completely different creature from the one that was terrorizing people a few minutes earlier.

I've learned from legal experts that it's a good idea to interview suspects immediately after a bite, not for the criminal case but for our own legal protection. The officers who are taking the report and doing the arrest can work at obtaining a confession from the suspect. That's not my concern at this point. Since my dog has sent this man to the hospital, I need to make sure this incident doesn't get twisted. In short, I need to act as Brag's attorney.

After praising Brag effusively, I drive to the hospital emergency room. Nine times out of ten, the paramedics are returning their equipment to their rig in the ambulance bay when I arrive and I quiz them about the bite. They always enjoy sharing the suspects' complaints about it.

Inside the emergency department – always bustling – I find the attending physician and ask if I can speak to the man with the dog bite. The doc tells me to have at it. I ask him if the bite is "life-threatening" and he laughs and says no. Outside of Reck's room I pause and prepare for my next performance. Pulling on a black SBPD baseball cap, I stroll into the room as if I'd never seen Reck before. Ten times out of ten when I pull this stunt, the suspect has no idea who I am.

"Hey, bud, how are you doing?" I ask cheerfully.

Reck gives me a guarded shrug. He's handcuffed to the bed so I don't try to shake hands.

"I'm investigating this incident. I understand you had a run-in with a police dog tonight."

Another shrug. He's playing tough. Perfect.

"Did the dog bite you?" I ask him, my face wearing an expression of wonder.

Reck looks down at the bleeding punctures in his calf. Now he's wondering what I'm getting at and why I'm downplaying the whole incident. He tried to kidnap his girlfriend at gunpoint and beat the crap out of her father with a handgun, and here I am acting like we're chatting at a bus stop.

"That looks like it hurts."

I examine the bite as if I'd never seen one before. But it's exactly what I want: four good punctures, which means Brag bit once and held on for all he was worth. Good boy.

"Out of curiosity, why didn't you just stop?" I ask. "You heard the dog, right?"

"I heard him."

"Didn't the cops tell you to stop?"

"One cop. He told me."

He has no clue that I was that cop. I shake my head in wonder, marveling at his courage. "You're crazier than I am."

Reck looks away. He's not interested in me or my opinion.

"So, you heard the warning and you thought you could outrun the dog."

He shrugs. I'm done. I turn around to leave, and Reck can clearly see "K-9" embroidered on the back of my cap. He stares at my hat, gears turning in his head. He'll sort it out in a minute.

The whole conversation is recorded and becomes part of my report. It's also outside of Miranda, which means none of it would be admissible against Reck in a criminal proceeding. But all of it could be used for rebuttal if he sues for an unwarranted bite resulting in mental anguish that affects his ability to earn a living working for a think tank. It's a game invented by attorneys, but I'll play along. I'll do whatever it takes to keep Brag and I ahead of all of them.

SMELLS

Cats. K-9 handlers don't like to talk about them, mainly because they can transform our highly-trained canine partners into wild-eyed hyenas in an instant. Every handler has a story of sneaking down an alley with their dog to arrest someone, only to have a cat streak out of hiding a few feet in front of the dog and leave a chaotic scene of barking and broken obedience behind.

Ignaz was a famous hater of cats. It was his belief that they should all be destroyed immediately. I'm the luckiest handler on the planet, because Brag can't be bothered to chase a cat. He's aware of them, he just doesn't care if they live or die. He does, however, object to their sneaky behavior, and shoos them away in the most effective way. Since cops are always looking for a quiet place to type out a report where it would be hard to surprise us in the dark (since we're staring at a computer screen), abandoned parking lots usually fit the bill. I have two lots that are my favorites. Both of them are always empty at night. But cats – nighttime sneakers – find this solitary car with a glowing interior light and murmuring police radio irresistible. A cat will often come into the lot to investigate, sometimes circling at a distance, a tactical approach. After watching for a few minutes, curiosity usually gets the better of the cat and she saunters closer to get a better look. Somehow – even if he is fast asleep behind me – Brag always knows the cat is out there. Maybe he smells her, or hears her quiet footsteps, but every time he rises to his feet behind me, peering out of the cage to locate the interloper. If that cat is within view, Brag will bark. But it's not the bark he uses for people or other dogs. It is the dog equivalent of bellowing "GET OUT OF HERE, CAT!" and it is hilarious. A mashup of canine vowels with no consonants. The instant that cat gets blasted with that sound she wants nothing more to do with either of us and disappears.

This brief interaction ends with what I have termed the Snort of Utter Contempt. Brag completes his wordless challenge to the cat and when the cat runs off, he stares for a moment and SNORTS once, as if he is expelling the odor of that irritating animal from his nostrils. It's the most dismissive sound in the world.

On many occasions, when I get out of my car without Brag on a late-night call and pad quietly toward the address, usually stopping a short distance away to observe the surroundings, I am investigated by a cat. Cats find cop behavior fascinating, perhaps because it resembles cat behavior: walk, stop, look around, walk, stop, listen.

An orange cat with an inquisitive expression sits on a low wall when I arrive for a call of a man yelling in the dark at an apartment complex. This is a "415" call, which means it falls under the catch-all CA Penal Code section 415: disturbing the peace. In reality it means "we don't know what this call is but someone is screaming so you'd better go check it out." It's the call where many cops get injured because it's so commonplace: someone hears yelling and stuff breaking so they call 9-1-1. When you arrive you have no idea what's happening. If you rush into it, you might regret your hastiness. Which is why I take it slow, listening and keeping in the shadows. It doesn't cost anything or take much more time than marching around shining my flashlight all over the place, and it's a hell of a lot harder to ambush me. The darkness is your friend. By the way, so are cats.

As I move quietly down the sidewalk the orange cat follows me, mirroring my steps. He stops when I stop. He knows the game is afoot, he's just not sure what it is. When I meet with the primary officer on the call, Morton, he grins at my feline companion.

"Did you trade Brag in for a cat?"

I nod. "It would be a lot quieter."

The cat continues to shadow us as we locate the apartment and knock on the door. The man inside is throwing a temper tantrum but he's not doing anything illegal so I ask him to close his windows and try to keep the shouting to a minimum. He demands to know my badge number, threatening to have my job for knocking on his door at this late hour. I point out – as I have a hundred times – that my badge number is printed on my badge. When he asks to borrow my pen to write it down, I refuse politely and Morton and I leave, rolling our eyes in unison.

The cat is waiting for us and follows me back to my car, wanting to see more late-night prowling. But Brag has been watching.

As I pull out my keys at the car door, Brag bellows "GET OUT OF HERE, CAT!" and the cat shoots away like an orange rocket. I get into the driver's seat, shaking my head.

"You enjoy that, don't you?"

Brag snorts at the vanished cat and pretends he doesn't hear me.

Cats may represent a frustrating distraction to K-9 handlers, but they do not bring the promise of a ruined evening like a skunk. Skunks emerge from their lairs at night when only cops and crooks and delivery truck drivers are awake, so most people never see them. They make no sound, they don't run away when confronted, and they will drench your dog with their foulness at the slightest provocation. Unfortunately, they also love the grassy field at the showgrounds where I take Brag late at night to exercise.

One cool night while throwing the Kong ball and letting Brag trot around and mark his spots, I notice that Brag has his ears up as he approaches some dark object on the grass. From where I am it looks like a black trash bag but suddenly a fuzzy, white-striped tail shoots straight up when Brag gets within about ten feet. Before I can shout a warning, Brag puts on the brakes and shakes his head. The skunk ambles away as Brag slides his face on the grass, trying to wipe something off. The smell hits me and I know he's been sprayed. He trots back toward me, licking his lips with displeasure as I curse my fate and all skunks in general. I try to wipe him down but the stuff is invisible and has penetrated Brag's double coat.

When we both get in the K-9 car the smell is overpowering, nauseating. After a couple of hours of driving around with all the windows down, the reek diminishes and I don't feel sick to my stomach anymore. I'm sent to help another officer take someone with an arrest warrant into custody at the hospital emergency room and when I walk past the nurses' station a nurse says, "Wow, there must be a *big* skunk out there." The other nurses agree and one of them wonders aloud if the skunk has come into the emergency department. I don't say a word. When I meet with the arresting officer and go into the examination room to put handcuffs on the wanted subject who has been medically cleared by the doctor, the arrestee screws up his face and asks, "Who got skunked?"

"Neither of us," I respond.

The arrestee snorts. "Well, one of you STINKS!"

Months later I take Brag in for a shampoo and blow-out at the only dog grooming place in Santa Barbara that can handle him. The owner, despite being covered in biker tattoos, is as patient as a pre-school teacher with the dogs that come through his door. Josh has also known Brag since he was a puppy and is the only person other than me who is able to wash Brag without risking life and limb. It's always dicey because of the other dogs around; Brag disapproves of all of them. His reactions to a dog that gets too close varies from an alpha stare-down to a chain-rattling display worthy of King Kong on a Broadway stage.

"Oh, Brag," Josh says when Brag snarls at a goofy Lab getting a bath. "That's enough."

Brag tolerates the washing but vocalizes his objections to the blower. A swirling cloud of amber fur swirls around the room, dusting all surfaces with Brag's fine undercoat. Josh sniffs Brag's head.

"Skunk," is all he says.

Odors define my world now. A car passes me on the road and I can smell the driver's cologne. After a call I'm chatting with an officer in the dark on the sidewalk and I am suddenly, acutely aware of the scent of another human being nearby. A moment later a man who had been standing in the dark thirty feet away steps out onto the sidewalk. It wasn't anything specific, just the smell of a person.

This is not accelerated evolution. My sense of smell has not improved, I just don't ignore it any longer. I live in a world of odor now. The movement of the air and the scents it carries are everything to Brag and therefore equally important to me. I used to place odor into two categories: good smells and bad smells. Dogs don't do that. They embrace the entire scent world without prejudice. The smell of a broiling steak is attractive, but I've seen more than one dog roll over the rotting carcass of a dead animal. I have no idea why. But it serves to show how differently dogs process the myriad scents that define their world.

I embrace this new super power granted to me by Brag. It really is nothing more than awareness, but in law enforcement that means survival. As the saying goes: hunt smarter, not harder.

I show up for briefing at the beginning of our week and bring Brag in so he can play tug-of-war with his favorite cops on that watch. There's always at least one or two of them in briefing that will play tug-of-war with Brag and he shoves the tug into their chests if they ignore him, practically forcing them to grab it and fight. After allowing a few minutes of growling and whipping his head back and forth, I'll take the tug away from Brag and put him on a down in the back corner of the room. He used to watch me the entire briefing but now he lays flat on his side, legs pushed straight out, and content as can be.

The watch sergeant informs us that the night before a wanted parolee stabbed another man in a city park. When the first cop arrived on scene, the suspect brandished the knife and fled into the densely wooded area on the other side of the creek bed that runs for half-a-mile down one side of the park, shouting "You're going to have to kill me!" It was dark and the cop was alone, so he didn't go after the suspect. Smart. The cop is a former K-9 handler as well, so he knew how bad his hunting odds were at that moment and decided not to pursue on foot.

There's also another factor in play in this scenario, and in a lot of scenarios like it. California has a native plant that grows in abundance in shady creek beds: poison oak. It can cover a hillside and grow in dense stands up to ten feet high. It's characterized by clusters of three oily leaves that turn red in the fall. If you're allergic to poison oak, and most humans are, contact with the waxy leaves or sap causes oozing blisters and horrendous itching that lasts for weeks. The oil is invisible and designed to stick, so it's difficult to wash off. The rash keeps you up at night and spreads when you scratch. Firefighters sometimes suffer life-threatening respiratory reactions after breathing the oils in smoke from wildfires. I waded into muddy floodwaters up to my chest once to look for stranded people in drowned houses and within two days I was blistering underneath my Kevlar vest. The poison oak leaves and oils washed down from the hillsides were mixed in the floodwater. Since everything below my chest was underwater, the horrible condition extended down below the gun belt as well. Suffering ensued.

Searching this wooded area is not a good option, especially since a day has passed and the suspect has likely left the area. But Kushner calls me after briefing and says the suspect was spotted an hour ago in the park, headed back up into the poison oak. Kushner wants to search for the suspect and asks me how I'd like to do it.

I remember Jim Corbett's hunting stories about using groups of people making noise to flush out tigers hiding in heavy brush, and I suggest that tactic to Kushner. He likes the idea. He and the other gang unit cops will make a big show of arriving at one end of the park, then walk slowly toward the creek area. I will park out of view at the other end and approach with Brag up the creek bed. It's an ambush that a man-eating tiger would appreciate. But I know something a tiger doesn't know: the man we are hunting will never smell us coming.

I put Brag in his harness and when Kushner and his partners arrive, Brag and I creep unseen up the mostly-dry creek bed toward them.

Kushner comes over the radio: "We just spotted the suspect moving in your direction."

Brag trots in front of me, not sure what is happening exactly except that he knows we're hunting someone because I'm moving in a crouch. Then the wind shifts and the scent of the suspect hits Brag in the face and his entire body changes; he raises his muzzle and surges forward, his tail quivering like an arrow that has just struck its target. I'm trying to hold onto the long line and keep my feet as we scramble over boulders when suddenly the suspect comes creeping around a bend in the creek directly toward us. He's in the same crouching position I am in, and he is looking back over his shoulder in the direction of Kushner and the other cops.

Brag sees him and lunges like a sled dog but I can't release him until the suspect is properly warned. The suspect faces forward again and beholds Brag bearing down on him. Slack-jawed with surprise, he throws his hands up and himself down onto the boulders, faster than I can complete my shouted warning and instructions.

Kushner and Gonzales come around the bend a minute later, smiling with satisfaction. Handcuffs click and Brag goes crazy, barking insults at the suspect. Kushner removes the knife from a sheath on the suspect's waistband. Easy hunt, ideal outcome. No one got hurt. I have no doubt that once Brag had the suspect's odor it would have been firing a guided missile to release him for a bite, even if the suspect was never in view. But I want nothing to do with that poison oak covering the banks of the creek. I'd prefer to meet a dozen skunks.

I catch myself smelling the air at work all the time. I've come to realize that I can discern a lot about who lives in a house by the smell of their laundry detergent (or absence of it). Our culture has deemed it okay to ask people questions based on their surname, appearance, and habits but has deemed it rude to ask anyone a question related to any odor attached to them. Unless you want to compliment someone on their choice of perfume, and that can be dangerous territory as well. Dogs aren't concerned with these social restrictions. The crotch sniff may be the most complete identification check available to a dog, but people don't like that much either. Brag doesn't do it to people mainly because I don't ever let him get that close to anyone except a suspect, but Brag's got such a good nose I know he gets most of the information he needs from a few feet away.

My phone rings as the call is going out on the radio: three suspects with guns burst into a house on the Mesa – an area of town with a lot of college students – and rob the residents of handfuls of cash from marijuana sales. A neighbor sees the three, ski-masked suspects run out and jots down the license plate of the suspect vehicle. By the time I'm on-scene, Chad Hunt and another SWAT team member, Mitch Jan, have already identified the primary suspect and his residence. It's less than a mile away. We head over there immediately, calling for three more police units on the way.

There's always a funny moment when four or five police cars roll up silently and park on a street as someone is out watering their lawn or engaging in some other innocuous outdoor task. If it's a neighborhood we rarely go into – especially a more affluent one – neighbors will approach us right away to ask what's going on. In the more troubled neighborhoods people hardly notice you. If cops emerge with rifles, they might call their kids back into the yard, but usually not. I don't know if it feels routine to them or if they just can't be bothered or if it's their way of not ruining our element of surprise (least likely), but the indifference is always odd. The best reaction happens when we inadvertently park across the street from a house where people are partying. The drunken commentary is priceless: "Whoa! One, two, three, FOUR cop cars! And a K-9! Check out that dog! He's ready to bite someone's ass!"

I follow Hunt and Jan to the front door of the two-story apartment where one of the suspect's roommates lets us in, telling us the suspect is not home. That, by the way, means nothing in police work. I don't care if the sweetest grandma you ever met offers you a plate of fresh-baked cookies and swears her gang-member grandson isn't there. If you don't check for yourself, you'll never catch anyone. People who wouldn't cheat the government out of one dollar on their taxes will hide their murderer son and lie all day to the police.

I make an announcement and Brag translates it into dog. His bark is so loud people are emerging from other apartments to make sure we're not talking to them.

Since I don't have much of a floorplan and I'm not certain there isn't an open window somewhere, I keep Brag on the long-line. We search methodically: downstairs living room, kitchen, bathroom, downstairs bedroom. Then we move up the stairs – always an uneasy moment because stairs are not a good place to be in a shootout – and Brag clears the landing and then another small bedroom. Now the suspect's bedroom is all that remains. Brag wanted to go up there first, which tells me that he's already picking up on some odor.

I make another announcement because I'm going to let Brag go into the last room off-leash. I can see there is a half-sized closet door that leads into a storage space with a low ceiling beneath the steep pitch of the roof. That's where I'd put money on the suspect's hiding place.

I let Brag go and he pads into the bedroom, circling the bed. He forces open the small closet door with his nose and his tail vanishes into it behind him. Silence, then a rhythmic swishing sound, like someone shaking out a comforter. Silence again. It's so quiet I can hear Hunt and Jan breathing next to me as they peer down the barrels of their AR-15's.

Brag emerges from the closet with a big pillow in his mouth. He looks right at me and gives the pillow a vigorous shake, making that same swishing sound I heard a moment ago. Chad and Mitch and I look at each other. *What in the hell…?*

"*Voran!*" I tell Brag, wondering why he is playing with bedding when we're supposed to be searching for an armed robbery suspect. Brag cocks his head at me and gives the pillow another enthusiastic shake. He looks like he wants me to chase him to try to take the pillow away. Hunt snorts, suppressing laughter.

"What now?" Jan asks me, doing his best to stay professional. None of us believe the suspect is here anymore, but we have to make sure.

"Finish searching by hand, I guess," I tell them.

Hunt and Jan move past me as I put Brag on long line again. They peek into the closet. No suspect, but he does live in there: it's crammed with his clothes and a nasty futon cushion on the floor to match the filthy pillow Brag has in his mouth.

"*Aus*," I tell Brag and he drops the pillow. I'm so annoyed with him I don't know what to do. I prod the pillow with my boot, hoping for some clue that would grant me understanding. Still not satisfied, I poke my head into the storage closet and I'm immediately slapped with the sour, pungent odor of unwashed bedding and clothes. The suspect has been living in that tiny space for months at least. No windows, no ventilation. And definitely no laundry detergent.

"Fifty-five, we're Code Four. Suspect not on-scene," I tell the dispatcher. As we head downstairs, the other cops are waiting for us.

"Do you think the suspect came here after the robbery?" one of them asks.

"He may have taken a nap," Hunt quips as he goes out the door.

Brag doesn't seem the least bit disappointed on our way to the K-9 car. But we're going to have a chat, he and I.

"What were you doing?" I ask him when we're alone. One amber eye looks at me through the bars, and I can't help but laugh. "You attacked a pillow. Have you lost your mind?"

There is, of course, no reply. But that doesn't mean there isn't an explanation. Then I remember the blue tarp: we hunted that wet burglar who hid underneath one. Brag bit the tarp and I pulled on the long line and the tarp became a man. Brag didn't try to lift the tarp or tunnel into it, he just found the highest concentration of odor and bit. Brag knew the robbery suspect wasn't in the apartment by the time we got upstairs, and he knew he wasn't in the funky closet. But he was hunting for odor, and in lieu of the suspect he bit into the object most impregnated with the suspect's odor: his pillow.

But it's not only that. There's something else I have to face, that I've been denying for a long time: Brag has a sense of humor. He is the fearsome Werewolf, the hater of people on skateboards, people wearing hoodies, people who make eye contact, people who approach his K-9 car, people who walk funny, people who holler at him, and anyone else who is more than twelve years old and doesn't wear a police uniform. But despite his deadly seriousness he bit that pillow because he thought it would be funny. And it was.

I don't know what this all means.

By the next training day Ted has already heard about the call.

"Hedges!" he hollers from the training field where he brandishes a whip and a bite sleeve. "Bring out your terrifying pillow-shredder!"

TRIAL BY FIRE

The Great Grinding Wheel of Municipal Bureaucracy has granted me a new K-9 handler partner to replace Claytor. His name is Tyler Larson, a cop who has more years on than I do. Whatever possessed him to want to join me in this insane endeavor is a mystery, but I'm glad to have a human partner again to help me plan training days and stem the tide of chaos on patrol. A large man with a huge heart, Tyler also has earned his reputation as a hard worker in the street crimes unit. I first met him when I was a brand-new cop and we went on a late night 9-1-1 hang-up call together. A woman answered the door with a strange look on her face and when Tyler asked her if she was all right, she suddenly raised a kitchen knife and tried to stab him. We wrestled her to the ground, both astonished at the absence of any warning or indication of violence. These jarring moments bind cops together, long after you don't think about them anymore.

Ted orders the new police dog and he arrives at LAX in a crate. He's a black German Shepherd, two years old, and has a twinkle in his eye, as if he's about to say something funny. I like him immediately. His name is Hondo.

Tyler and Hondo hit it off. They both have a youthful exuberance that they're going to need to get through their initial training and the first year of figuring each other out. Watching them struggle through some of the basic training scenarios reminds me how far Brag and I have come together. A K-9 unit with only two handlers means you'll always be taking bites during training from the other handler's dog, which means at some point you're going to get bitten for real by the other handler's dog. Hondo isn't as big as Brag but he is incredibly fast. He develops an immediate dislike of Ted, because Ted plays a nastier bad guy than I do. Ted grabs at the dogs' feet, simulates hitting them with a stick, and blows in their faces when they bite – all actions they despise. But these behaviors are necessary for the training of the police dogs, since suspects will not politely submit when they are bitten. The dogs must be prepared to be in a real fight with a larger animal. They learn that if they stick with it, they always win. It's a bit of a lie; sometimes the dogs don't win. But they must believe that holding the bite and fighting on is the only way. Good police dogs enjoy it.

During one training scenario at a closed hospital, Brag locates Ted hiding on the third floor and bites him. Ted writhes on the ground until I arrive to take Brag off of the bite.

"Your dog is stabbed!" Ted yells at me. This is part of the scenario. "Get him out of here before he bleeds out!"

I run toward the stairs with Brag on leash beside me.

"He can't walk!" Ted shouts after us. "You gotta carry him!"

He wants me to pick this enormous dog up and carry him down three flights of stairs?

"You're not serious," I reply.

"HURRY - he's losing blood!"

I crouch beside Brag and gingerly scoop him up. Bewildered at this bizarre twist, Brag tries to wriggle free until I straighten up and double-time with him toward the stairwell.

God, he's heavy. But he stops struggling, looking around at the dingy hospital walls as we go down the hall and into the stairwell. He is perfectly content to be carried out and this is so out of character that I'm laughing and I can hear Ted laughing behind me and this is making Brag feel even heavier because I can't catch my breath.

We burst out through the doors to where the other handlers are waiting, and as I hurry past them carrying my relaxed werewolf, they all laugh as well. I nearly drop Brag when I reach our car and he hops into the back. I collapse against the trunk, trying to catch my breath.

Ted comes up. "That was the funniest thing I've ever seen. He liked being carried."

"I would not have expected that," I said, still panting.

"Me neither; I was pretty sure he was going to bite you in the face," Ted says casually, then turns to the waiting handlers. "Next dog!"

The crow is back on the wire, watching me. This time I have a handful of walnuts and I walk down my driveway and drop the walnuts in the gutter and crunch them beneath my shoe.

"Those are for you," I tell him and walk back into the house.

I peek out the window and watch as curiosity gets the better of him and he swoops down to investigate. He picks out the edible parts and calls to his mate. She hops over, sharing the unexpected boon. They look out for each other; no one else will. I'd give them more to eat but I have to go to work. Brag waits in his spot at the back gate.

It's a busy weekend, with a warm breeze blowing the wrong direction down the canyons toward the ocean. Tyler is certified and works patrol with Hondo now. This is an overlap day so we get to meet and talk all things K-9. While we're chatting, Tyler points up at the oak and chaparral ridgeline above the city, where a thin ribbon of gray smoke unravels up into the sky. From this distance, it looks like it could be a burning structure, but it's a wildfire. The hills are dry as stacked kindling and the wind is all wrong.

"That's bad," I say, stating the obvious.

An hour later the thin ribbon has become an ominous stack of churning smoke, possessing an immense solidity, as if it were carved out of some poisonous matter.

We keep answering emergency calls, with one eye on the hills above the city, knowing what's coming tonight. The winds howl down the canyons from the warmer, drier regions beyond. The fire grows – pushed by the hot winds – and charges downhill.

A dozen of us are dispatched to the Command Post set up in a parking lot on the north end of the city, where we will receive our areas to evacuate. The Command Post is a fancy motorhome modified with telecommunications equipment and some other bells and whistles to serve as a control center in an emergency incident.

Tyler meets me in the lot. He and Hondo have been dispatched to assist with evacs as well and we take our dogs out individually for pee breaks while keeping an eye on the widening smoke. More cops arrive: California Highway

Patrol officers and Santa Barbara County Sheriff's deputies and everyone else that they've managed to call in on a mutual aid request. But we're all standing around waiting.

I get restless watching the monstrous fire grow so I poke my head into the Command Post to see how close we are to receiving our area assignments. The CP is manned by an administrator and at this moment the man is furiously vacuuming the Command Post carpet. This guy is killing me. I watch him for thirty seconds, dumbstruck by the intensity with which he tidies up while a growing, monstrous wildfire eats everything on its way down to the city.

It's getting darker now; the smoke has spread across the sky like a shroud, and cops aren't joking around anymore.

A sergeant calls us over for our evacuation maps and I grab it and head to my car before studying it carefully. These wildfires move so fast that residents often aren't aware that the flames are closing in until it's too late.

Ash drifts down – gray snowflakes that stick but do not melt – and Brag stares intently out of the windshield as we drive up to the foothills. I know the area we're going into reasonably well; it's in the county and outside of our jurisdiction. Problem is, the roads up there are winding, narrow, and mostly dead-end.

Within a few miles of the fire's edge, we plunge into a darkened world. I roll the windows up and run the AC, hoping to filter out some of the smoke. We pass dozens of fire trucks parked all over the roads, the firefighters moving urgently as they prepare to meet the blaze head on. Houses are burning already. People are fleeing with their trunks and backseats packed with their most important belonging, or at least whatever they could grab quickly.

I hit the first few houses on my evacuation map, pounding on doors and yelling to make sure there's no one inside. Brag thinks I'm yelling at a suspect so he barks from the car, trying to help. This is a mandatory evacuation area but if someone refuses to leave there's little I can do but note the address and let dispatch know so they can pass it on to whoever is running the evacs. You can't force people to leave, but you have to try to make sure they understand what they're up against. Death by fire, mostly.

We reach the end of the road and turn back. But the way out is toward the fire, and the visibility is reduced to zero. The ash *ticks* as it blows hard against my windshield. Suddenly the road doesn't look familiar anymore and I'm wondering if I made a wrong turn. We pass another fire truck and the firefighters on it look like wraiths, gray and indistinct in the half-light.

The wind is howling now and I can barely see the edge of the roadway. I curse under my breath and place my palm on the inside of the windshield. Hot. I push aside a growing sense of panic. This is how firefighters burn; they get stuck in a bad spot and the fire comes on too fast and their vehicles won't run because engines need to be able to pull in clean air to operate. Oddly, I recall my grandfather teaching me about the internal combustion engine when I was fourteen. *It's not a gas pedal*, he explained, *it's an air pedal.*

The scenario is getting worse by the second. If the engine dies Brag and I will have to abandon the car and run for it. But trying to outrun the fire is a foolish gamble since the flames can move faster than you can run and they push a blinding torrent of smoke and embers in front of it. The same maelstrom we're driving into at this moment.

I slow to a crawl. If I can't outrun the fire, I'll have to let Brag go. He can outrun it. But I don't know a command to tell him to leave me. We don't train for that, and I'm not sure he would be willing to leave me behind. I look back through the cage at him.

"Get ready to run, Brag," I tell him. He looks at me quickly then back out at the tumultuous brown world outside.

I know we're close to a bend that will turn us away from the fire, but it feels like we should have rounded it by now. I wonder if the fire has already jumped the road.

Shit. This is how people die. I stop. I can't see the road enough to turn around.

A firefighter in her gear suddenly appears at my window. She's wearing a breathing apparatus and pointing up the road toward the fire. I can't roll the window down because I'll get blasted by the hot wind so I mimic her pointing and she nods, snapping her hand forward as if it to say *you gotta go now!*

Trusting the firefighter, I drive toward the fire. Ghostly, flashing lights appear in the smoke in front of me and I pass the fire rig. The firefighters are bent silhouettes as I go by. They're battling the blaze by hand, facing a gigantic, enveloping enemy that destroys all life. Crazy, brave people.

The road bends and the scorching wind blows hard against the driver's side windows. We're turning away from the fire front. I can see mailboxes now and I just aim to go past the next one and the one after that until the smoke thins out and I can see both sides of the road again. We're clear of the burn zone.

I exhale with relief, driving back through the neighborhood I passed through a few hours ago. It's all burned. Small, lazy flames dance in patches on the charred ground. Some of the blackened oak trees wear crowns of fire.

I roll down the windows as we drive and kick up a swirling tornado of ash inside the car. When I pull over to the side of the road to take a moment to deal with myself, I open the back door to check on Brag. He's puzzled, but fine. I run my fingers through his coat, picking up a layer of fine ash grit. A gray film covers the water in his bowl.

"That was a close one. You okay?"

Brag looks back toward the fire. It's impossible to tell what he's thinking. We spend the rest of the night monitoring the evacuated areas, alerting dispatch whenever it jumps a road.

The fire burns thousands of acres but only dozens of homes. Memories are lost, but no lives. When Brag and I are released to go home it's daylight and the winds have abated so it feels like the fire is beaten. It's not. It's waiting for the winds to kick up again later and it will come to life again. I drive past the road closure signs and parked fire trucks on Highway 154, winding up into the hills through the burned zone. As I round a curve a fifty-foot column of flame leaps up beside the roadway from the canyon below.

I slam on the brakes and turn back, stopping at the fire truck I passed two minutes earlier. Brag's so tired he doesn't bother to bark when a sooty-faced firefighter comes to my window.

"Is it safe to drive up the pass?" I ask the firefighter.

"I wouldn't," he says. "Still pretty hot up there."

I laugh and thank him. I want to ask "why didn't you stop me?" but I'd driven around their barricades with such purpose that they figured I had somewhere important to go. Who stops a cop car?

I glance in the rear-view mirror at Brag's steady amber gaze. Suddenly it hits me: if we'd had to run for it, he would have refused to leave me behind. I can't picture him galloping off and consigning me to the flames.

I ask myself: would I leave *him* behind? I let the question tumble around in my mind, even though I know the answer is never. This is a problem; I don't want to get close to this dog.

I haven't been entirely honest, with myself or Brag. It's not the tactical and professional risk I'm worried about, it's personal. I already had a dog once. His name was Beowulf.

BEOWULF

Growing up in a household with two brothers means few things are truly yours. Bikes are shared and passed down, as are clothes and just about everything else. The family dogs fell into this category as well; they belonged to none of us individually.

It would be decades before I got my own dog, after I'd begun my career as a cop. My friend Steve called one day and said his female Border Collie was about to have puppies and asked if I would like one. I said yes immediately and within a few weeks the mama dog gave birth to a litter. The pups were mongrels, but half-German Shepherd, which meant they would be intelligent and bold, the best traits for any dog to possess.

I told Steve I wanted the largest male in the litter. I shared the heroic name I'd already picked for the dog, so Steve and his wife held a naming ceremony, where they plucked the pup out of the tumbling mix of siblings and announced to the world that this dog's name was Beowulf.

On Christmas I got my puppy. It would be the best gift anyone had ever given me. Beowulf was all black, with a white blaze on his chest and white socks on his feet. If you said his name, he cocked his head.

Beowulf grew into an intelligent, handsome dog. I was a bachelor; he was my family, my alter-ego, and my best friend. We ran together and hiked together. An unspoken communication developed between us. He needed no leash. In the evenings he chewed bones for hours on the floor beside me in my office. If my hand dropped down to my side he would shove his muzzle into it, a silent demand for affection. He slept in a crate beside my bed. We were inseparable.

Beowulf loved to run at my side. He lived for it. Our favorite place to go was up a trail that followed a wandering ridgeline above the valley where we lived. The first time I climbed that trail, Beowulf was a puppy. He was so small I had to carry him when he got tired. I never hiked there without him; he knew every bend, every patch of shade. We rarely came across other people up there, but when we did, they always asked the same question: "What breed of dog is that?" Beowulf seemed to be his own breed, as if he were a dog designed by a child with only a black crayon.

Late afternoon was our favorite time to go hiking, when the sun cast long shadows across the ridge. Beowulf loped ahead of me, mindful of my ponderous gait, and stopped every time he was about to slip out of view. He would look back at me, urging me on. At the top of our climb, he would trot to the bowl-shaped depression in a rock, waiting for me to pour some water in it for him to drink. He never begged; he simply knew I shared whatever I had with him.

It was common for us to go for an entire hike without my uttering a word. There was no need. Our silent companionship seemed like the only thing in the world as we ran back down the trail, veering off here and there through the waving grass to find new routes. He never strayed, never fell behind. He was a good dog.

Countless miles rolled beneath our feet. A decade passed without notice. Beowulf's muzzle was dusted with gray. He slowed, but still loped far out in front of me on our hikes, still chased deer for a hundred yards or so before turning back with his tongue hanging out, grinning, as if to say *did you see them run?* I would shake my head in mock disapproval.

One day, Beowulf started limping. The limp grew worse, and soon he wasn't using his left rear leg at all. I took him to the vet and she felt the knee problem could be corrected with surgery. She called me a few days later with bad news: the surgeon looked at the x-rays and said the dog had cancer. They couldn't fix him; Beowulf's running days were over. They wanted to take his leg. How could I do that? I agonized over it, but Beowulf never complained. He was waiting for his leg to get better so we could run. Within a few days he was putting weight on that leg again. I wondered if the vets were wrong, but when I took Beowulf for a short walk, he could barely keep up with me. At one point he tottered and nearly fell over. I cut the outing short, and heard him whimper when I lifted him into the truck. The look on his face was apologetic, and I could see an overwhelming weariness in his eyes.

That night Beowulf wouldn't eat his dinner. The next morning he couldn't get up. I had to go to SWAT training that day, so I took him to the vet. The blood test showed cancer had spread into his marrow. There was nothing anyone could do for him; he was suffering far worse than he had let on. I decided I would bring him home after I finished training, sleep with him downstairs, and put him down in the morning. I had no idea how I was going to do such an impossible thing; I might as well have pointed at the moon and announced I was going to leap up and touch it. Where had the time gone? This was the puppy in white socks that I'd brought home not so many years ago. We were inseparable. How could I separate us, even for compassion's sake?

The impossible thing never had to be done, because in his typical fashion – without complaint – Beowulf died. At the vet's office I had stroked his muzzle and told him I would see him that evening. He let go of his life a few hours later.

He'd been holding out for that last walk we had the day before, I think, to confirm his suspicion that he would never run again.

He lived to run with me. When he couldn't, there was no more reason to live.

Beowulf was gone, just like that. The trails were still there, the sun was still casting long shadows across the hills, and an empty dog food dish sat on the kitchen floor. These things were now symbols of my abrupt solitude. I moved through the rest of the week like a man pushing through deep snow. I did my job, met my responsibilities. But in the quiet moments I suffered. It was only a dog, right? Why did it feel like something had been torn out of me? Like nothing would ever be right again?

I knew it was wrong to sit around and feel sorry for myself, so I went for a run. The silence was profoundly different. Far into the run, when I was sure there was no one for miles, I called Beowulf's name as loud as I could. It seemed reasonable that out there, alone in the hills with no one else to witness and question how such a thing could be possible, Beowulf would come bounding out of the woods and join me. I struck a quick bargain with the Almighty: if he would allow Beowulf to appear and run with me when no one else was around, I would never speak of it to anyone, ever. As part of the deal, I also wouldn't say a word to Beowulf, but just run beside him. I would never break the spell by touching him; his loping at my side would be good enough. At the end of our secret runs, Beowulf could vanish in a flash of sunlight, or disappear behind an oak, until next time.

It is an unavoidable truth that those who wish to bargain with God usually have nothing to bargain with. I let the childish wish go and ran on, lonely and miserable.

How strange that an animal could so thoroughly become a part of me. His love of running and deep appreciation of the wild places mirrored my own. I would still catch glimpses of him out of the corner of my eye, on the floor of my office, holding down a bone with his white socks. There seemed to be no other reason for his existence than to be my fast companion. Intellectually, I understood the natural order: my dog grew old, got cancer, and died. But an unreasonable grief still filled the quiet moments. I thought about how Beowulf must have felt the cancer tightening its grip, draining his vitality and robbing him of his greatest joy until he gave up on this world entirely.

Time passed, pushed Beowulf's death away by months, then years, but the wound never healed. My best friend went away. I won't go through that again.

Brag and I can hunt together, fight together, but that's it. He is city property, like my Ford Interceptor, my badge, and my handgun. If I make a mistake – even an honest one –

Brag can be taken from me forever by a bullet or a two-sentence email sent by an administrator.

This is how the game is played. Brag and I will catch as many bad guys as we can. Defense attorneys will scour my reports, searching for unchecked emotions and legal missteps. Bad guys will arm themselves and hide in darkness, hoping I care for my dog and refuse to send him.

We will disappoint all of them, because I will never love this police dog and he will never love me.

BENNY DREADFUL

Blood in, blood out. Once you're jumped into a criminal street gang, you don't simply leave. You must take your beating – and bleed – to get out. The more ruthless the gang, the more severe the beating. An Eastside gang member told me, "We hate Westsiders, but we hate your gang more." I'd never thought about them considering cops to be a rival gang, but in their limited point-of-view it makes sense; we are always in opposition to them, threatening them with violence, trying to break up a social system that makes them feel strong. Throughout history, opposing armies often emulated their enemies. Even members of the U.S. military fighting in Iraq and Afghanistan adopted the *shemagh* scarf of the Muslim mujahedeen as an addition to their own battle uniform. Wardrobe practicalities aside, it is a nod of respect to an enemy's commitment to their cause. Even when the only manifestation of that cause is violence.

Blood out. Brag and I are also bound by this oath; it will take blood to stop us. A lot of it.

I'm thinking about this as I pull out of my garage in the K-9 car. Brag sits in silence behind me and I wonder if he's envisioning the coming night and its chaotic promise. We are both up against a number problem: a minimum of three, ten-hour shifts a week, with an unknown number of high-risk calls coming at us in no particular order with infinite variables, each loaded with critical legal and procedural concerns, with no allowance for fatigue or error. How can we run a perfect lap, every time?

I turn on the AC and the smell of smoke fills the car. At least it doesn't reek of skunk anymore. I stop by the city yards and the mechanics pull the air filter; it's clogged with ash and it looks like it's been buried in the ground for a year. These folks try their best to keep my car up and running; they know that it's one of only two K-9 cars and I can't work properly with a regular patrol vehicle with those slippery plastic back seats. I also get a flat tire at least every few months because I'm always driving where you're not supposed to drive: on the railroad tracks, down the emergency lane on the freeway, across abandoned lots. Add lots of high-speed maneuvering to that equation and you go through plenty of tires. By policy I'm not allowed to change a flat, which sounds ridiculous but it's so I don't put on a directional tire facing the wrong way and then lose control and crash. Liability is on everyone's mind. They'd have to send me to a 40-hour Tire Changing Course before they could authorize me to do it. In the meantime, I've gotten to know all the tow truck drivers pretty well.

That night Brag and I run a perfect lap. More searches, more finds. Another apprehension. Brag leaps out of the car the same way, every time. His muscles straining on the long line are comforting, consistent.

In the morning my phone buzzes with texts and calls because there's a wanted subject who may be barricaded in his house with a firearm. I haven't shaved but I rush out and bring Brag into the garage and put him in the car. Something isn't right; the K-9 car lists to one side. I squat down and discover the right rear tire is flat.

No time for tow trucks. I grab my bicycle pump and pump the flat tire furiously while Brag watches me from inside the car. My arms burn, I'm panting, and when the tire looks like it will roll I jump in the driver's seat and back out into the street. I drive the eight blocks as fast as I can to the one gas station in town. After hearing my breathless explanation, the gas station attendant Silverio jacks up the K-9 car, pulls the tire off, patches it, and puts it back on in about ten minutes. A one-man pit crew. Brag doesn't bark at Silverio, who refuses any money from me because he knows I'm rushing to a call. I arrive in time to use Brag to search the house for the suspect, who fled before police arrived. He is arrested blocks away by a cop on traffic control who looks up and sees the suspect sauntering past him. That's how it goes sometimes. My arms are sore for days after the event and the next time I see Silverio he teases me about the SWAT bicycle pump.

Brag and I have a real driving rhythm now. He never loses his balance on turns and I have learned to accelerate smoothly without banging him into the metal cage. He's so big that when he stands up in the middle of the cage, I can't see anything in the rear-view mirror except a forest of sable fur. He also communicates to me when he needs a potty break, giving me a short whistle while turning circles. How he manages to spin around back there so easily is still a mystery. I never make him wait – it's part of our agreement.

The narcotics detectives have an arrest warrant for a drug dealer named Benny Manteca. He's a long-time Eastside gang member and it's odd that I've never run across him. The narcs call me in because Manteca is legendary for his ability to fight and escape. When I walk into the narc office it's packed with cops in various states of professional-appearance decomposition. Some of them have long hair, some have goatees, and none of them are in uniform. The cops from the state agencies who work only narcotics take their deconstructed appearance to extremes since they don't have to meet patrol grooming standards. One of the Department of Justice agents has a long beard braided with beads and dangling down from his chin. Everyone calls him "King Tut" which I'm not sure he appreciates. I don't bring Brag to these briefings because I'm concerned that since these cops look more like bad guys Brag might decide one of them needs straightening out.

Someone hands me Manteca's photo. He looks like two-hundred pounds of lard stuffed into a one-hundred-pound bag. This guy is a master at escape and evasion? I scan through his criminal history and that gets my attention because it reads like a scavenger hunt of California Penal Code violations: felony battery, possession of a deadly weapon, conspiracy, domestic abuse, burglary, armed robbery, smuggling narcotics into a correctional facility, terrorist threats, auto theft, assault on a peace officer, and rape. But his one conviction that stands out for me is "penetration with a foreign object." I ask the room if anyone knows the story behind that one.

"He violated a young woman with a beer bottle," one of the detectives explains.

What a vile man. I can't wait to introduce him to Brag.

Several narcs are out in cold cars watching Manteca's residence right now, waiting for him to leave to make a drug delivery. Cold cars are cars that have been seized through asset forfeiture and now serve as nondescript conveyances so cops can follow drug dealers. None of the cold cars are Ferraris or Range Rovers. That would be so obvious that you'd get burned before you tailed a suspect for one block. The narcs prefer ten-year-old sedans with oxidized paint. One of their favorites is a mini-van with tinted windows because you can squeeze a bunch of cops into the back, turning it into a law enforcement clown car. None of the license plates on these vehicles are registered to the city, so the drug dealers can't associate them with the police department that way. But some are so clever they do counter-surveillance and watch the narcs leave the building to see which cars they get into in the surrounding neighborhood.

Benny Manteca's been in this game for a long time so he knows all the tricks. He's also looking at doing some real time for this parole violation so there's no way he's going to go easily. The plan is to wait until he gets on the road and then make a traffic stop and take him into custody. He will likely run and fight, so I'm going to move into the front position when they tell me to move up and make the stop. Brag will be the push of a button away. A week ago, Manteca led the CHP on a wild vehicle pursuit and escaped on foot, leaving only a box of ammunition behind. So, he's likely armed as well. I hope Manteca runs and fights, because he will get Brag's business end.

Many people ask me who gets bitten and who doesn't. The truth is, it's up to the suspect. They get plenty of chances to surrender, even if everything they've done up to that point is felonious. My response to the question is "we don't bite people who deserve it, we bite people who demand it."

One of the detective's phone buzzes. Manteca's on the move. We rush out to our cars and caravan toward the freeway, preparing to get in behind Manteca as he travels north to make his drop. There's a wrinkle: a woman is driving the car and Manteca is the passenger.

We jump on the freeway and speed to catch up. Brag turns circles in the back because he can tell by the way I'm driving that we're going after someone.

Manteca's car – a red Honda – gets off the freeway. I'm the only marked unit and still a quarter mile back and as I exit I realize that there must be at least six narc cars in front of me. This doesn't look right at all; a drug dealer exiting the freeway with six plain cars immediately behind him. He can't see me yet but he will when I get closer.

The red Honda turns off of the off-ramp and the narcs are calling for me to move up and make the traffic stop. But the Honda is moving pretty fast and I'm sliding around turns and passing narcs and trying to get close without crashing into somebody.

We're burned. Manteca knows the narcs are behind him. The Honda accelerates, making turns at every block and the narcs are backing off and I'm rushing to catch up and I turn a corner and find the red Honda on the side of the road with the passenger door wide open.

Manteca is gone. The red Honda drives forward slowly with the door open and as I turn on my emergency lights to make the stop, I realize that Manteca has jumped out of the vehicle at a walkway that leads between houses into a hilly park.

The woman rolls to a stop and sticks her hands up. I want to go after Manteca but I have to wait until someone takes control of the woman before I can grab Brag.

A half-dozen narcs are already running into the wooded park – guys with tattoos and beards and beanies running around with guns. People in the park stare. It's surrounded on three sides by houses, giving Manteca all kinds of opportunities to jump a fence and disappear. The narcs fan out as Brag and I jog into the park, hoping to catch Manteca's scent but there are so many people running around that Brag can't distinguish which scent trail we're supposed to be following. We jog all the way to the other side of the park before I realize Manteca is gone. Cursing, I go back to the red Honda because we have to search the car.

Brag knows I'm upset; his dope searches are terrible. He's clearly got the aborted hunt on his mind, and keeps looking back toward the park. I'm stunned at how quickly Manteca got out of that car and escaped. Now I realize that I misinterpreted that stare in his booking photo. It wasn't a blank look; it was a look of cunning determination. I underestimated him.

The narcs try to ping the location of Manteca's phone off a nearby cell tower. Soon we have a possible location less than a mile away, but it's an intersection so it could mean he was in a car driving by or in a backyard or in the overgrown creek bed. We search anyway, and Brag has a scent trail for a while but it peters out. By the time I call the search off hours later, it's well past end of watch and everyone is done.

Brag is exhausted from all the searching but he doesn't lie down in the car on the way home. He knows we lost and he doesn't like it. Manteca is still out there, laughing at us. Often these suspects disappear for months after an escape like this. I'd love to say it solves the problem to have him gone but it doesn't – he'll just commit crimes somewhere else.

When I feed Brag in his kennel, he eats with no enthusiasm at all. I scramble up some eggs and they taste like salted cardboard. To fall asleep, I put in my earbuds and blast some metal, music that no one should be able to fall asleep to. But I do, which says a lot about my state of mind. Brag is just as grumpy, it turns out.

"Did you two have a bad night last night?" Rachel asks me when I come downstairs later.

"Who told you that?"

"Brag," she says. "He was a jerk this morning."

The sun drops low in the afternoon sky. Brag holds his vigil at the gate, waiting for me to appear. He picks up the Kong in his mouth and when I unlock the gate he sprints to the garage, letting the ball drop and bounce alongside him as he skids to a stop. He has no further use for toys tonight. He wants to hunt men.

Last night's failure is still on my mind as we drive the highway to work. When my phone rings I see it's Danny McGrew calling. I can't answer fast enough.

"You and Brag on your way in?" he asks.

"Got something good for us?"

"Benny Manteca," he says. "He's holed up on Pueblo Street. We're there now."

"Ten minutes. Don't move."

He hangs up and I pull over to yank on my vest and uniform shirt and gun belt and I slip Brag's harness on him as well. He doesn't lie down again as we drive to the apartment complex to meet McGrew and the other detectives. Brag looks calm, like he knew this was coming.

"Ready to catch that bad guy?" I ask him.

His amber eyes slide over to meet mine for a second and it occurs to me how rare it is for him to make eye contact with me. It's not evasiveness, it's a sign of respect. He doesn't take his eyes off of me if I'm any distance away, but he never returns my gaze when I'm beside him.

We stop on the street outside the apartment complex where McGrew said to meet him. I bring Brag with me on the long line, coiled up to keep him tight against my leg.

Several detectives are questioning a glum-faced fellow sitting on the curb so I don't approach with Brag. McGrew hurries over to me, nodding his head toward the guy on the curb.

"He's on parole. He says Manteca is hiding inside his apartment."

I know there's a creek bed behind the apartment complex and I'm already picturing Manteca bailing out a window. McGrew smiles. "There's no back door or windows. He can't get out."

"Does he have a gun?"

The parolee says no. I study his face to decide if he's being truthful. He looks like he wants no part of this whole mess. But even if he says he didn't see a gun it doesn't mean Manteca doesn't have one. He did have a box of ammo in his car.

I join the six narcs at the front door, which includes Feller, one of the best SWAT operators on the team. They have their guns out, ready to rumble. I don't. I'm running the long line with two hands and that's okay because I trust these guys to shoot around me if they have to. Now I'm looking into the empty living room of the cluttered apartment. I can see the tiny kitchen and a doorway leading into the bedroom. Somewhere past that door, Benny is hiding. The longer we wait, the more time he has to develop a counter plan, to barricade, to arm himself.

Brag's eyes are glazed and he works his jaws open and shut like he's eating the odor pumping out of that tiny apartment. I nod at McGrew and he shouts into the doorway, ordering Manteca to surrender or be injured by the police dog. Brag barks. Silence. Feller yells for Manteca to come out and show his hands. More barking.

A male voice yells from inside the apartment – muffled, unintelligible. Both McGrew and Feller repeat their instructions, but Manteca does not come out with his hands up. I don't like this. Our advantage is slipping away, but we must follow the rules and give him every opportunity to surrender.

"Manteca, come out RIGHT NOW!" I shout. Nothing.

He's barricading or buying time. I'm not waiting any longer to send my partner in there alone. Each second that passes is distinct, worse than the one before it. The long-line is taut as a bridge cable, cutting off the circulation to my fingers.

Time's up. I unclip the long-line and send Brag with a single bite command.

Brag vanishes into the bedroom, his nails digging into the carpet. A crashing sound. Scuffling. A man yells in pain. Brag's back end reappears, bucking and straining – he's on the bite and he's dragging whoever it is back toward me. Good boy. Good, good boy.

We move into the apartment and I can see Manteca, shirtless, covered in abrasions, writhing on the floor with Brag attached to him. Feller shouts at Manteca to show his hands. Brag is biting Manteca on the inside of his upper right arm, trying to pull him through the doorway. He gets frustrated and switches directions, twisting Manteca's body the other direction. I step over Manteca and grab onto Brag's collar with both hands. I can feel the power of the bite; Brag's neck feels like a tree trunk trembling with electricity. He's not going to want to come off of this one. I straighten my back and bend my knees like a power lifter, readying to lift him off.

"*Aus!*" I say as firmly and clearly as I can. Brag's eyes are wild, bloodshot. He's in the bite fugue, or as Ed Olsen puts it so aptly, "the blood fever." These dogs know they are hurting a bad guy. They bite these men's souls.

Brag spits out the bite, leaving ropes of bloody spittle. Holding him up on his back legs I retreat from Manteca's twisted body to prevent a second bite.

Manteca howls. I lean back, restraining Brag as he barks at Manteca. My face might be expressionless as stone but inside I am relishing the sound of Manteca's pathetic yodeling. He knows now what it is to feel agonizing pain and helplessness, like his victims. The difference is, he chose this moment. We don't bite people who deserve it, we bite people who demand it.

There's more blood than I anticipated, and it streams down Manteca's arm into the carpet. He's blubbering now. McGrew and Feller usher the handcuffed Manteca outside and plop him into a plastic chair. More blood. McGrew jams his gloved fingers into the bite, clamping it down. Manteca doesn't look good; his skin color has turned a mottled gray.

The medics arrive in an ambulance as I jog with Brag and put him in our car. He's got blood dripping from his tongue because he bit through it during the struggle with Manteca. It must hurt but he's unfazed as I run my fingers through his mane and press my forehead against his.

"Good job, Brag. You got that bad guy."

Brag doesn't pull away. I'm breathing in the hot, coppery air he breathes out. It's only a few seconds that he lets me lean into him like this, enjoying my praise and letting me violate the sacred space of an intact alpha male canine who has just obliterated a dangerous adult male human in the span of six seconds. I admire Brag's merciless drive. He's hard to handle, but these moments make it all worthwhile.

When I get back to the apartment the medics are loading Manteca into the ambulance. The man's eyes are panicked, bulging with fear and pain.

Feller rides in the back with Manteca to make sure he doesn't attempt another escape on the way to the hospital. But there's no need for concern: Brag severed Manteca's brachial artery, the main artery running down the inside of the bicep. Without direct pressure on it and medical treatment Manteca could have bled to death. Feller follows Manteca's gurney through the emergency room and into surgery.

Because Manteca is rushed right into the operating room, I don't have a chance to do my hat trick and ask him questions about the bite. It's just as well. I'm not sure I could have played nice with a man like that.

When Manteca is finally booked into jail a few days later, he's got rows of stitches in his arm and leg, where they borrowed some artery to repair the one shredded by Brag's crushing canines. Manteca is also covered in oozing, angry blisters from the night he fled on foot out of the red Honda and got away – poison oak. The plant may be my dreaded enemy in most cases but it is my ally in this moment of comeuppance.

If Manteca had surrendered when I tried to stop him in the car he would have gone to jail in perfect health. I picture him blubbering on his cot in jail, cursing me and my police dog as he scratches at his sutures and his rash. In addition to being a rapist, he's infamous for getting even with those who cross him. I'll take that fight on a moment's notice. But I'll have to get in line behind Brag.

FENCES ARE THE ENEMY

Before the 9/11 terrorist attacks in 2001, the many federal, state, and local agencies tasked with security and law enforcement rarely interacted with each other. It wasn't that we didn't get along with each other, we just had few protocols to encourage information sharing. But once the twin towers fell, many of the invisible walls between agencies toppled as well.

The U.S. military bases took a hard look at themselves and found they were much softer targets than they wanted to be. Vandenberg Air Force Base is an enormous complex an hour north of Santa Barbara, occupying thousands of acres of sandy hills rolling down to the Pacific Ocean. The Air Force realized that the off-base housing complexes were not secure enough and began moving families onto the base where they could better protect them. Once new housing was arranged, the people living outside the gates up and moved en masse. An empty neighborhood was left behind: houses, sidewalks, schools, backyards. This became a rare training opportunity for K-9 handlers trying to perfect the art of the suburban man-hunting.

There's something unsettling about an abandoned suburb: row after row of silent houses, yards still featuring rusted swing sets and plastic slides. The dogs are indifferent to it, but Tyler and I always feel like we're training in a Post-Apocalyptic ruin. Dried-up hoses coil beside forgotten lawns. A Crayola rendering decorates the wall of an empty child's bedroom.

It is here that we learn to let our dogs work scent properly. Street intersections are difficult and it's always too easy to pull your dog off of the odor he is trailing. Streets are problematic enough because odor doesn't always stick well to the asphalt but collects against curbs. We lay trails down mazes of streets, through houses, out rear sliders, and over wooden fences. No one likes to talk about fences in the K-9 handler world because we struggle with these deceptively simple structures. They are rarely over six feet high, which sounds like it should be no problem at all. But it is. It's easy enough to get your dog over a fence. I could tell Brag to jump over and he'd do it with ease but I can't allow him to unless I know what's on the other side. If it's at night and the neighboring yard is lower in elevation, Brag could land wrong and break a leg. So I have to look first and then get him over. Now he's on the other side, trying to follow the trail while I try to control him and climb over myself. Sounds simple: put him on a down and climb over. But fences don't like two-hundred pounds of gear-laden cop. They're not built for scaling; they're built to discourage it. And often shrouded with trees and brush. Add the danger of moving from a mostly-secure area into an unsecure area where there might be a dangerous suspect lurking and you've got a tactical problem.

Some handlers go back out to the street and try to pick up the scent again by walking into that new backyard to the point where the suspect went over. This works sometimes, but may mean you find yourself trying to work the odor the wrong direction. Dogs can usually tell the difference, and it confuses the hell out of them when we force them to go the wrong way. For those of us with virtually no sense of smell this is hard to grasp, but dogs can tell which way the scent trail goes. If you approach a suspect's odor trail from a ninety-degree angle and the dog has the choice to go right or left when he reaches the scent, he will work out which direction the suspect went. He may need to investigate either direction a short distance but if you let him work it out and not interfere, distract, or put too much pressure on him, he'll get it every time. I don't know how this works exactly, but it does. Even if one odor trail is mere seconds newer than the other, the dog can tell. Voodoo magic. Call it whatever you like. It's real.

Brag's uncanny ability to work out this kind of problem quickly is nothing short of astonishing. It's nothing I've taught him – dogs are born to hunt and Brag was born to hunt men. He's so determined that he ignores all distractions. I've learned to leave him alone and let him work it out with as much long line as I can safely give him. It's not uncommon for him to range back and forth as far as he can or do a wide circle or two around me.

Ted finds the abandoned training neighborhood to be liberating. He climbs trees. He throws articles of clothing one direction and runs another. He goes across rooftops, climbs into attics. Every training scenario is designed to beat the dog, just like real scenarios. I love Ted's competitive, wily personality and I love using Brag to beat him. His faux screams of terror and pain when the dogs find him echo down the silent streets.

The fences remain a problem. In the end, Tyler and I decide that fences suck. We approach each one individually because no one system works for all of them.

During an alarm call one night I send an agile cop named Shawn Hill over a chain-link fence that has sharp metal edges running across the top. I can't send Brag over because the pointy parts will slice him if he drags any part of his body across it. Shawn stares at me, wondering what I'm going to do, then realizes I don't have a plan. He holds his arms out toward me like a forklift.

"You serious?" I whisper.

He nods. He likes Brag but I'm not sure Brag likes Shawn enough to be manhandled by him. With a shrug I bring Brag close to the fence and bend over and scoop him up. Brag turns his massive head to look at Shawn with disbelief.

We make the transfer. Shawn lowers him down to the ground on the inside of the fence and Brag pulls as far away on the long line as he can, as if to say *let's pretend you didn't just do that*. Shawn and I laugh our way to the back of the building. It ends up being a false alarm, but Brag's tolerance for his fellow cops has reached a new level. A year ago I would never have entertained the idea of picking him up and handing him to another cop. Brag's reluctant acceptance of me as his partner is now extended to the people we work with.

Later, I give Brag a potty break at a business park parking lot enclosed on one side by a building and two sides by barbed-wire fencing. One of the fences runs along the railroad tracks, where a swampy area is all that remains of a tidal marsh. The lot is a good place to let Brag off-leash to trot around and pee, since the space is contained and no one is ever there late at night.

Brag stops by the fence near the railroad tracks, his entire body stiffening as he sniffs the ground along the fence-line. His tail wags and he looks over at me with a grin on his face.

"What are you doing?" I ask him, which makes his tail wag harder as he hops on his front feet with excitement.

I spot what he has discovered: a fresh-water turtle that has crawled out of the swampy area and is resting beside the fence. Brag is fascinated with the creature. He looks up at me as if to say *isn't that the coolest creature you ever saw?* I can't help but laugh.

Brag barks at the terrapin playfully and it pulls its head and limbs inside the shell. I can't tear Brag away from it; I've never seen him so intrigued with an animal before. When I go back to the car, Brag stays by the fence, watching me.

"No, Brag," I tell him. "We can't bring it home."

He lowers his head and returns to the car like a disappointed child.

The savagery and suddenness of a gang fight would shock most people. It takes three words or less. One gang member, whether in line at a fast-food joint or in a car at a red light, asks someone "where you from?" There is no right answer to this question. The gang member is not inquiring because he is interested in meeting new people. He is finding the quickest reason to attack someone simply because they're not from where he is from. The area in question could be the size of Los Angeles or it could be less than a square mile. It is a mindless challenge that serves only as an excuse for immediate violence. Two men flashing different gang signs at each other need never utter a word.

This is the case with some Eastsiders and Westsiders that confront each other in a fast-food joint on Milpas Street, a place well within Eastside territory. The fight spills out into the parking lot where knives and baseball bats appear.

I'm close, close enough to drive up on it as a gun comes out. Rullman rolled up on such a confrontation in his patrol car recently by pure luck only to witness one gang member draw a handgun and murder another in a parking lot and run off. The dying victim's pitiful moaning was as clear on the radio as Rullman's surprise at witnessing a murder resulting from the exchange of less than three words. The suspect was captured a few blocks away and seemed more inconvenienced by the arrest than remorseful about taking a human life.

Brag's looking through the windshield as I drive into the midst of the chaos. The combatants scatter. I select one using the same method a predator would use to select a fleeing ungulate from a scattering herd: I pick the one who looks the most surprised by my arrival. Within seconds I discover I chose poorly because when the young man sees the patrol car closing in behind him, he shifts into higher gear and sprints across the street and turns behind a row of closed businesses like an MLB base-runner rounding first on a double.

When he reaches the end of the alley he hurdles a fence and I slam on the brakes and kick open my door and run after him, hitting the door pop button on my belt. I can hear Brag's nails scraping on the asphalt behind me as he gets up to speed and as I go over the fence Brag is sailing over it past me.

The suspect has already leaped over the next fence. Brag crosses the yard and leaps that fence before I reach it and as I go over, I can see another fence. I'm falling behind.

I call Brag back to me. He makes an abrupt U-turn, wondering if I am in trouble. When he sees I'm just slower than he is he bucks like a horse, frustrated at my pace. Now the suspect is out of sight and I'm not sure exactly where I am and I'm afraid of losing Brag so I hook the leather lead to him and run beside him and we both go over the next fence together.

Brag's nose lowers to the ground on the other side and we emerge onto a dark street and he pulls hard left down the sidewalk, his muzzle coming up as we close in on the suspect. I can hear sirens but we're alone and as Brag pulls down a deep driveway a shadowy figure leaps over a pile of junk and engine parts and scrambles over an eight-foot fence into yet another back yard. Dogs bark on the other side. This is one fence we won't go over.

I get on the radio to set up a hasty perimeter. Since there are obviously dogs in that yard I can't go in with Brag. The gang unit arrives and the homeowner brings them through the house to the back, where they can hear someone yelling for help. They find my suspect cowering inside a dog house. Two agitated pit bulls bark and circle as the gang cops extract the suspect and take him into custody.

I walk Brag back to the car and put him away, praising him for coming back to his bipedal handler and we drive to the arrest location to see who it was I was chasing. I know him: William Vacio. He's known on the street as "Psycho Billy" because of his propensity for over-the-top violence. The other Eastside gang members revere him for it.

An ambulance rolls up and I wonder if Vacio is stabbed or shot. I can see he is holding his left arm as if it is broken.

"What happened to him?" I ask Gonzalez, who has a satisfied smirk on his face.

"One of the pit bulls bit him," he says. "It's ugly."

I shine my flashlight on Vacio's forearm and see there is a section of skin about the size of a dollar bill that is missing. It's a bloody mess but hardly life-threatening. Vacio is cooperative now so he lets the medics irrigate the wound and then wrap a bandage around it.

After a few minutes of conferring with the gang unit I learn we have no cooperative victims from the fight and no way to attach Vacio to the abandoned knives or baseball bats. He did flee from me after I ordered him to stop, a clear crime in this case. But if I arrest Vacio he gets to go to the hospital and have his injury treated before he goes to jail. That will take hours and the city will have to foot the medical bill. Vacio would be released from jail within an hour anyway.

I come up with a solution that the gang unit appreciates: I write Vacio a misdemeanor ticket for resisting arrest. He signs it and I tear out his green copy and hand it to him. The ambulance drives away.

Vacio blinks at me, confused. He thought he was going to get his arm wound treated at the hospital and that we would pay for it. Wrong.

"Aren't I going to jail?" he asks.

"No," I reply. "Your court date is on the citation."

"But what about my arm?"

"You should probably get that looked at."

Blood is already seeping through the hasty bandaging. He looks down at the green copy of the ticket in his hand.

"Vacio, don't you think it's funny?" I lob back at him as I head to my car. "You got bit by a regular dog while running from a police dog."

Vacio's cold stare tells me he doesn't agree. Brag barks at him as we drive off.

I'm walking through the police department when a patrol sergeant stops me in the hallway.

"Has the staff questioned you about how many bites you and Brag are getting?" he asks.

I feel my spine stiffen. "What do you mean?"

"Brag is biting a lot of suspects. Just wondered if anyone on the third floor is concerned."

"I hope they interpret it as a sign we're doing our job," I reply curtly.

I'm suddenly reminded that not every cop in this building wants to catch bad guys, and some of them resent the cops who do. I should feel grateful for the reminder. I've forgotten that the third floor of the building is a bastion for obstructionists.

I go out to my K-9 car and open the back door, letting Brag out to say hello to Epstein, who asks for a brief game of tug-of-war with his buddy. These two are friends. Because Epstein is such a good cop, they go on a lot of calls together. As I watch the two of them mock-fight, a feeling replaces the hollow one that I felt a moment ago. It's a warm feeling. I respect these two cops, one on four legs and the other on two. They're the ones who go into danger every day and try to do the right thing.

I glance back at the squat building behind me and think about the men sitting in their wood-paneled offices on the third floor. They don't matter. They've forgotten what it is to want to do a job so much that you'll risk your life doing it just because it's right. It may not be fair to label them cowards, but they don't deserve to be called courageous.

I pull a wire brush out of my trunk and brush out Brag in the parking lot while chatting with Epstein. Brag endures the tedious grooming because he has a tug in his mouth and because Epstein is there and might engage any moment in another rough-and-tumble game.

When a call of a robbery in-progress comes over the radio, Epstein and I jump into our cars, nearly colliding with each other as we race out of the lot.

Brag looks past me out the windshield, eager, the embodiment of everything I wanted to be when I decided to become a cop so many years ago. I am grateful to him. He has given me the gift of purpose again. His desire to do police work is unapologetic. Once upon a time, I assumed that police dogs only did what they were trained to do, without any real understanding of the job. Now I know otherwise.

Although he cannot do his job without me, Brag's will is separate from mine. He's not motivated by blind obedience; he's driven by something deeper, a need to matter. He knows he is doing police work. I don't understand why a dog would be so interested in the world of humans, with all our senseless violence. But he is.

Blocks away from the robbery call Brag presses his nose to the window screen and inhales deeply. He can already smell the suspect. But that's impossible. I grab the radio mic.

"Fifty-five, K9-1, any info on the suspect's direction of travel?"

"Suspect is on a bicycle. Fled south on Hope Avenue five ago," is the reply.

We're on Hope Avenue, south of the crime scene. Brag smells him. This dog.

I make a U-turn and try to do something we've never trained to do: trail an unknown suspect riding away on a bicycle when there is no perimeter. It doesn't work. Brag can't tell me when to turn right or left so I'm guessing, observing Brag in the rear-view mirror and watching for the suspect on his bicycle in front of us. After fifteen minutes, I realize it's pointless to continue.

But that doesn't lessen the significance of what I just witnessed: a police dog catching the scent of a bad guy before we even arrive on-scene. I shouldn't be surprised. This is Brag, after all. He knows exactly what we're doing out here.

Weeks later I'm on the north end of the city when I hear an officer make a traffic stop on Haley Street between the Eastside and State Street.

"Foot pursuit!" the officer's voice yells over the radio. "Hispanic male, white shirt, running westbound!"

Brag leaps to his feet; he knows the sound of a foot pursuit. But we're on the wrong side of the city and as the suspect vanishes over barbed-wire fences and more cops arrive I know that my odor trail is getting trampled in the worst way. Normally I would tell everyone to wait but since it's going to take me at least ten minutes to get there, I don't. By the time I arrive, cops have stomped down alleys and shone their flashlights into every dumpster. The suspect is gone.

I get out and speak with the cop who made the stop. He's found a handgun in the car and the driver of the car admitted that his passenger who fled the traffic stop was Johnny Basura, a gang member who has been wanted for murder for eight months. The U.S. Marshals were looking for him in Oxnard – a gang-riddled suburb thirty miles south of us – but their latest information was that Basura had fled to Mexico.

The cops who got to the traffic stop first and searched the area haphazardly get back in their cars and leave. It's over.

I drive through the area slowly. We're about six blocks from the ocean and even when there appears to be no wind whatsoever, I know the ocean always pushes the damp air inland. I go up a block from the foot pursuit and wind my way in and out of parking lots, behind buildings, down alleys. Brag lays in the back, lost in his own thoughts. As I pass behind a building, he stands up, pressing his nose against the driver's side rear window.

I drive down that alley to the next street and continue on. After a minute, Brag lies back down. I make a loop and repeat that route, cruising slowly behind the dark building again, and at the exact same spot Brag stands up and presses his nose against the left window.

I stop and get out. There's a six-foot, barbed wire fence with a fabric woven through it so the view is obscured, but when I look over the fence, I can see all the way across a scrubby, abandoned lot to Haley Street. I look down and see a pair of bare, tattooed legs in shorts sticking out from behind a stack of old wooden pallets. Basura is three feet away from me.

I back away from the fence and whisper into my radio that I see the suspect hiding in the lot. Police cars come screeching in and cops scramble over the fence. When a cop yells a challenge at the suspect, Brag blows up in the back of the car. Realizing he is surrounded and hiding mere feet from an angry police dog, Basura sticks out his hands and is arrested without a scratch.

Brag caught a murderer without getting out of the car. And no one was bitten.

We call the U.S. Marshals to let them know that the suspect they've been seeking for eight months was captured in eight minutes. I take Brag to the park and play a game of Kong toss, telling him over and over what a good police dog he is. He knows he caught that man, and seems amused at how easy it was.

I can't help wondering how many bad guys I drove past because I was looking at my MDT screen or blabbing on the radio instead of paying attention to my partner.

Won't happen again. Now I know how good he is.

When we arrive home later it's one of those perfectly still nights where you can hear the owls hooting a mile away. In the backyard Brag and I go pee at the same time, standing side-by-side in the starlight.

ANIMAL KINGDOM

The crows have a young one. She's got a short tail and she hops around awkwardly and they bring her to eat the peanuts I put out. I've named her Frendo, and because she's known me since she left the nest, she's much more relaxed around me than her parents, who know human beings better than she does. Once, a cat slinked up while the three of them were eating and they flew up into the trees to scream accusingly at the intruder. When I heard their hoarse calls I rushed outside and chased the cat away. The crows watched in silence. After that they behaved differently toward me. That was the moment they knew for certain I was their ally.

I blame Brag for this shift in my understanding. I see less of a distinction between human thought and animal thought. Every day I pair my conclusions with Brag's conclusions. You can't do that if you consider animal intelligence to be "lesser." Brag's memory is certainly better than mine, and he possesses a temper as incendiary as my own. Our similarities outstrip the differences.

Brag sits up when Rhyne calls me for a search on Haley Street. This street runs across the lower portion of the city and has always been an epicenter of bad behavior. It's the street where I once witnessed a homicide, where the prostitutes ply their trade nightly, and where violence has visited every address.

In this case, Rhyne and Merrett are looking for a wanted subject at his girlfriend's apartment at the corner of Haley Street and Bath Street. She's cooperative, insisting that her boyfriend has not been around. The neighbors tell a different story but she's given us permission to make sure he's not inside. Since he has a history of violent resistance and weapons charges, I bring Brag out on a long line and announce ourselves at the screen door. No reply. Brag barks into the apartment but doesn't seem particularly agitated, so I'm pretty much going through the motions, putting him in each tiny room and then letting Rhyne and Merrett double-check beneath beds and behind hanging clothes in closets. I no longer wonder if Brag might have missed someone. I wouldn't say it's impossible, but it is so unlikely that I turn my back to a room once he's come out of it. I suppose he could make a mistake, but his nose doesn't make mistakes, and at least his body language would tell me someone was somewhere inside somewhere.

When we get to the bathroom, I hear movement inside. Brag cocks his head. I open the door and a rustling comes from behind the smoked-plastic shower door. I yank open the door and two young cats hiding inside the shower – now hopelessly trapped – jump straight up in the air like repeatedly-popping popcorn kernels.

I slam the shower door shut on the spitting cats. Brag looks up at me as if to say *those cat-things are weird.*

On the way out I ask the suspect's girlfriend why she didn't mention she had two cats as I went into her apartment with an enormous police dog.

"I put them in the shower so they'd be out of the way," she says.

She obviously has no idea how many suspects I've found hiding in showers.

Although I have never subjected Brag to a DNA test, he is most certainly a dog. On more than one occasion suspects he has bitten have claimed otherwise. I do agree that he looks different from most German Shepherds: he's larger than average, his head is blockier, and he carries himself in a way that is unnervingly feral. To me – and the cops who admire him – Brag will always be the Werewolf, a wonderfully canine curiosity with a hint of supernatural menace.

The darkness is your friend. I remind myself of this as Chad, Little, Officer Kerr, and I slip into the back door of a State Street clothing store in the middle of the night. The motion sensor alarm went off inside the building a few minutes earlier, then was activated again in another part of the store. The store manager meets with the first responding officer outside, describing a man who was behaving suspiciously inside the store earlier in the day. He'd made her uncomfortable. I always advise people to trust their instincts; we have them because our ancestors trusted them and survived. The instinct-ignorers sank in tar pits and were spitted on the horns of woolly rhinoceroses. Nice people, I'm sure, but they just wouldn't listen.

So, this sounds like a commercial burglary-in-progress to me. This guy picked the wrong night for this, because four hunters and the Werewolf slip inside the back door and stand in silence inside in the absolute darkness, letting our eyes adjust. Listening. Studying the interior.

I shout the K-9 warning announcement into the store. No reply. Brag barks, translating my words into dog-speak. He moves with an urgency inside that tells me he is getting a noseful of suspect odor. I choke up on the long line and head upstairs first because the most recent alarm activations came from that part of the building.

Buildings take far longer to search than outdoor areas of the same size, for one simple reason: ventilation systems. Nature does not build walls and install air conditioning ducts inside them to suck up odor and deposit it in another place. The wind may be an ever-changing phenomenon but it is much easier to work with when it comes to hunting men. Most buildings have automatic air movement systems that turn on and off of their own accord, making it more problematic. An experienced police dog will work this out, but it can be a scent-based hall-of-mirrors. The more a dog searches buildings, the better they get at it. Once Brag is hunting – especially if he is off-leash – he would much rather solve the problem and get a bite than get frustrated and bark for my help. And when he's on the long line I can tell a lot by the way he crosses a room and how hard he pulls.

Chad and I clear the attic storage space, crowded with teak furniture and boxes of exotic oddities. Brag is telling me there's less odor up here and I realize I chose the wrong location to start. We come back downstairs to where Little and Officer Kerr hold the main floor and I send Brag off into the darkness, happy to let him work away from me. It's faster and safer, but it requires absolute silence because I must be able to hear if Brag is on a bite.

Brag gallops away down one side of the main floor. He's working out the scent in the building, which may take a few laps along the walls. There are counters, dressing rooms, displays, offices, and other architectural peculiarities to worry about clearing in a few minutes. In some cases it's a great idea to turn the lights on inside the building, but in this instance, I don't like it. The suspect is not that much more familiar with the place than we are, and the store is half-a-block long and filled with mannequins. They look like cops to the suspect and like suspects to us, but to Brag there's no human odor so they're just mannequins. He doesn't need light to search, and it's far more nerve-wracking for the hiding suspect to hear the K-9's toenails scratching across the floor somewhere in the dark.

Trying to make the search area smaller, I ask Little to move forward. This is a tactical mistake on my part, because we move into an area that Brag has not cleared yet and Little takes no more than a few steps before he illuminates a pair of shoes and some jeans peeking out from a display case.

The suspect is hiding mere feet in front of us and Brag is on the other side of the building, working out the forced-air odor problem.

I call Brag and he comes streaking back, his eyes glowing in the flash lit darkness. I grab onto his harness, pointing him toward the display where the suspect is hiding. I shout at the suspect to show his hands but he thinks I'm bluffing and doesn't move. Brag was working the odor out and I've interrupted him; he doesn't see the suspect's legs because they're motionless.

I reach out and grab onto the corner of the display and pull it, and the whole unit comes crashing down, exposing the suspect. I send Brag and he fires at the suspect like a missile.

He's on the bite and throws it in reverse, pulling the man from beneath the clothes. He's bitten the suspect on the side between the ribs and the hip and as the man is yanked out from his place of concealment Brag does something that astonishes me and the other cops in the room: he picks the suspect up in the air – like a backhoe picking up a scoopful of earth – takes a few steps backward, then slams the man down onto the floor again. I'm not sure what I just witnessed, but it was a feat of strength worthy of a wild animal.

The man's face is twisted in agony and I know there's no fight in him now. I grab onto Brag's collar and straddle him in preparation for the out. Brag's muzzle has to be under absolute control because there can be no second bite if it's not warranted.

Brag comes off the bite and I backpedal us away from the suspect as Chad snaps cuffs onto the man. Brag barks challenges at the suspect but the man is finished. He grimaces as the cops walk him into the rear alley so the paramedics can examine him.

Little comes over to me in the alley, an incredulous smile on his face.

"Did you see Brag pick that guy up?" he says. "I didn't know he could do that."

"Me neither," I admit.

Brag and I trot victoriously back to our car, parked in the shadows down the street. Every cop we pass says "Good job, Brag," like a teammate congratulating a batter who has just crushed a fastball into the upper deck beyond the center field wall. Brag smiles the whole way.

At the hospital I put on my baseball hat disguise and change my demeanor from Werewolf Handler to Officer Friendly. I find the suspect handcuffed to a gurney in an examination room, awaiting his medical clearance to go to jail. He has four clean punctures on his side, two in front and two in back. By tomorrow hideous, purple bruising will spread out across his torso. He doesn't feel much like talking, but I try to chat with the suspect for a few minutes anyway. I just want him to admit he heard the warning, that he knew the dog was searching for him and that he decided to stay hidden anyway. I need him to verbalize his non-compliance for the recording. He does.

As I'm leaving, I turn back for one more question, one that satisfies my curiosity more than eases any concern for liability.

"When the dog bit you," I ask, "what did it feel like?"

The suspect thinks hard for a moment before answering.

"A shark attack," he says.

Brag and I go straight to the empty showgrounds for a game of double-Kong toss, burning off any excess anxiety from the bite. The report can wait until later. I'm throwing two Kong balls, picking up one as Brag runs after the other and then throwing it the opposite direction when he returns with the first ball. He drops the one in his mouth when I throw the other, so I walk ten feet each direction while he streaks back and forth at a dead sprint.

As he barrels toward me I turn to throw the ball the other way and I lose my balance on the wet grass, stepping wide to my left. Brag – who was passing close by me at top speed – clips my left leg and sends me airborne. "De-cleated" is the proper term; both of my feet fly up toward the sky and the first part of my body to hit the ground is the back of my neck. I lie there like a rag doll for a few seconds, looking up at the stars and realizing that the ones that zoom around aren't real.

Brag returns with his Kong and stands over me, sniffing my face with curiosity because he's never seen me lie down on the wet grass before.

I sit up and look around for any witnesses to my de-cleating but it's the middle of the night. Brag flops down beside me, gnawing happily on his Kong ball and seeming pleased that I have learned to enjoy the cool dampness with him.

The next morning a garish purple bruising is painted across the back of my left leg and my knee complains the entire way as I make my way downstairs for a bowl of cereal.

Just another day. In a few hours we'll do it all again.

Auto theft is technically a property crime. Suspects who steal cars usually do it when the owner isn't around. Like most burglars, they want to avoid a confrontation. Carjacking is another story; that's a crime against a person because the suspect is forcibly taking a vehicle, often at gunpoint. Suspects do sometimes steal cars to "joyride," but they also steal them to use them in the commission of more violent crimes, such as armed robbery. Robbery crews generally do not take over jewelry stores after double-parking their personal vehicle in the loading zone. It's a stolen car. Once the crime is committed and witnesses have scribbled down the license plate of the fleeing vehicle, the suspects abandon the stolen car someplace out of the way and get into another one. Because of this tactic, any time a cop runs across a stolen car driving down the road that cop is understandably nervous about interacting with the driver and occupants. Also, nine times out ten, when you try to stop that car, the driver has no intention of pulling over. A pursuit is almost guaranteed. Things get crazy after that.

Officer Kyle Lowry is a new officer and a go-getter and he has spotted a stolen car occupied by four gang-member-looking knuckleheads on the mesa. Lowry takes one hard look at the car and – not surprisingly – the chase is on. Before any other cops can get close enough to join in, the suspects abandon the still-moving vehicle and scatter in all directions. Because he is young and vigorous and still does not understand that the bumblebee cannot technically fly, Lowry captures two of the passengers by himself. I want the driver because he is the one most likely to answer for the crime. He was last seen vaulting a fence into a residential yard.

I take a couple of cops with me and go to that house and knock on the door. The occupants say they did see a young man in baggy jeans running across their backyard, which they found suspicious. They add that there is no need to search their backyard because the young man was clearly running through the yard with the intention of going over the next fence into the neighbor's property. Three years ago, I would have accepted this explanation – not wanting to trample someone's geraniums unnecessarily – but today I want to confirm one particular detail.

"Where *exactly* did you last see the suspect?" I ask the homeowner.

He walks to the back window and points to the exact middle of his backyard. "Right there."

That's where my search begins. I put Brag on harness and long-line and take my cover officers into the backyard and tell Brag, "Search." Brag's nose goes down; he zig-zags, heads back toward the fence where the suspect entered the yard, and then pulls me hard to a wooden shed barely a dozen feet from the fence he came over. One of my cover officers tries the handle. Locked. Brag is frozen at the shed door, his body shivering with anticipation.

"Get the key," I tell one of cops beside me and he retreats back to the house. It is five minutes before he returns.

"The owners never lock that shed door," he whispers.

He puts the key in the door handle and turns it, unlocking the door. But it won't open. Another cop named Payne and I make brief eye contact. He nods; someone is pushing the door shut from inside. Time to announce.

"Suspect in the shed, this is the Santa Barbara Police Department K-9 Unit! Come out with your hands up or you will be injured!" I shout.

As usual, there is no reply. I repeat myself.

I can picture bullets punching through those thin wooden walls and taking us all out. The suspect knows we're out here. He's not coming out. He demands to be bitten.

"Kick it," I tell Payne.

Payne drives his boot into the door and it flies inward. Brag fires into the dark shed as I repeat "*Packen, packen!*"

A struggle. Tools tumble down and pots shatter. The nylon line in my hand gyrates and I pull as hard as I can. Brag emerges backward with a suspect's arm in his mouth, pulling the man flat onto the grass. The suspect tries to show his hands as best he can while being savaged by Brag and that's good enough for us so I take Brag off as the cops grab onto the suspect.

I trot with Brag past the wide-eyed homeowner watching from inside his house. He gives me a thumbs up through the window. I smile and nod at the favorable review.

At the hospital I find the suspect lying quietly in his exam room. I can tell the instant he looks at me that he doesn't recognize me, despite that fact that the entire arrest occurred in broad daylight. His injuries aren't life-threatening, they've just delayed his trip to jail by an hour.

I quiz him about the bite, and when we get to the moment where the shed door was kicked in, I ask the suspect what happened.

"The cops told me to come out but I didn't," he says. "Then they kicked the door and sent a bear in to bite me."

I raise my eyebrows. "Are you sure?"

"Officer, it was bear. His head was HUGE."

I've played the Straight Face Game so many times that I can relish this moment without ruining it. I click my pen shut dramatically. "Well, you have a good story to tell your homies when you get out of jail."

I go out to the K-9 car and open the back door, ruffling Brag's mane and laughing with him. It's time to take this grizzly somewhere for a play break. But before I do I call Ted and accuse him of duping me for years. Now I know why this animal took so long to warm up to me: he's a police bear. It all makes sense now.

TERRIBLE DEEDS

I'm standing in my kitchen, looking out across the garden and past the metal gate where my nine-year-old son Strieker wanders around the dog yard. He can speak, but has so much trouble forming sentences and processing conversation that he prefers not to. Social interaction is usually too much for him. As a baby he would howl and squeeze his eyes shut when a stranger walked directly toward him and made eye contact. After years of examinations and evaluations he was diagnosed as autistic, which sounds like an explanation but really is the absence of one. It is also irreversible; my son will forever be struggling to reconcile his inner world with a confusing, terrifying outer world.

He's alone out there with Brag. When they first met, Brag stood taller. Not anymore; Strieker has shot up. Brag follows him around the yard, being nosy, watching the boy's every move. The dog understands that Strieker comes out for quiet so Brag gives him space. Occasionally, Brag will drop a Kong ball, ever hopeful, but he knows that Strieker has no interest in any game that doesn't take place in his own imagination. It's all but impossible to penetrate that inner world, and Brag respects that. I couldn't say with any certainty when I knew that Brag would never harm my son, but I know. He and Strieker are friends, and there is no need for them to ever utter a word to each other.

Having a child with crippling developmental disabilities often opens a window into other people's souls that I wish would have remained closed. I doubt people who smirk at my son's hand-flapping realize how satisfying it would be for me to slap that smirk away. It's a constant struggle. I'm always balancing the urge to apologize for Strieker's panicked outbursts and the desire to burn the faces of those who mock my son into a book that I will keep to the end of my days. I would prefer not to carry the burden of this book, but I do.

I am often equally surprised by the kindness of strangers, people that I would have expected to have the opposite reaction. Once while boarding a delayed flight when my son was five, I struggled to calm him as the passenger line stopped on the jet-way just shy of the cabin doors. Strieker writhed and shrieked in my arms, realizing we were about to enter this confined metal tube with hundreds of strangers. A gruff-looking man traveling alone turned around and saw me trying to soothe my child. I recognized that look as the man realized there was something not quite right about this child and the sounds he was making. I expected an eye roll or a grimace from the man.

"Hey, buddy – look!" the man said, smiling and placing his hand on the red and blue fuselage. "The airplane is the same color as Superman! We're going to fly like Superman!"

Strieker went quiet, puzzling out this unexpected input from a stranger. The plane was undeniably the same color as Superman. The man smiled warmly at my son and then at me. I remember his face. It goes in a different book, the one I should keep.

On the lower East Side there is a liquor store owned by a man from Syria. He came to this country years ago and realized the American dream, opening up a shop that allowed him to work hard and take care of his family, which included his developmentally-disabled adult brother. The brother was high-functioning enough that he could walk by himself to work at the store and make his way back home again after it closed. But the shop owner always kept close tabs on him, often keeping him on the phone as the disabled man walked alone across a neighborhood that wasn't exactly safe – the lower East Side.

One night as the two talked on the phone, the disabled brother paused in the conversation to respond to an unknown passerby on the street. While the store owner listened on the other end, a male voice asked a muffled question.

"I am talking to my brother," the disabled man replied. The line went dead.

Worried, the store owner went looking for his brother and found him lying bloodied in a gutter, beaten to death for no reason whatsoever.

Cops swarmed into the area and the gang unit immediately contacted the usual suspects, finding some Eastsiders at a residence only blocks away standing around a fire pit and drinking "40's" of malt liquor. One savvy gang cop saw a bit of clothing burning in the fire and yanked it out. The bloodstains were still visible on the unburned fabric.

My phone buzzes. Tyler – on his way in to work with Hondo – gives me the rundown. Three gang members are in custody but the final suspect is still outstanding: William Vacio. Yes, "Pyscho" Billy, the same man who fled from Brag only to be bitten by a pit bull. Vacio was the ringleader in this latest deadly assault: he'd laughed while he stomped on the unconscious man's head. Cops had gone to arrest Vacio at an apartment after receiving an anonymous tip but Vacio escaped and fled into a brushy creek bed.

Tyler tells me a perimeter is set and cops are pretty sure they have Vacio contained in a narrow but difficult-to-search area.

Brag sprints ahead of me to the garage door, sensing my silent urgency. He doesn't mind that it was our day off. In this case, I don't either. I would love to say I'm looking forward to apprehending a murder suspect and bringing him to justice. I'm not. If Vacio gives me a lawful reason, I'll put some holes in him. But I wonder – would I feel bad afterward? Would Vacio's accusatory shade visit me at 3:37 a.m.? Or would I sleep more soundly knowing the world was a better place? This anger inside me is a volatile element.

Brag doesn't lie down in the back as we drive over the pass into the city. He feels the tension and keeps an eye on the road the entire time. When we arrive on-scene, I repeat the same phrase I always say to him as I put on his harness and uncoil the long line: "Let's get that bad guy." He barks once in agreement.

Tyler and I split up. He takes Hondo and holds one end of the creek and I take the other. Brag and I creep silently into position, wrapping darkness around us like a cloak. As more cops arrive and tighten the perimeter, a college student who lives next door to the apartment where Vacio was hiding comes out to complain about the number of cop cars in the complex parking lot. When he doesn't get a satisfactory response from anyone, he and his friends go out onto the second-story balcony to drink and provide an obscene commentary on the police activity below them. They know who we're looking for. One of them opines about how much force is being marshalled against one man. Forget about the fact that the man is a murderer.

A hostage negotiator arrives on-scene and it's his show for now. His job is to try to reason with a man named "Psycho" Billy. Good luck. The negotiator gets a bull-horn and about fifteen minutes. Then, we hunt.

"Billy, we know you're hiding in there and you need to come out. Billy, we don't want anyone else to get hurt. We don't want you to get hurt, either. Come out and we can talk."

It goes on and on. It's a quiet, cold night and the negotiator's voice bounces across the narrow canyon. Unless he's got his fingers stuffed in his ears, Vacio hears every word. Brag and I wait and each second that passes means I'm closer to doing this my way. I'll hunt this man down and for the first time in a long time he will be afraid of something in the dark.

Time's up. The negotiator tells Vacio the dogs are coming.

Tyler and Hondo and their cover team move slowly in our direction from their position upstream. If Vacio breaks and runs he'll end up right in Brag's jaws and my sights. Minutes pass. Brag and I crouch and listen, inhaling the night. Brag stays silent – he knows we're laying an ambush.

Suddenly there is shouting up the creek bed. Brag gathers in a deep breath. Someone yells for Vacio to show his hands and Brag explodes into barking, half in frustration and half in release. Hondo's excited barking echoes back at us and then Tyler's voice breaks the radio silence.

"Code Four," he says flatly. "One in custody."

No bite; Vacio surrendered. I curse under my breath and lead Brag back toward our car. Brag cranes his neck behind us at the dancing flashlight beams emerging from the brush. I put him in and shut the door as the arresting officers march Vacio past the place where we were hiding moments ago.

The people up on the apartment balcony spy Vacio being led away in handcuffs.

"We love you, Billy!" they shout. "Fuck the police!"

I can't listen any more. I get in my car and log off, vanishing from everyone's computer screen. I have no interest in a de-briefing or a high-five. It's wrong. The murderer lives on to boast and be fed and feel clean sheets and watch the newest cable series and lift weights. An innocent man died in a gutter without ever knowing why. I wanted Vacio to feel that powerlessness, even if only for a moment.

Brag turns restless circles in the back of the car. There's nothing I can say to calm him. As we drive up the highway and there is only the winding road in the headlights, he knows it's over so he collapses onto his elbows and his sigh is more like a groan of frustration.

At home I put his steaming food bowl onto the cold cement tile in his kennel. While he eats I place my hand against his ribs. He doesn't mind. When he's finished, he licks his chops and goes out into the darkness to check the yard and be alone with his thoughts. He looks back at me once before vanishing into the night.

I go inside to the refrigerator and stare at a picture my son drew of an airplane, a cross-section with stick figure passengers seated row upon row. The sun outside the plane is the only thing in the crayon drawing that has a human face, but its expression is blank. A perfectly straight line for a mouth.

I wear that same expression right now. Beneath it an angry, molten core spins and spins.

PACK LEADER

Humans are animals. We juggle different drives – some lofty, some base – and this balancing act determines the course of our lives. Laws and social accountability keep many of the more destructive human urges in check. Mostly.

Dogs don't have laws. Their actions are pure instinct. And yet Brag has revealed himself to be a living puzzle. Once upon a time, I was certain that police dogs did only what they were trained to do; the more trained and obedient the dog, the better the results. One-hundred-percent wrong. When Brag rides behind me, he looks out the window with undisguised intensity, evaluating all that he sees and smells. Cascading thoughts are visible behind those amber eyes. I still don't know exactly what drives him to take such an interest in this violent world of men. He cannot tell me and it may never be proven by science, but somehow, he cares. There is no term in dog training for this invisible ingredient, though every handler asserts that their dog has special qualities no other dog possesses. I believe it is because we glimpse that ghost inhabiting the machine. A soul, perhaps. Brag and I spend so much time together that I talk to him as if he were a person. Because, well, he is. I tell him things I wouldn't reveal to anyone else. Maybe that's one reason we stay so close together, even during meals. Since I've been partnered with Brag, I've eaten inside a restaurant during my patrol shift less than half-a-dozen times. I don't like being separated from him. If I can't see the K-9 car or if I'm too far away to hear Brag barking I get uneasy. We're partners – there's no other way to say it. The restaurant food doesn't taste good anyway because I eat too fast. The answer to this dilemma is trunk dining. I park somewhere out of the way, like a large parking lot behind a business – helps when you work nights and weekends – and eat my lunch standing at my trunk. I never miss a radio transmission this way and I'm always ready to jump in my car and take off. It's also pretty hard to ambush me in that scenario. It's a sad state of affairs when a cop has to think about getting shot while he eats, but it happens. I eat my dinner on top of my trunk and looking over the top of the light bar. Brag never watches me eat because I have never once shared my food with him. When we park and I get out and open my little cooler, he doesn't raise his head. He likes human food as much as any other dog, but he has the most fragile intestinal tract imaginable. A few bites of my food would probably throw his stomach into total revolt. If you think a steaming, wet dog in your car for eleven hours on a rainy night is bad, try diarrhea dog in your car for the same length of time. It's awful. When Brag's stomach acts up, he gets frustrated because he knows he's missing out on good calls to take bathroom breaks. I try to be understanding because his digestive difficulties are stress-related. He feels pressure, like I do. He worries about me when he can't see me. And when he barks he does it with every fiber of his being. Too many barks create the same condition as too much people food.

On a sweltering training day, a stomach issue appears without warning. Brag is barking his head off in the back of the car while we work some other dogs on the training field. I go to get Brag out for his turn and find what could best be described as a crime scene in the back of my car. Liquefied dog doo is splattered on all surfaces, even Brag's face. Cursing, I bring him out and he stands as still as he can while I hose him down. The look on his face is such a mix of disappointment and embarrassment that I have to laugh, just like the other handlers are laughing at us right now.

"Come on," I tell Brag. "Let's break up this party."

I trot him over into the middle of the group of handlers and Brag takes that opportunity to shake the water from his coat. The handlers scatter.

The street crimes unit calls me to do a narcotics search of a parolee's room in a half-way house occupied by a number of people. I bring Brag in through the kitchen and go directly to the parolee's bedroom to conduct the search. Brag searches unenthusiastically. No dope. As he and I make our way quickly back through the house, we pass the same kitchen trash can we passed ten minutes earlier. Brag did not react when he went by it the first time, but he clearly remembers what was in there because as we pass by the trash can a second time he sticks his head into it as quick as a cobra and comes out with a slice of pizza. Before I can utter a reproach or grab it, Brag swallows the slice whole.

The cops who witnessed the pizza snatch are amused by this dastardly side of Brag. I'm not.

A few hours later we go to help Gary Gaston who tried to pull over a suspicious-looking character in a car, only to have the man jump out and flee into the darkness. Being a wise cop, Gaston didn't give chase but stayed with the car until it was determined that the car was stolen. He asks for me to come help locate the suspect.

There aren't enough cops to set up a perimeter – it's too busy – so our only hope was that the suspect fled a short distance and then went to ground on his own. I bring Brag out on long-line and let him work the odor from the stolen car and the search is an immediate disaster. Brag looks uncomfortable and oddly confused by what we're doing and it's so quiet I can hear his stomach gurgling as the oily pizza slice works its magic on his digestive tract. Within fifteen minutes I realize that we're going in circles in the same yard and I apologize to Gaston and head back to the K-9 car at a brisk walk.

Brag won't look at me. He's so ashamed at his performance that he hangs his head. I know he doesn't feel well and it's a cheap shot but I'm annoyed with him so I say it anyway: "I hope you enjoyed your pizza, because you let a bad guy get away." I pull off his harness and we head out of the city. End of watch.

Brag lies down quietly in the back of the car but we're not halfway home before he turns fast circles behind me, whistling through his nose. That means he has to go. Right now. We end up stopping twice so he can relieve himself. I stand beside him on the side of the highway, keeping his leash out of the smelly mess he's making, watching his legs tremble as he voids. I can't stay mad at him so I pat his neck and tell him it's okay and when we get home, I mix some rice and pumpkin into his meal, which always helps to settle his stomach down.

The next day at work Brag and I come out of briefing in the police station to find an empty pizza box on the hood of the K-9 car.

Cops.

I'm brushing Brag out so he'll look especially beautiful for a demo. His thick undercoat produces an endless supply of fur. Curiously, I like K-9 demonstrations now. I think I enjoy interacting with people more in this setting because they're enthusiastic about police work with a dog. Let's be honest, no one really cares as much about the handler. All eyes are on the dog. I've come to realize that Brag isn't a mascot of the police department, he's symbolic of the *idea* of police work. He's also a beautiful animal, with an undeniable presence that makes people step back in fear and lean forward with interest.

There's a moment I love during K-9 demos. I always start the event by addressing the group without Brag first so they'll get some information about the dog while they're still paying attention to me. It's also an important opportunity to warn people about what NOT to do around the dog, because if you don't tell them up front, someone will always do it. Folks have tried to kiss Brag, offer him chocolates (poisonous to dogs), bring their pets close to "meet" Brag, and even – believe it or not – try to startle Brag on purpose to see how he reacts. After I admonish my audience to do none of these things, I get my dog. When I come back into the room with Brag, my favorite demo moment happens: Brag strides through the door and the room goes dead quiet for a full second and then people "ooh" and "ah" and I'm reminded how lucky I am to be paired with this incredible creature. Brag is affected by the excitement of these demonstrations, too. I am reluctant to call him a show-off but I think he is becoming one. When we hold a large fundraiser in the Santa Ynez Valley, Brag seems aware that there is a much larger and electric crowd than usual, hundreds of people waiting to see him do his thing. When I hit the door-pop to let Brag out for a bite as Ted simulates attacking, Brag hits Ted and slams him into the K-9 car with such violence that I'm certain Ted is injured and the car is dented.

I put Brag back in the car as the audience applauds. Ted stands by the trunk, wincing.

"Brag's never hit me like that before," Ted tells me, prodding his rib cage tenderly.

"Are you all right?"

He grins stoically. "Ask me tomorrow."

I check the car: no dent, just a scratchy smear where another human being was humbled by the Werewolf. Brag looks out the window at the adoring crowd, a smile on his face.

We finish out the week with a call-out on the ocean. A man holds his girlfriend hostage on a sailboat and I bring Brag out to where the SWAT team waits for us on a larger Harbor Patrol launch. Brag whines with joy when he spies the green

SWAT uniforms, thrilled to discover that this is not a pleasure cruise but real work. We rescue the hostage and forcibly tow the suspect's boat into the harbor with him hiding inside. Faced with the land shark I threaten to send below decks to retrieve him, the suspect gives up. Afterward, Chad declares this to be his favorite SWAT call-out because we resolved it by cutting anchor and taking the sailboat as a prize – a very Napoleonic-era naval tactic. No one was hurt; the hostage fell into the sea but was plucked out immediately, and Brag's enraged barking secured the suspect's surrender. The four-legged scalawag is as useful on water as he is on land.

There is so much technology available to law enforcement, it's hard for cops to understand how the police K-9 fits in. When I began this career the only technology I carried out of the patrol car was a portable radio on my belt. It was the size and weight of a brick. Now there are GPS-guided Mobile Data Terminals in every police car that not only provide all the details about an emergency call, they show you where it is on a map and where the other cops are, in real time. I have a video camera attached to my dashboard and one clipped onto the front of my uniform. I exit my car, with all of this technology, and open the back door. Out comes a canine at the end of a rope – still the most efficient way to hunt a man. But only if handler and dog hunt effectively as a pack.

There's an exercise we do once a month at K-9 training. All the handlers put their dogs on a down on the field and walk away. Six dogs watch us like sphinxes while we vanish as a group around the corner of a building. One by one, the handlers call their dogs to them. The remaining dogs must not break their down, no matter how badly they want to not be left behind. Brag – one of the most experienced dogs on the field – is usually last. He waits, alone, for the sound of my voice.

This is an "obedience" exercise, but that word doesn't work well anymore, as it implies subservience. I am not Brag's master, I am his pack leader, a relationship that has no satisfactory translation into human speech or thought. But I know it on an animal level, somewhere deep inside my brain that has slept until now. There is no him without me, and no me without him.

I call Brag and hear the sound of his toenails across the asphalt as he runs to me.

SECOND CHANCES

O n several occasions, I've run across suspects Brag and I arrested years earlier and had cordial conversations with them. One or two of them were willing to show me the scars from Brag's bites, usually after expressing an understandable reluctance to re-visit that experience. I try to approach these encounters from a "that was a crazy night and there's no hard feelings" direction. Cops and suspects usually fall into this type of relationship once the dust has settled. After an adrenaline-soaked car chase, foot chase, and sometimes a fight, we both must move on to the legal and procedural minutiae necessary to conclude the event, beginning with the trip to the county jail. There's a strange moment where the cop, now disarmed of his handgun and sans all other weaponry (a legal necessity before entering the jail), stands with the suspect outside the locked series of doors, awaiting entry to continue the booking process. It doesn't take long for a rookie officer to realize that during this phase the crazed, combative criminal of an hour ago has more often than not been replaced by a subdued individual who is only interested in getting a sack lunch from the jail staff. Since county jail is a non-smoking facility, the brutal reality of spending the next few months without tobacco is often the most pressing personal concern for the arrestee. With this in mind, when you know an arrestee is going to be locked up for any extended period of time and they've been respectful, it is a gesture of ultimate coolness to remove the handcuffs for a few minutes in the secure jail parking lot and let the arrestee smoke his last cigarette. It's a curious tableau. The cop – weapons locked in the trunk – leans against the car while the suspect smokes wistfully. Quiet words are exchanged, and never in anger. I wish I'd recorded all of those conversations. They're usually about life, family, or some obscure philosophical concept. Suspects who've been granted those few precious drags of a last cigarette before a lengthy incarceration never forget that act of kindness, especially with the knowledge that it is technically a violation of policy. But is a human thing to do.

Since I have a K-9 partner occupying my back seat, I don't take arrestees to jail anymore. Another cop always takes the arrest and the paperwork, leaving me free to bring Brag to another call. It's just as well; Brag does not want to make nice with suspects. For him, you're either a good guy or a bad guy. Children are always good guys. Cops are usually good guys. People on the street are bad guys until proven otherwise, and suspects who are arrested – especially the ones who need to be hunted down by Brag – remain bad guys. How long does he remember them? I have an opportunity to find out this summer evening while I'm cruising the Eastside.

"Fifty-five, K9-1, subject with a handgun at 1200 East Ortega St."

"K9-1, Code 6 area." Which means I'm there, but the dispatcher already saw that on her screen. I'm three quick turns away and Brag's on his feet the instant he feels the engine kick up. When I arrive in that block I'm confronted with a scenario that's not uncommon to police work, especially during the day when there's a lot of humanity moving around; there are people on the sidewalk, pointing. The suspect has fled on foot. I follow the pointing fingers, turning onto another block in time to see another resident in their front yard who has divined from the urgency of my driving that I'm looking for the man who just ran past them. So, they point.

The suspect description is a Hispanic male adult with a heavy build in his forties, an unusual description for an armed person loose on the Eastside. He's running mostly downhill, and fast. He can probably hear my engine.

"Five-five the suspect is running south and east." More units are rolling in, and I want to tighten the noose. I spy another witness on the street who is eager to point out where the suspect turned. I slow down, looking up an empty block. No one. There are at least twenty residences on each side of this block, many of them with converted garages and apartment additions. The suspect has run into one of these properties. I think he's winded and wants to lay low.

"Suspect last seen in the 400 block of Voluntario," I tell the responding units over the radio and I can hear them placing themselves into perimeter positions. Good. It's still light so it's going to be particularly hard for him to break perimeter.

I stop in the area where he was last seen and harness Brag up and clip the long line to him. Since I don't know exactly where the suspect ran last, I let Brag out with the whole fifteen-foot line in the middle of the street. He knows what that means and he trots urgent circles at the end of the line, his nose hovering above the asphalt. Every once in a while his head comes up and he takes a look and opens his mouth to gulp in air. Four cops join me for the search, guns drawn, ready to meet fire with fire if the suspect decides to shoot it out. I still make no attempt to search with my handgun out. This admission will likely make a lot of K-9 handlers cringe, but they're not partnered with Brag. I just don't find it possible to work this dog properly with a gun in my hand. Yes, I know how to index, how to operate a safety, how to keep a gun at low-ready. I've never had a negligent discharge in my career and I intend to keep it that way. I definitely don't want to get shot in the face. There's no right answer, just one that is less wrong for me. So, I have two hands working the long line, pulling and sliding the nylon through my palms.

Suddenly, Brag's on the scent. He yanks the line taut as he surges down a driveway mid-block, back toward a duplex tucked behind an old orange tree in the rear yard of the property. I can smell the ripe oranges as I duck beneath the low branches. Brag pulls me to the front door of the apartment and I tell the cops with me that we've arrived.

"Are you sure?" Sergeant Lazarus asks. Brag snorts at the door like a wild boar.

"One-hundred percent," I tell him, and he sends officers either direction from me to cover the back and sides of the duplex. I pull Brag away from the door, not easily.

Not looking totally convinced, but trusting Brag enough to not argue with me, Lazarus knocks on the door. A young woman answers, her face registering the sudden sight of serious-faced cops and a mad werewolf. There's one second of awkward silence where the cops are no doubt questioning my surety. But Brag is incensed now that the door is open. He lunges for it and it takes all my strength to restrain him. He's so maniacal that I don't try to put him on a down – Brag is behaving as if the suspect were standing behind that young woman and waving his arms.

"Santa Barbara Police Department," Lazarus says, stating the obvious out of legal necessity. "Is there anyone else in the house?"

"No," the young woman replies woodenly, her eyes wide.

"Pull her out," I tell Lazarus. "He's in there."

Cops reach for the woman to remove her from the doorway but she needs no encouragement and bolts out to us, leaving the door open. Now we have a few minutes to decide our next step. The suspect will have a hard time getting out. We're not sure if he's barricaded, but he was armed so the worst move we can make would be to rush in immediately and get in a surprise gunfight.

Brag is losing his mind. He's gone full werewolf. There's no way I can discuss our next tactical step with Lazarus while my dog's behaving like this.

While Lazarus and I try to communicate over Brag, I hear the unmistakable sound of a man shouting. Brag had already heard this, which is the reason he was reacting. Now it's louder, and we can all hear it. The cops freeze, listening. There it is again: a man yelling. It's urgent, full of panic, but I can't make out the words. Then through the open door I see a form writhing across the floor of the front room in the duplex: a grown man moving like a worm toward us, his hands spread in front of him. He's Hispanic, forties, soaked with sweat.

"I give up!" he shrieks. "Please don't send the dog!"

I haven't even made my K-9 announcement yet. The man undulates toward us, his face a rubbery mask of terror.

Then I recognize him. It's Benny Manteca, the career criminal who nearly bled to death when he fought with Brag a year-and-a-half ago. Benny looks nothing like the imposing person from his many booking photos where he glares into the camera with the dark menace of a playground bully-turned-adult sociopath. He looks like a pathetic man-child, his mouth wide and downturned with fear. Tears streak his cheeks. I almost laugh.

"It's Manteca," I tell Lazarus, who orders Benny to keep crawling out to where we are, the soundest tactical conclusion to that scenario and the only one that will save Manteca from a werewolf attack.

I grip Brag's harness with both hands as he explodes with rage. His eyes bulge, red and wild, and spittle flies in the air toward Manteca's frightened face. Cops creep forward to make the arrest. The handcuffs go on and I backpedal with Brag at a forty-five-degree angle so the cops can walk Benny down the driveway. Manteca, the infamous escapist and fighter, looks relieved. Once Manteca is out of sight, I take Brag in to search the duplex to make sure there's no one else hiding in there. There isn't. We call Code Four and I put Brag away, walking him past the patrol car where Manteca sits in the back. Brag pulls toward the car, smelling his nemesis. Benny doesn't look at either of us.

I put Brag in our car. He's panting, his eyes still bloodshot and crazed.

"Good job, Brag," I tell him but he's looking past me toward Manteca. "You got that bad guy. You knew who he was."

On my way back to the scene, I pass Officer Lowry, who will be booking Manteca on a list of charges, including holding the woman against her will in her house while we were outside. He didn't know her; he forced his way in when she cracked the door open to see who was knocking so urgently. I don't know if he planned to harm her or not. Doesn't matter now, because he can't.

"He wanted nothing to do with Brag," Lowry says.

"He remembers the last time they met."

Lowry grins. "He told me 'that black-faced dog bit me last year and I almost died. I'm not going through that shit again'."

I look past Lowry at Manteca seated in the back. Sweat streams down his face. I resist the urge to speak to him. He won't look at me or Brag, which is exactly how I want this to end.

Brag knew the man he was hunting. He'd carried disdain for that human, stored in his canine brain. Brag might've killed him this time. He wanted to, and maybe he would have been right to do it. To most people, murder, robbery, and rape are nothing more than sensational headlines. For me and Brag these are physical events, with real human victims and gruesome crime scenes that are often the starting point of our hunt for the suspect. All of these crimes are perpetuated by a dark will to harm, one that must be stopped with a stronger will.

This call is over; it won't make the news or change anyone's lives in any way that they can perceive. But Manteca is done making more victims for now. I walk back to the duplex where the young woman weeps as she describes to one of the cops the breathless terror when she was trapped inside her own home with a man who had soulless eyes.

When she spies me, she asks, "Was that your police dog?"

I nod, not wanting to interrupt the primary officer's investigation.

"Tell him thank you from me," she says. I promise her that I will.

Brag and I don't have time to go chase the Kong ball right now. It's too busy. But hours later I park in an empty lot and open the back door and run my fingers through Brag's mane.

"Now I know, Brag. You remember everything, don't you?"

He meets my gaze and I have my answer.

SWAMP THINGS

As a K-9 team, if the call isn't hot, we won't go. I love this constant action, but I suspect it's grinding me down emotionally. It's just not healthy to point a gun at someone every night, to view the world through a predator's eyes. I'm worried I'm becoming less human. Professional and efficient, but not approachable. Maybe even feral.

This newest phase of my vocation has also all but ruined my casual social interactions. After a night of wading through chaos until 3 a.m., I can't wake up and behave like the person next door. I fake it, but it feels like people can tell. It's like wearing someone else's skin. Even the polo shirt I wear to barbecues and birthday parties on the weekend feels like a disguise. I can't relax and drink one beer because I have to go to work later and it's already on my mind as I try to make small talk. But in reality, I don't care about the NFL or the weather. And every barbecue conversation carries with it a creeping dread that someone will share their "unfair speeding ticket" story or ask my opinion on whether or not their cousin's arrest for public intoxication was a case of excessive force. My response is always, "Hard to say; I wasn't there."

Brag dislikes our days off. He goes into wait mode, sitting by the gate every afternoon with the faint hope that we'll get called in. I'm certain he always knows what day of the week it is. He's always ready for a savage game of tug, even if it's just to kill time. When people come over and try to interact with him, he walks away. He and I both look for reasons to avoid small talk with humans.

I also dread the jarring 3:37 a.m. wake up to a jack-hammering pulse and the certainty that someone – or something – is moving through my house. It's every night on my days off, so I get a pass when I'm working because I'm never in bed before four in the morning.

I put this issue off as personal maintenance to be addressed at a later date and continue on. The calls keep coming in. The phone keeps ringing. You can't stop it, and you can only hunt one person at a time. Hunting isn't the worst part, it's the best part.

Another confession: vehicle pursuits are fun. In every car chase there's a good chance someone could be seriously injured. It is difficult to explain how anyone could be having a good time knowing that something terrible could happen any second. Part of it might be that a bad guy has declared that he intends to escape at any cost. Things seem surprisingly simple when ambiguity is eliminated.

When I hear cops go in pursuit of a stolen car one night, I activate the Extrapolometer. This particular suspect is making quick turns, which tells me he's looking for a place to bail out soon. I'm still ten blocks away when he does just that, leaping out of the still-rolling stolen SUV and leaping fences in the dark. The Extrapolometer tells me he's going to turn right more often than left and favor a downhill if presented with any slope. He's running in a block that has a slope, so that helps vector me in. By the time I've decided where he's going to pop out, I'm slamming the car into park and throwing open the back door and latching onto Brag's collar with the lead as Brag is leaping out of the car. We jog past two residences and I hear yelling somewhere mid-block and then suddenly there's a dark figure sprinting out of a driveway directly in front of us and before I can say one word Brag is airborne and clamping his teeth onto the man's right buttock. The man stops like he was attached to a bungee cord, hitting the ground with his limbs still spinning. It's over, just like that. Two breathless cops come clambering over a fence at the end of the driveway to find the suspect in cuffs and Brag barking at the prone suspect. I get on the radio to call off the responding units, who are all in an understandable hurry to get here. One of the officers involved in the pursuit and foot-chase, Nelson, stares at me incredulously as he catches his breath with his hands on his knees.

"Where the hell did you two come from?" he asks, looking for my police car which is parked out of view around the corner. From his perspective, Brag and I materialized out of thin air where the suspect was about to emerge from the wacky obstacle course of fences.

"Short cut," I tell him, stabbing my thumb over my shoulder. I don't mention the Extrapolometer, because it's not an actual device and it's pretty hard to explain. But once you have one, there are short cuts all over the place.

The suspect is barely injured: four clean, shallow punctures on his butt cheek and some scrapes from the foot chase. Since he's cooperative and his injuries are minor, the medics clear him to go to jail. No emergency room wait. It doesn't get any more efficient than that. We're back in service and immediately drive to the scene of a felony hit-and-run with a parolee driver who fled down a steep hillside. With the firefighters and curious onlookers studying my every move, I bring out Brag and we creep down the wet embankment.

Two steps down Brag pulls too hard and I slip and tumble down the slope on my backside, coating my uniform pants with mud. I glance behind me and see my sergeant, Mike McGrew, doing his best to suppress a laugh. It takes me a full minute to scramble back up to him. I decide I was only doing this to satisfy the audience, so we're going to cruise through the neighborhood instead. Inexplicably, Brag has hardly any mud on his coat. It's so near to the end of our shift that I don't bother changing clothes.

When Brag and I arrive home, I slip out of the crusted patrol pants in the garage and walk Brag out in my boxer shorts and unlaced boots. Brag finishes eating and trots off to find the Kong ball, so I duck behind a tree. When he reappears, ears erect to locate me, I leap out and surprise him and he chases me with the ball in his mouth. We race round and round the tree, two idiots in the dark.

I'm listening to the radio traffic on this particularly cold night when I hear Officer Nelson dispatched to the scene of a crazed subject running in traffic down by the Bird Refuge, a wide, brackish pond near the beach. When Nelson says the suspect just hurled a metal trash can at a passing vehicle, I hurry to my car. Brag is already on his feet.

When I arrive, the suspect has lumbered across a green belt beside the road that curves around the marsh and descended into the mangrove-looking trees along the shore. I can hear him raging as he moves in darkness in the shin-deep water among the tangled roots.

I harness up Brag and clip on the long line as Danny McGrew and two more cops arrive. The flashlight beams illuminating the suspect – a stocky, wild-eyed man covered in tattoos – only manage to incense him further. My guess is he's high on meth, which means not only will there be no reasoning with him but he'll also possess super-human strength.

Until you have experienced the strength of an adult human being under the influence of certain drugs, it is hard to understand the experience. It's shocking. Officer Feller and I once fought with a suspect on a sidewalk and after we got him onto his stomach – with both of us on top of him – he simply stood straight up with us still on his back as if we weighed nothing. The man had over four-hundred-and-fifty pounds of cop and gear on top of him and he just got up to continue the fight. The danger of these struggles is that a person who is stronger than you now has access to your tools and your firearm. Many cops are murdered by their own service weapons; handguns work for anyone who pulls the trigger. This is another benefit of the police K-9: the suspect cannot use the dog against you. It's the only police tool that has an opinion.

The suspect rages on in the dark mangroves. The water is only a foot deep, but going into that freezing, fetid swamp to arrest this man would mean an epic struggle where someone would probably be injured, equipment would be lost, and we'd all end up covered in muck. I have a better idea: wait until the suspect crosses between two trees and then send Brag on the long line. Brag has already demonstrated a deep desire to remove suspects from their hiding places and bring them to us, so with a long-line attached we should theoretically be able to bring this shrieking lunatic out of the swamp. McGrew asks me how I intend to do that.

"I'll hold onto Brag. You hold onto me," I tell him. He nods and without any hesitation wraps his arms around me and plants his boots in the grass at the edge of the mud.

I give the suspect a K-9 warning but in the dancing beams of light I can see he's putting on a heavy Pendleton to protect himself from the dog.

"Send your dog!" he bellows, clenching his fists. Brag barks back, lunging. I've got him on a foot of line and he's pulling so hard it's cutting off the circulation to my fingers.

"Ready?" I ask McGrew.

He tightens his grip. "Yes."

"*Packen!*" I send Brag in for the bite, dropping the coils as Brag sprints away from me and splashes through the cold water. He bites the man on the side, below the ribs. They struggle as the man fights back, hammer-fisting Brag on the head. "Good boy!" I shout, encouraging Brag, but knowing he's not on the correct bite for me to be able to pull them both out.

Brag comes off the first bite and clamps his teeth onto the suspect's wrist.

"Pull!" I tell McGrew.

A wild tug-of-war ensues, with the suspect thrashing away from the edge of the swamp. The long line vibrates with tension and it feels like the tendons in my shoulders are tearing so I can only imagine what Brag's jaws must feel like. The suspect moves sideways, entangling himself in low branches but Brag doesn't come off and for an instant we're stuck, not moving either direction until a branch breaks and the suspect loses his footing and goes down into the muck.

Now he's beaten. He still struggles but it's like a fish on a gaff. Brag yanks and McGrew and I backpedal and the suspect slides heavily out of the mud and up the grassy slope and I pull Brag off of the bite and I realize I am panting as loud as he is.

Dazed and spent, the suspect lies still; the savage monster of a few minutes earlier is gone. He steams in the cold night air. When the ambulance arrives, he remains docile as he is handcuffed to the gurney and driven away. None of the cops have so much as a scratch.

Since it's late at night I decide to give Brag a unique break; I take him to the beach. He turns into a pup immediately, galloping at the end of the long-line, sniffing clumps of kelp on the sand. There's no need for a Kong ball here. Brag gazes out at the waves and pulls hard until I finally relent and let him walk in the water. He's going to smell like wet dog and the Pacific Ocean for the rest of the night, but he deserves it.

We walk down the beach and I don't say a word to him; no commands, no chatter to fill the silence. I turn off my radio. It's just the two of us and the wet, tearing sound of the breaking waves and the occasional cry of a startled seabird. Brag deserves to forget he is a police K-9 for a little while.

During the day this sunlit beach teems with people. Now, in the middle of the night, it is an empty stretch of sand that belongs only to a dog and his human.

As the shift winds down I turn my Interceptor north and check my computer to see if there are any calls holding on that end of the city. Just one: BEAR. I've never seen a call with that title so I ask the dispatcher to send it to me and discover that a cab driver reported a loose bear on De La Vina Street. Suspecting that the cabbie is overtired and hallucinating, I head in that direction. It's on our way home. Brag is already half-asleep, lying on his side.

When I turn onto De La Vina – devoid of moving cars at this hour – I find the lane in front of me blocked by a large black bear lumbering up the street. I'm not sure what I'm supposed to do, so I turn on my overhead lights like I'm making a traffic stop. The bear lumbers on, not interested in me at all. The red and blue lights illuminate his fuzzy backside.

The scent of bear suddenly hits Brag and he leaps to his feet and stares in disbelief through the windshield at the animal in front of us. Brag explodes.

"GET OUT OF HERE, BEAR!"

The bear kicks it into top gear, startled by the barking dog behind him. Veering off of the roadway, the bear throws himself clumsily over a fence in the direction of the foothills.

Brag snorts with utter contempt at the vanished trespasser. I tell dispatch the bear was last seen heading thataway.

Homeward bound, all of us.

FAIL

Whenever I see the California Highway Patrol on a traffic stop on a city street, I pull in behind them. They usually wave me off, but I get out anyway and ask them if they need a K-9. Once they see my partner search, they realize I have a dog who doesn't care what color uniforms he is working with as long as he is working. Brag and I magically locate more dope, get more apprehensions, and have found ourselves in high demand. Task forces call for us before their operations, essentially booking a reservation with Brag instead of waiting until they need us and running the risk of him being unavailable. Brag's become used to working with these people who act like cops but look like drug dealers. I hate getting up that early but Brag loves it; his unbridled joy at being awakened hours before dawn to go serve a warrant makes me feel less grumpy, even if it doesn't make me any bubblier during briefing.

The result of all this inter-agency Never Saying No is exactly what I'd hoped: the CHP asks for Brag all the time now. Mike McGrew, my current sergeant – who also happens to be one of the best cops in the building – feels it's our duty to help everyone out. He calls me one afternoon and says "instead of coming into the city can you go help the CHP at the termination point of a pursuit?" Brag and I are on the road ten minutes later.

When we arrive I find out why they called me: the suspect they were pursuing ditched the car, fled on foot, went into a woman's home and held her at knifepoint while CHP officers and Sheriff's Deputies scoured the area for him. Unaware the suspect was hiding inside, they'd knocked at the woman's front door and – getting no response – bypassed the house. There was nothing to suggest the suspect was inside. Shortly afterward, the suspect fled out the back door into the night. This is a real bad guy and I can see that the CHP are not happy about being outfoxed by a suspect who held a woman against her will in her own house. I uncoil the long line and harness up Brag, asking him the same thing I always ask: "Ready to get that bad guy?" He barks once, high-pitched and eager, and when he hears the long line clip onto his harness he pours out of the car past me, his mouth working as he gulps the scents around him. A circle of CHP officers stands behind me. Brag does a quick pass among them, inhaling their individual odor so he can eliminate it from the scent of the suspect. I never taught him to do this; he taught himself.

We search down the long driveway leading to the woman's house. I can see the woman inside, talking with a CHP supervisor. She looks shaken, her arms wrapped tightly around herself. I feel sorry for her but I'm not here to comfort, I'm here to catch the suspect. If Brag and I can't do that, we're no use to her.

I pull Brag away from the front door and we make our way around to the back. We search the yard, moving on to another house and that yard, and so on. When Brag indicates that he's hitting human odor, I look up and see the blinking red light of a police radio on a deputy's gun belt in the darkness ahead of us. He and another deputy are walking all over the scent.

The deputies are grumpy; they've been poking around in the dark for an hour. "This dude is long gone," one of them grumbles. They watch while Brag and I circle that large backyard but by the time we work our way back around, they're already leaving. I can hear police cars starting up and rolling away. We keep searching.

Another hour crawls by. We've gone in a big circle and ended up at the victim's house again. The CHP officers who were with us dissolve away. Their sergeant leaves as well. I turn around and there's just one CHP officer left, a young cop whom Brag and I have helped on several occasions.

"Do you mind searching a bit longer?" I ask him.

"I'll stay as long as you need me to stay," he says.

We start over, the three of us, following the same trail that at least a dozen cops have trampled. We work through the same yards, checking the same sheds, pausing under the same window where a television's glow from the inside tells us the resident is inside.

Our flashlights are dying but we make another circular search of the last yard. Brag looks spent. He's slowing down, no longer trailing on the ground or working the scent high. I squat beside him, patting his side.

"Brag, I know you're frustrated. Let's go around one more time."

I hold onto his harness tightly until he looks at me.

"You want to get that bad guy?"

He barks once in agreement and I release him, letting the nylon line slide free through my hand as he goes down the driveway of this last residence, pulling hard again, not wanting to let me down.

We pass the same parked cars. Suddenly, Brag jerks hard to the right, pulling me back into the carport. He runs his nose along a small car with a car cover wrapped tightly with bungee cords stretching beneath the undercarriage. Brag works his nose all over the car urgently.

"Did you check this car?" I ask the CHP officer.

"We couldn't get the cover off," he says and I see why: this cover was put on a car that isn't going to be used any time soon. I grab the bottom of the cover and pull on it, stretching the bungee. The cover only moves a few inches away from the car. I don't know how our suspect could possibly be inside it, but Brag is insistent. He barks, the deep bark he makes when he's found the bad guy. I nod at the CHP officer.

"He's in there," I tell him.

"You sure?"

"One-hundred percent."

The CHP officer unhooks one of the bungees and wrestles with the car cover, peeling it partially off. His flashlight beam illuminates the face of the suspect crouched in the back seat.

Brag goes nuts, challenging the suspect to a death match and burning out on the concrete to get at him. We pull a door open and the suspect surrenders without a struggle, as surprised as any of us that he was located in the best hiding place ever. He still has the knife with him.

I have no idea how he managed to open a car door and squeeze inside with the bungee cords so tightly in place. But he did it. Once again, logic fails and the Werewolf nose wins.

CHP units who heard the radio traffic come speeding back down the driveway toward us. The CHP sergeant scratches his head when he sees the suspect prone on the ground.

"That's our guy," he confirms, looking utterly bewildered, as if the suspect had fallen out of the sky. The officers walk the suspect away.

"You need anything else?" I ask the CHP sergeant.

He laughs, then looks at Brag.

"Tell your dog thanks," the sergeant says.

"He heard you," I reply.

The lone CHP officer who stayed follows me and we shake hands.

"You get your coffee yet?" he asks, reading my mind.

We meet at a place where the CHP always get their coffee, near a freeway on-ramp to the US 101 and well beyond the city limits. It's like being invited into the secret club house by a member of another club. He pays for my latte and I realize the last time I shared a cup of coffee with a CHP officer he went to a late-night road hazard call during a terrible rainstorm and drove off of a broken road into a swollen river. They found him and his partner the next morning, still seat-belted in their CHP unit, upside down beneath the cold, muddy torrent. That was over a decade ago.

I raise my cup. "Here's to Officer Stovall."

The CHP officer nods, realizing I knew the man. We pass the next few minutes in silence while we sip our coffee as an endless river of cars flows past us on the freeway.

Four months later on a warm summer night this same young CHP officer goes in pursuit of a wanted subject. The wanted driver crashes and bails out into an avocado orchard. The CHP officer calls our dispatch and asks if K-9 -1 is available and gives me a grin when we show up.

I harness up Brag and we start our search at a trot, kicking through dead leaves in the orchard and then dropping into a creek bed down a dirt trail. When we near the creek, Brag pulls me to it. He steps gingerly into the shallow water, lowering himself and paddling across a wide swimming hole, a look of contentment on his face. I play out the long line to give him slack. He turns half-way across and paddles slowly back while four cops stand on the bank, watching.

"Is he tracking the suspect in the water?" one of the CHP officers asks me.

"No," I answer. "He's just going for a swim."

Brag climbs back out, shakes water all over all the cops standing there, and resumes trailing the suspect, pulling me down the dirt path that skirts along the creek.

"He loves water," I explain.

The cops fall in behind me again and I can hear my CHP buddy chuckling.

We keep searching, but the suspect is far out in front of us and decides he's not going to get bitten so he surrenders to perimeter officers in a parking lot a quarter-mile down the trail. The suspect is dry as a bone; he never went in the creek.

I don't know why Brag had a lessened sense of urgency on this hunt. Could he smell the suspect's intention to surrender? I doubt it. But I can't be sure.

My car smells like wet dog for the rest of the night. I don't mind it at all.

It is time for our yearly patrol certification. This used to stress me out, since a failure removes a handler/dog team from the street – at least temporarily – and becomes permanent record. Just like you can't "unsee" something, you can't "un-fail" a K-9 certification.

At the training site, the evaluator shows up with his clipboard and shakes hands with everyone. He's a former SWAT and K-9 Sergeant from Oxnard and he was on-scene when a SWAT friend of mine was shot and killed during a warrant service years ago. In typical cop fashion, we've never spoken about it.

Everyone is bent over their trunks, readying equipment. Handlers are understandably nervous. I'm not. Brag knows this training day is different, and important; he can feel it in the way I move, hear it in my voice. He's been through these specific scenarios enough times to know exactly how they go.

Our turn. Brag and I work through the pages on the Evaluator's clipboard. Brag is crisp, exacting. The last test scenario requires that he call off of a bite. This used to be a worry, because Brag didn't seem to want to listen to me. Not anymore. The scenario begins and I send Brag and he's running on the field and the agitator – in a full bite suit – turns to attack me and in his enthusiasm, he accidentally steps on my foot while I'm backpedaling and I topple backwards in an awkward heap and I can hear the collective GASP of the handlers watching as Brag rockets toward the man who knocked me down.

"AUS! AUS!" I yell as I try to right myself on the ground. A sable blur flies through the air over me and Brag hits the agitator at full speed, knocking the man off of his feet. I'm up and yelling for Brag to out but his teeth are buried deep into the bite suit and he thrashes back and forth savagely.

Brag won't release the bite. Grabbing onto his collar, I lift him off of the wincing agitator. Despite Brag's enraged barking, I'm keenly aware of the awkward silence from the onlookers. I back away, holding onto my police dog who has become a wild animal.

We failed the certification.

I walk Brag to the car and I can tell he's confused. I'm flushed with embarrassment. Brag hops in back and I slam the door behind him. I can hear him turning nervous circles inside.

I'm thinking about the email I'll have to write my boss to explain how we failed the yearly cert and that we'll re-test in a week or two. But that isn't the worst part.

Ted and the Evaluator break up their whispered huddle and Ted strides over to tell me it was the agitator's fault for accidentally altering the scenario. We get another go at it, right now. I open the back door and kneel down in front of Brag. He's still panting but his eyes aren't wild like they were a moment ago.

"Brag, we're going again. You've got to be perfect this time."

He is; we run the last scenario without a misstep. When I put Brag up in the car again, I turn around to find Franklin, a San Luis County Sheriff's Department K-9 handler, standing behind me with his thumbs in his belt loops and a grin on his face.

"Did you see the look in Brag's eye?" he asks.

"No, I was too busy untangling myself on the ground."

"The second you went down he ran to check on you, and when he saw you were okay, he went at that agitator like he was going to destroy the man."

"I wasn't sure I could get him off."

Franklin nods with understanding: "These dogs would die for us."

When the certification day ends the K-9 handlers all shake hands and zoom off. I'm the last one to leave and instead of taking the highway home I opt for a meandering road that takes twice as long but winds through undulating hills covered with oaks and grapevines. I stop at the same place every time we take this route, a grassy spot along the road where Brag can take a break.

When I let him out, he trots off to mark his usual spots but keeps his eye on me. He sprints back when I say his name. I toss him the Kong and he flops down onto the cool grass and holds the ball between his front feet, content.

Brag is an excellent police dog – a trustworthy, fearless man hunter. But today he ignored me, and not because he wanted to be disobedient. He thought I was hurt, and then he refused to listen because he wanted to punish the person who knocked me down. This is a complication I'd hoped to avoid. This is how mistakes are made on the street, when emotions rule your decisions. I was worried about getting too close to this dog, but I never worried about him getting too close to me. I never saw this coming, and it is the most inevitable thing ever. The force that drives Brag isn't anger, it's love. There's no denying it anymore.

Some part of me already knew this strong-willed dog would be willing to die for me. I just hadn't realized that I would willingly die for him, too.

Training with SWAT. Brag became their favorite negotiator.

Best friends, after all.

(photo courtesy of Michael Brian)

Brag and Ted. Friends? Maybe...

(photo courtesy of Jessica Maher)

Brag and me, as always, attached by long line.

(photo courtesy of Craig Rullman)

PART THREE

IMMORTALS

There was a time when our myths teemed with animals. Not surprisingly, humankind revered – even worshipped – the fearsome predators. We learned to survive by watching them hunt, invented tools that mimicked their superior attributes. But never, in the ensuing millennia of mechanical progress, did we best them. I am witness to this, as I am witness to the unavoidable truth that every creature, no matter how formidable, can get stuck in the weeds.

Mitch Jan calls me to search for a suspect who fled from a burglary scene across a vacant lot adjacent to an apartment complex. It's July, so there hasn't been any rainfall since February. The lot we're going to search is covered with what looks like millions of long, yellowed teeth – dead grass grown knee-high and so desiccated you can grind the stalks into dust in your palm. But along the stalks grow the most innocuous-looking devils of the plant world: foxtails. These little bastards are Mother Nature's answer to nine months of no rain each year, seed pods shaped like barbed medieval arrowheads and the size of the writing end of a pencil. They are the bane of dog owners because when they attach themselves to a dog their barbs propel them slowly and painfully into flesh.

There's a period where the foxtails are at their most plentiful and sturdiest, which makes them stick to anything. That time is now.

I don't want to say no to Mitch, but I don't want Brag to inhale one of those little monsters. I decide to skirt around the edge of the lot as best I can and get downwind and see if Brag reacts to any odor. I put him on the short leather lead instead of the harness to keep his head up and even so we must cut through the foxtails to get downwind.

Brag scents the suspect and barks like mad and we call the man out to us. Thankfully, the man complies. I jog with Brag back to the car and kneel down to run my fingers through his fur, looking for foxtails. He's covered in them. Cursing, I put my small flashlight in my mouth and start plucking them out, one at a time. The only way to do this is to re-direct the point outward and push. If you try to pull it out the twin tails break off, leaving the barbs on the point to push the foxtail forward into the skin.

Brag knows I'm doing some sort of necessary grooming so he tolerates it. I stop counting at a hundred foxtails, and I'm still not close to being done. An hour grinds by and I have to tell other cops I'm not available on the radio. I check every inch of my dog, running my fingers between his toes and pads and also into that delicate space between his back legs and his dog goodies. He endures this ignoble treatment, and when I tell him we're done he leaps into the back of the car with undisguised relief.

A week later we're at training in Paso Robles with the San Luis County K-9 Unit – a great group of deputies and dogs that came to us a few years ago and asked for help in re-forming their K-9 program after it had been discontinued for several years. Most of these new handlers have deep street experience so they are immediately on board with our training regimen.

In one scenario, a suspect – Ted, not in his underwear this time – flees from a car at the end of a simulated pursuit. Because these events happen quickly in real police work and there's never time to bring our dog out and direct him toward the now-vanished suspect, we are practicing hitting the door pop and directing the dog in the direction of the fleeing suspect with a simple point. The K-9's learn to mirror whatever direction you are running and shoot ahead if you point your arm out. Hopefully, they spot the suspect and lock on. If they don't, the handler needs to be able to call back the dog and re-direct him.

When it's our turn Brag leaps out when I pop the rear door and barrels past me, his eyes scanning past my outstretched hand toward a dirt road where Ted runs away with the sleeve.

But Brag is too clever. Instead of making a hard left on one road and then a right on a second (the route that Ted has run), Brag knows he can angle to the right across a field and cut off the fleeing suspect. The only problem is that Brag has not noticed – or does not care – that there is a barbed wire fence between the route he has chosen and the road that Ted runs down.

As Brag closes in, I suddenly realize that he is on the wrong side of the fence. Before I can utter a word, Brag veers left and goes airborne, passing impossibly between the second and third strand of barbed wire and leaving a cloud of black and tan fur behind.

Brag fishtails in the dirt but keeps going. The barbed-wire strands behind him undulate from his bulk passing through them and I sprint as fast as I can, wondering how bad he is hurt. He bites Ted on the sleeve and Ted holds him there while I rush up to check.

When I get to Brag and click on the leather lead, Ted slips the sleeve. I kneel down and run my hands along Brag's ribs, checking his thighs. He chomps down on the sleeve, pulling away from me to carry it back to our car in victory. I feel for wounds and bleeding with my fingers, looking for any blood on the ground or on his coat.

There isn't a mark on him. How he hurled his huge body through that narrow gap of barbed wire without slicing himself open is an absolute mystery. I check him again.

Ted kneels beside me. "How bad is he cut?"

"He's not. He's fine."

Ted's face breaks into his characteristic grin. "Only Brag could do that," he says.

I'm laughing but it's out of pure relief. I let Brag carry the sleeve back to the car while Ted and I talk about adjusting the scenario so that can't happen again. The other handlers rib me about my misusing city equipment but when Brag went through that fence, I heard their collective gasp. I know how much each one of them loves their K-9 partner.

Brag jumps into the back of the car and drops the sleeve. I walk around and open the other door and retrieve it, pressing my forehead against his.

"You're a nut," I tell him. "Never do that again."

Brag smiles in my face. If a dog could shrug, he would do it now.

I'd assumed for a long time that this story was going to end happily but lately I'm less certain. We're beating the odds every day, but sooner or later you're going to hit an unlucky number. If our run ends suddenly and badly, I think I'd rather Brag and I left this narrative at the same time. How could I work without him? Or he without me?

Brag has broken all records. He's done more searches, found more narcotics, tracked more suspects, and apprehended more criminals than all the previous police K-9's combined. He's bitten hot-prowl burglars, a homicidal stalker, and plenty of other suspects who mistakenly thought they'd made good their escape. He chases a robber down a busy street one afternoon, dodging cars and dogs on leashes to bite the man in front of a taco joint. By the time I catch up, people are already calling 911 to report a "gigantic dog attack," unaware they are witnessing a police K-9 capturing his quarry. I call Ted after each bite, regardless of the hour, and he always answers his phone.

For each suspect who demands to be bitten, there are dozens who surrender when they see or hear Brag. His bark shakes walls, rattles windows, and shatters criminal resolve.

My sergeant sends weekly reports of our work up the chain of command to the Chief of Police. The Chief sends encouragement back down, careful to address Brag in his praise. The administrators go silent. They no longer matter; the fight isn't in the building, it's on the street. Brag shows no signs of slowing down; when he receives seven staples in his side after a cyst removal, he paces the back yard with such agitation that I bring him back to work after a single missed shift. When I dislocate one of my fingers badly during a struggle with a suspect, I tape it up to the neighboring finger and keep going, out of respect for Brag's ethic if nothing else. My neck and back are disaster zones from working this enormous dog as much as from lack of sleep and tension. I can't turn my head more than a few degrees in either direction. But the danger is in front of us most of the time, or should be if I'm doing my job right.

The pace is blistering. Our training days could easily be relaxing but Tyler and I still feel the need to push harder. We want to get better, to never lose. We arrange helicopter training with the CHP, which requires me to muzzle Brag and squeeze both of us behind the pilot and observer while we buzz over empty fields to where Ted hides in a creek bed. Brag doesn't love the muzzle but it's necessary because if he bites the pilot mid-flight, we're going to have problems. Landing safely, for one. Once Brag figures out that we're flying in that incredibly loud airship to go bite a suspect, he's all for it. He waits patiently while I tighten his leather muzzle and then pulls me toward the helicopter for his second scenario. Some dogs are uneasy about aircraft because the experience of flying is uncomfortable. Brag sees it as a necessary evil. I'm so proud of his work ethic I don't mind that he smacks me in the face with that muzzle when he spies

Ted on the ground far below us. The fact that Brag was scanning the ground below the helicopter for a suspect proves to me that he understands exactly what we're doing.

A lot of police dogs are accidentally killed during training. The places where we train are usually abandoned or in some state of disuse; empty warehouses, shuttered hospitals, closed processing plants. They have to shimmy through sewer pipes, climb into attics, jump through bus windows, and stop on a dime when we tell them to. We also must expose dogs to the sound of live gunfire so they don't react to it. Training days smell like gunpowder and dust and rust and fetid water. Tyler, Ted, and I laugh most of the way through them, soaking our uniforms with sweat, wincing from our stiff joints. If you are not suffering you are not training properly, we remind ourselves.

As Brag and I arrive first at a call of an armed robbery, Brag spots the suspect going over a chain link fence. I try to put this info out on the radio, but Brag isn't waiting; he pulls me hard and I skid behind him for ten yards down the gravelly road on the soles of my boots with my one free hand behind me, getting filleted on the rough ground.

When Josh Morton arrives to help, we leap the fence and follow the suspect's trail into a concrete flood channel that runs beneath a highway exchange. The radios don't work down there so it's just the sound of us panting in the dark as we run and Brag's toenails *click-clicking* on the concrete. Part of me wants to let Brag go; I'm certain he could catch up to the suspect in the dark. But I might not be able to find them in the branching tunnels. Or is it because I can't stand the thought of losing Brag? We emerge from darkness in a different neighborhood on the other side of the exchange, in a steep ravine overgrown with poison oak. The suspect is gone. We turn around and Brag guides us back the way we came and I never doubt his memory of the return route for a second. Josh remarks that we could make a wrong turn and be lost down here for hours. Minutes later, Brag leads us out into the night again, a few feet from our patrol cars.

Things happen fast in police work. You usually have seconds, sometimes less. Minutes are luxuriant. Once things are in motion there's no pause, and no reverse. Despite all our training I wasn't quick enough to catch this robbery suspect in the tunnels. Brag doesn't hold it against me.

At night I dream about police calls. In one recurring dream I can't find Brag and I'm holding the long line that isn't attached anymore and calling for Brag in the dark and there's a rising sense of panic because I can't remember when I released him or why. Then I wake up. It's 3:37 a.m. and I calm down again because I know he's outside. He's okay. Sometimes I can't recall what day it is and fall asleep trying to figure it out. It's as effective as counting sheep. I'd rather not dream at all. My dreams are often populated by unspeakable horrors. At that hour of the night, it feels like the bad guys will just keep coming in waves until we are overrun.

Then I hear Brag barking outside, a deep, staccato warning that trails off when there is no response from whatever enemy he is calling out.

If Brag's still in the fight, then so am I.

The CHP chase a stolen vehicle from Santa Maria at speeds of over 120 miles per hour. The suspects are gang members and when they reach Montecito, they abandon the car and the driver escapes both the CHP airship and the ground units. The driver – also wanted for a plethora of violent crimes in Santa Maria – was last seen running across the fifth fairway of the Montecito Country Club, the most unlikely place for a wanted gang member with neck and face tattoos to find himself. He vanished into the estates beyond the golf course.

By the time Brag and I arrive the excitement has faded. The witnesses are gone. The CHP helicopter has left to fuel up and will likely not return. Most of the perimeter units have cleared to go answer the emergency calls that have been holding.

I find the CHP officer in charge. We've worked together before, and he's apologetic about the time delay and conditions. Behind him, wealthy country-clubbers play through as if nothing had happened. Everyone thinks this call is over. I don't, and neither does Brag.

"Where was the suspect last seen?" I ask him.

The CHP officer points across the fairway. "Over there."

"The witness?"

He shrugs. "He left."

"Can you bring him back?" I ask.

"If you need me to."

I do. We wait. The witness – a teenager – returns with his parents. He points to where he last saw the fleeing felon but I make him walk with me and point out the exact location on the clipped grass of the fairway. It's over one hundred feet from where the CHP officer told me it was. That's why I need the witness. Time to get Brag out.

Brag pulls me off the golf course, up a creek bed, through several estates, down a driveway and then across a private road where two CHP officers have set up the containment perimeter. When we cross their perimeter line, they seem annoyed at the suggestion that they've had their back to the suspect for two hours. But they have. We keep going past the perimeter and they get in their cars and leave. Can't really blame them; it's been three hours since anyone saw the bad guy and he didn't appear that he was going to stop running any time soon.

This is the difficult part. Brag is trailing the suspect, working odor on the ground and in the air. The odor swirls around, rises up in the heat, and gets pushed by the wind. If there were no people or roads or cars and I didn't need to be with Brag when he found the suspect, I could let him go the minute he was trailing the suspect's odor and he would find the man every time. But the complications ruin that. I can't move like Brag can move, there are countless dangers, and there are other people that are always going to appear in the search. Dogs don't know that people have such a pathetic sense of smell. If I try to control Brag too much, he'll defer to me as the alpha, thinking I must be following odor he's not getting. Once you pull a dog off of odor it's difficult to get him back on it, especially if you're not sure where you pulled him off.

To make matters worse, this suspect is beyond the perimeter. If he's escaping at three miles per hour and we're trailing him at three miles per hour, we will never catch up to him. I'm banking on him trying to find a place to hide until dark. Like all humans he is still an animal and I've hunted enough of them to guess that he will go to ground when he feels he's safely out of range. But in the meantime, I am letting the long line out and coiling it back in as Brag works, watching his body language, watching for dangers ahead, trying to be as invisible as I can while still controlling him.

Four more overgrown yards later, it's only Brag and me and Laz and Mitch Jan and one CHP officer. The "perimeter" is far behind us. We're at least a half-mile from our cars and the only one paying attention to our search on the radio now is the police dispatcher who logs the address into the call when we advise her. Even she sounds bored.

Brag is tiring. It's so much harder than it looks – trailing a suspect through a populated area – especially when he has to pull me along. I can see the frustration in his eyes as the quarry seems to get farther away.

"One more property," I tell the cops with me, which in this neighborhood means another couple of acres. "Then we'll call it."

Brag knows what I said, and works the ground even harder. But despite his efforts it looks like there's no scent left at all until we pass a cobwebby shed and Brag suddenly snaps his head to the left and takes a deep sniff beneath the door. His tail wags and his whole body stiffens. The cops around me nod as I point at the door – silently confirming what they already knew.

I choke up on the long line and back Brag up. "Call him out."

Mitch calls the suspect out, warning him that he'll be bitten if he doesn't comply. It's a formality. The suspect knows we're there and knows we have a dog. He decides to bluff.

Someone goes to get the key from the homeowner and I call out the suspect one more time. "You'd better open that door because my dog is coming in and you're going to wish he didn't."

The door handle turns slowly and a pair of prison-tattooed hands appear. The suspect emerges, dripping with sweat, and keeps his eyes on Brag's salivating jaws while he's handcuffed.

I put out on the radio that we have one in custody. There's a long silence and I can tell the dispatcher is smiling when she repeats my radio traffic. I drive them to distraction with my stubbornness and self-dispatching to calls but they do love it when the K-9 wins.

As we march the suspect out to the road a former SBPD officer who now works as a deputy comes zooming up in his car and gets out with a puzzled grin on his face. Noel Rivas has been a cop for over thirty years and he demands to know how the hell we just did that.

"Voodoo magic," I tell him, inclining my head toward Brag.

Noel laughs and offers us a ride back to our patrol car, but Brag and I are going to walk. It's our victory lap. I sing a quiet song to him about what a good boy he is while we're walking and bury my face in his neck again once he's in back. He gulps a lot of water and it runs down the front of my uniform but I don't care. This kind of apprehension is worth a hundred late night awakenings. Maybe we are winning, one bad guy at a time.

The next day I fill Brag's little plastic pool with water in the backyard and he drops a toy in before lowering himself ceremoniously into the cool water. He soaks with a serene expression on his face, unaware of how hilarious he looks. I'm sure he'd love to have that turtle for company right now, but I'm not sure the turtle would enjoy it much.

NAKED PREY

For some reason, law enforcement means interacting with a lot of naked people. Clothing is the first layer of civilized behavior that is stripped away when a person experiences a psychological crisis. When you are dispatched to a call of a naked man acting irrationally, it is rarely going to end quietly. You don't arrive and walk up to the fellow dressed only in his birthday suit and say, "Sir, I feel obligated to point out that you are naked," whereupon he replies, "I shall clothe myself immediately. My sincerest apologies!" That never happens. In all likelihood, the cops will soon find themselves in a wrestling match with a nude combatant. Drugs, mental illness, or both are always on board during these calls. The most difficult part is trying to physically control a naked person while avoiding all contact with the more personal parts of their anatomy. It's pretty much impossible. That's where you earn your pay for the night.

Brag and I are facing down a naked man at this moment. The man just stabbed someone and now stands, hands on his hips, in the shower of his apartment. He is ignoring our commands to come out and ignoring Brag's enraged barking. We don't know where the knife is, and I can't see if it's with him in the shower. As far as I'm concerned, he's done stabbing people for the evening. It's my job to take him into custody. He gets to choose Easy or Hard. Also, he's standing in running water so the Taser isn't an option; electricity and water don't mix well.

I demand he show me his hands and come out of the shower – *right now*. He doesn't. Instead, the suspect turns away with a sneer and urinates. He then slams the plastic shower door shut in our faces. It is the worst decision he's made tonight.

We don't bite people who deserve it, we bite people who demand it.

I send Brag and he blasts the shower door open with his body and bites the man on the right thigh, yanking him out from beneath the water the way a Vaudeville stage-crook would yank a failed performer off of the stage. The suspect comes flying out and knocks the shower door off its hinges, sliding on his wet backside across the floor toward us in Brag's jaws. He's so overpowered by Brag that we easily take hold of him despite how slippery he is.

I retreat with my wet K-9 while Hunt and Lazarus slip a bright blue pair of undies onto the man so he can be taken to the hospital. By all rights they should let the fellow ride in the ambulance as naked as the day he was born, but common decency compelled them to pull on the underwear. The suspect offered no resistance for the rest of his treatment, in gratitude of this small act of kindness.

The marine layer rolls in after dark, cloaking the city in a dripping fog. Brag smells like a wet dog. I back up another officer on a traffic stop of a parolee and put Brag in the car for a search. No alerts. When Brag hops out onto the sidewalk he gives a small yelp when his left rear leg touches down. The other officer heard that and asks me if Brag is all right.

"Yeah," I lie. "He caught his foot in the seatbelt on the way out."

The jump down from the car to the curb was eighteen inches. I put Brag in the back of our K-9 unit and pat his side to ease his disappointment. No narcotics, no Kong ball.

It's time to face something: Brag is dragging his left rear leg. I can hear the top of his foot brushing the ground sometimes when he walks. He ignores it and no one else sees it. But I do. And I am thinking about Beowulf's limp.

The clock is ticking. Brag can't keep doing this forever. We've still got time, but how much? How will I be able to tell him he's done? Will Brag give up when he knows it's over?

Tyler calls me the next day to tell me he is retiring Hondo. Tyler will be rotating out of the K-9 unit and it will be months before a replacement is found and months before that replacement is trained and up and running. A green handler and a new dog. I'm happy for Tyler because he is transferring into the detective bureau – the only unit he loves as much as K-9 – but I am sad to lose him. We've spent a lot of long hours training our dogs together. No one understands the struggles and fears of a K-9 handler like another K-9 handler. On their last training day, we barbecue with Ted and the San Luis Obispo County handlers and laugh at stories of K-9 mishaps until our sides hurt. The day ends with firm hugs and handshakes all around and Tyler gets in his car with Hondo and drives out of the story.

Brag and I are alone again.

It would seem to the casual observer that Brag is utterly indifferent to affection. My son appears to possess this trait as well. Neither of them cares much for hugs, and too much praise only serves to agitate. The truth is, both of them do appreciate it. The difficulty is that they don't always give it back, which hurts feelings. I've learned from my time with both these unique beings to enjoy the rare moments when they are expressing affection, even in the subtlest of ways. These moments are always quiet, and always just between the two of us.

For Brag, a visit to the city yards represents a temporary full-stop during hectic work shifts. Since my Ford Interceptor burns gasoline like a monster truck, I have to fill the tank at least once per shift. During the day the city yards are bustling but at night it's a ghost town of warehouses. Brag knows nothing interesting is going to happen for ten minutes while I pump gas and clean the windows, so he lays flat on his side in the back.

The first time I realized this was an opportunity to hug Brag was when I opened the back door to get his Kong ball out and found it had rolled to the other side of the car. I didn't feel like walking around to open the other door, so I crawled half-way in and reached across Brag's supine form to retrieve it. Brag raised his head ever so slightly and licked my hand as I grabbed the Kong. I froze, then lowered my arms onto him, scratching softly at his mane. He didn't move. As I turned the scratching into a full hug, he stayed perfectly still and relaxed. This moment, a private location where there was no need to keep watch, was the only acceptable time to express this affection. And so, it became our routine. I bury my face in his mane and tell him he's a good dog. He licks my hand slowly. No one ever witnesses these moments.

For my son, a brief glance with eye-contact and smile means the same thing. These two beings live by their own rules, and it's all right with me.

Sergeant Johnson calls me into the station. He's my fifth supervisor and a good cop but he's got administrators breathing down his neck all the time so if he's calling me in off of the street it's probably at their behest.

He nods at the door behind me when I come into the office so I shut it and sit in my usual chair. "What is it this time?"

"The lieutenant wants you to come to briefing."

"Why?"

"He wants to see your face."

"He can access my car camera from his desk any time he wants."

I'm being argumentative, but Johnson and I have known each other for a long time so he grants me a lot of leeway. "He *is* the Watch Commander," he says with a shrug. I head out to my car, grinding my teeth. This Watch Commander is the same administrator who recently announced in briefing that he intended to change his leadership style to "lead from the front," and was going to use the non-fiction WWII book "Band of Brothers" as his inspiration and guide. Moments later he admitted that he'd never read the book and asked if anyone in the room could loan it to him. Moron. Now he wants me to drive across the city every day in my police car without responding to emergency calls so I can waste thirty minutes listening to him read aloud from the briefing binder that I read through in three minutes the day before.

I call Sergeant Johnson back and tell him, "I'm not coming to briefing."

Here's my plan: I'll clear on the radio when my shift starts and immediately be busy doing something. There are some homeless who live in the shrubbery alongside the off-ramp on the north side of the city and it's the first place I'll stop every day. Unless there's a call where Brag and I are needed, in which case we'll be ready to respond immediately.

The next day I go to the off-ramp the instant I clear on the radio. Two of my homeless friends – Susan and Cliff – are sitting in the shade of the scrub, drinking beers. They're startled by the sudden appearance of a uniformed cop until they realize it's me and are all smiles.

Susan holds up one finger, signaling me to listen carefully: "Buck did not read the newspapers, or he would have known that trouble was brewing..."

"The Call of the Wild," I answer.

Susan snaps her fingers, disappointed. She has a degree in English Literature and tries to stump me with opening lines from classic books. But that one was easy. Susan beats me more often than not, even when she's drunk.

I hand Cliff a short stack of used books; he grins, excited for new reading material.

"How's your dog?" he asks.

"Dangerous, as usual."

Susan has a sudden coughing fit and waves me off when I ask if she is okay.

"Hedges," Cliff says to me as I turn to go, "you and your partner be careful out there." It's a cliché, but he means it.

I stop by most afternoons to say hello to these two and bring a book or two to pass on. To be honest, I like these two homeless folks better than a lot of "normal" people.

Brag is watching for me when I return to the car. I know he doesn't like it when I'm out of sight, just like I don't like it when I can't see him. But he's always a push of a button away. He wouldn't stop searching until he found me. How many people are there like that in my life, I wonder, who wouldn't stop searching until they found me?

MORTALS

"**Y**ou should come outside," Rachel says to me from the bottom of the stairs and I can hear in her voice that there's something wrong so I come down two steps at a time but instead of pointing toward the back yard, she opens the front door.

A crow lies lifeless on the lawn, wings spread as if flying. It's Frendo, the young one.

I kneel down and stroke her feathers. There isn't a mark on her and she's so inky black and perfect it seems impossible for her to be dead. Her eyes still shine; she hasn't been lying here for long. But the crows don't roost in that tree overnight, they fly away with a large group every evening. Why is she here, a few steps from my door? Was she ill and hoped I could help her?

I don't want her parents to wonder what happened and search for her, so I don't move her. No sign of any crows the next morning. They already know. I suppose they are grieving in crow fashion: silent, stoic.

I bury Frendo in the yard and get ready for work. I'm trying not to dwell on it, but her death feels like a portent of doom.

It's one of those summer nights where, as the sun goes down, the temperature goes up. These warm, humid evenings mean a flood of calls. Fights. Traffic collisions. Robberies. Parties. It's all fun and games until somebody stabs someone.

"Fifty-five to K9-1 and all units, 245 with a knife, 229 Voluntario Street. Multiple victims. Suspect still on-scene."

"K9-1 enroute."

Here's the truth about bullets and knives: they're the same. A knife is a metal object designed to cut flesh. A bullet is a metal object designed to cut flesh. When a bullet enters the human body it severs arteries, penetrates organs, and causes catastrophic exsanguination. Same for a knife. The disadvantage of a knife is that the wielder must be within arm's reach of the target. But where you can run out of bullets, you can't run out of stabs. I guess at some point a person's arm gets tired, but by then the job is done. When people ask me if it's worse to be shot or stabbed, I always answer "all of the above." Whether you're shot to death or stabbed to death, it's the same dead.

Brag and I arrive to find the familiar chaos. There are two victims – Hispanic men in their 30's – sitting on the curb or lying in the gutter bleeding and there is broken glass and it smells like beer and dogs are barking over the rumble of the fire truck engines. This may end up being a homicide but for now the victims are still alive. Witnesses are pointing at an upstairs apartment, where Mexican *banda* music blares out of the open windows.

This suspect stabbed two people inside the apartment. I don't know what state he is in at the moment but it's safe to assume he may not be done stabbing people tonight.

Brag's pulling on the long-line and I'm stepping around blood splatters as he marches right through them and tracks bloody paw prints to the bottom of the stairs and a cop behind the building says on the radio that the suspect is still inside the apartment and looking out a back window. Up we go. Through the front door I can see upended furniture and holes kicked in the drywall and bloody handprints smeared all over, straight out of a horror movie.

The suspect is inside, still armed. Lazarus is with me and he makes a K-9 announcement in both English and Spanish, but I already suspect this man is not coming out. He had plenty of time to run before we got here, and chose to stay.

I ask Laz to make another announcement and he does and two more cops press in behind us, waiting to see what I'm going to do.

Brag's gone quiet. He's waiting for me to let him go and I don't want to do it. It makes no real tactical sense to do anything else; if we try to clear the apartment without using Brag and the suspect wants to stab one of us, he'll be able to get at least one of us. Tasers don't always work; both barbs must hit flesh and if the suspect drops and rolls like they practice in the yard in prison, the circuit is broken. Pepper spray is slow-acting. It takes a few precious seconds to work and that's assuming you score a direct hit in the eyes and mouth. If he holds up his hand and blocks it, it splashes back at you and also, he can wipe that super-hot sauce on you in a fight.

The rule of thumb for using Brag has always been if a cop has to go in to look for the bad guy, the K-9 should go first. If it's so dangerous that cops wouldn't go in if I wasn't there, I won't use my partner. It's simple. But I'm hesitating and Lazarus is looking at me wondering what I'm waiting for and Brag angles his muzzle up toward me with the same question.

I can't delay any more. I unclip Brag and let him go.

Brag vanishes around the corner past the kitchen, his tail smacking the wall as he goes. The *banda* beat thumps in lieu of that awful silence and I focus on a single thought: *do not stab my dog.* But then I remember, *he's not really my dog.*

I hear a struggle and we creep into the apartment as Brag and the suspect come crashing down the hallway toward us, locked in a desperate struggle. Brag's jaws are fastened on the man's arm and the suspect tries to break free so Brag pins him against the wall and bites him on the side. Now we're all in the fight as we try to force this man to the ground and when I pull Brag off, I see the blood splattered all over Brag's face and neck, dripping onto his paws.

That's when I spot the serrated-edge knife on the floor where man and dog were fighting a moment ago.

Oh no... I pull Brag into a corner of the living room and kneel down, lighting him up with my flashlight and running my fingers through the thick blood.

"Where are you hurt, Brag?" I search by feel, holding the flashlight in my mouth. Another cop realizes what I'm doing and comes over to help, illuminating Brag's face and neck so I can use two hands.

Brag looks more like a werewolf than ever; his tongue drips bloody saliva and his bloodshot eyes bulge, fixed on the handcuffed suspect who still spits curses and kicks at the cops.

"Can you get me some wipes?" I ask another cop who comes in and he hears the concern in my voice and sprints out to his car. He rushes back in and hands me the wipes silently.

I wipe Brag down, searching every inch of him for stab wounds. Nothing. I don't believe it so I hustle him into the kitchen where the light is better and check again. He's not stabbed; the blood was from the bitten suspect and the victims.

I can finally exhale and I plop down on the filthy linoleum beside Brag, taking a second to collect myself. I look around to find three cops standing behind me, afraid to ask if Brag is okay but waiting to see what I need. I nod at them and force a smile: "He's good."

Brag disarmed the armed suspect without receiving so much as a scratch. The man was lying in wait, hoping to stab one of us. He wasn't expecting a werewolf.

We trot downstairs and past the fire trucks to the K-9 car where I get more antiseptic wipes to clean Brag's face and check him over once more. This he endures with his characteristic stoicism and I open the back door and for the first time Brag does not leap in but hesitates a moment before climbing in slowly.

I squat down in front of him. His mane is still wet.

"Good boy, Brag. I'm glad you're okay."

He's tired. It was a short but intense fight. I go to the hospital emergency department and put my police baseball cap on to play that "we've never met before" game with the suspect and get the statements. But the man is still uncooperative. I wonder what I would have done if he'd stabbed my partner to death. I don't answer my own question, only because I don't have to.

At the showgrounds the grass is cool and Brag doesn't want to run much so he lies down near me and chews his Kong a few times before letting it fall. He looks at me expectantly. I'm doing the math in my head, to confirm what I already know: he's nine years old.

"You can't ever leave me, Brag," I tell him. It's an unfair request to make of him, even if he wasn't a police dog. I know Brag's got an opinion on this: he wants to work. He is well aware of what he's doing and he knows it's dangerous. But he's not finished yet.

We run more calls and at the end of the shift I drive to our empty church parking lot near the bottom of the 154 highway that goes up over the pass and takes us home. I strip off my gun belt and uniform shirt and vest and lay them in the trunk on top of Brag's stuff. My t-shirt is soaked with sweat so I'll be shivering by the time we get home but I'll warm back up with some scrambled eggs after I make Brag a hot dinner.

Brag usually sits in the back and watches me while I drop my gear in the trunk but tonight, he's already flat on his side and falling asleep. I drive home in silence as we wind around the curves that coil up the mountain while the city lights fade in the fog behind us.

THE ROCK

B rag has a rock. It's roundish, about the size of a bowling ball. He's obsessing on it, digging around the bottom to make it move, play-barking at it. He's convinced the inanimate object is resisting him. Why this highly-trained, intelligent police canine feels the need to move a stone around the back yard is a mystery. Yet he's doing it, and is thoroughly engrossed with the task.

I'm sitting outside with him, trying to read a book. The barking is making me read the same paragraph over and over.

"Brag, stop."

He looks at me but he knows if I really want him to stop, I will put him into his kennel. He decides my order to cease and desist is not going to be enforced, and continues to bark at his stone nemesis.

My son is walking around the yard as well, equally entertained by his own imaginary world. He is eleven. Despite the grim predictions of educators and other experts,

Strieker has learned to read. He doesn't read well and it took years and years of intensive tutoring, but he does read. He also learned to ride a bicycle. He has no interest in going for bicycle rides, he just wanted to prove he could do it. I ran behind him for weeks, gripping the back of his seat with four fingers while he pedaled around the empty playground and made the micro-corrections necessary to create the neurological paths that would ultimately result in his riding away from me on his own. His face was pure joy the first time he did it – despite the fact that he was at least five years older than most kids who master that skill – and there were some families playing at the school who realized what was happening and cheered for him. It was just in time too; my back was screaming at the awkward angle necessary to run behind and hold him upright and I don't know how much longer I could have done it. Brag may be aging faster than me, but I am definitely aging.

This gets me thinking about all of the things Brag and I weren't supposed to do. We weren't supposed to have any association with SWAT and now we're called out with the team every time. We weren't supposed to go this hard, this long. We've already beaten the odds and I still don't know how it all ends. I watch him trot around the yard, and every few steps I see that back leg drag. He's not in pain – the vet confirmed this – but Brag can't quite get the limb to work like it used to. Whatever neurological system it is that operates a dog's back legs is failing. I used to lament how my son's neurological systems were broken at the start of his life, and now I feel like some of his systems can be rewired eventually. Some of them are better; not healed, just re-routed. Brag won't get better. He and Strieker are passing each other in opposite directions. My son is climbing over each hurdle to improve while Brag is slowing down. There will come a time, sooner than I'd like, when my partner cannot continue at this pace.

At training I mention the back leg to Ted and he says, "Yeah, he's been dragging that foot for a while now." He doesn't miss much when it comes to the police dogs.

I ask him how much time he thinks Brag has left to work.

"You'll know when," Ted says. "Trust your instincts. No one else knows this dog like you."

When he's hunting and when he's fighting, Brag looks as strong and fearsome as he ever did. But at the end of the training day, he snores all the way home. He used to watch out the window while I drove. Today he is too exhausted.

"Remember, Brag, when we were immortal?"

He stops snoring at the sound of my voice but sleeps on. When we get home, he doesn't rise until his dinner is ready.

I scan the MDT screen in the K-9 car constantly; if a call sits for even a minute we could miss an opportunity to catch someone. But in most cases the dispatchers let me know something is happening before the call pops up on my screen. In this case, the call is a stolen vehicle.

A bad guy just stole a work van with the ignition keys in it, so he believes he has at least a few hours of driving around anonymously – plenty of time to commit a robbery – except for one wrinkle in this case: the van owner's iPhone is under the front seat. Within minutes there are four police units converging on the suspect vehicle as it drives around. There's a slight delay in the reported location, but as we close in it's a matter of time before one of us spots the van. I turn on my Extrapolometer and choose an intersection and I don't even put the car in park before the stolen van appears. The suspect pretends not to see me as he drives through the intersection.

I follow behind him and we play the "does the cop know it's stolen?" game for a few blocks but when Mitch Jan pulls in behind me in another police car the suspect takes off. Now we're in pursuit on the US 101 freeway.

Your pulse rate, breathing, and decision-making are all affected by a pursuit, especially in the first few minutes. The more pursuits you have under your belt, the faster you can bring that pulse down and regain total command of your thought processes. But you have to work at it: deep breath in, hold it, long breath out, pause. If you make the extra effort to communicate calmly and clearly on the radio it helps too. Any time a cop is yelling on the radio I get worried.

The suspect gets off of the freeway and speeds up Highway 154, the same winding road that Brag and I take home every night. There's no way this guy is going to lose me on a route I could drive in darkness with no headlights.

Ten miles later the CHP take over the pursuit. I stay in the chase, ready to deploy Brag if the suspect foot bails. Another ten miles brings us to the Santa Ynez River bridge, a natural narrow point in the road where the CHP vehicle in front of me suddenly slows down, giving the suspect space. I know what's coming: the spike strip. The suspect doesn't see it until too late and goes right over it. The CHP officer lying in wait yanks the strip out of the roadway and we close the distance as the suspect's tires come apart immediately. Direct hit.

The suspect rolls slowly for half-a-mile, which to me means he's cooking up some plan, one I'm not going to like. It usually doesn't take a few hundred yards of slow driving to surrender, so I tell the other cops on the radio not to chase the suspect when he runs.

The van grinds to a stop on rims. There isn't much on either side of the highway but miles of rolling, grassy pastures. He can't get away from Brag; he won't make it a hundred feet. The suspect opens the driver's door as the CHP give him commands to surrender. He doesn't, and instead brandishes a knife, shouting "Kill me!" Each time he yells, Brag bucks in his harness.

This man wants us to shoot him. If we wait long enough, he'll charge at one of the cops and seal his own fate and maybe take someone with him. Brag can beat this guy, I know it. There's not going to be a shooting, or a stabbing. This ends now.

Brag and I backtrack around to the right side of the CHP unit directly behind the stolen car. I grab one of the officers for cover, and the three of us creep up out of sight behind the van.

Brag peeks around the left side of the van and sees the suspect's left arm hanging out of the open driver's door. I send him for the bite; Brag streaks forward and hits the suspect's arm. The knife goes flying as Brag yanks the stunned man out of the driver's seat and onto the asphalt and then I pull on the long line with all my might and a second later the suspect is on his back behind the van and cops grab his arms as I lift Brag off of the bite. Done. Anyone who blinked missed it.

The CHP officers all breathe a sigh of relief that they won't have to shoot the man, grinning at Brag but giving us a wide berth because Brag is still incensed and trying to get at the suspect. For Brag, as long as the suspect is in view, he is still our mortal enemy. The barking isn't annoying to cops, it's reassuring in its exuberance.

Best of all, the dragging limp that ghosts Brag's every movement has vanished during this incident, as if willed out of existence by the purity of Brag's drive. It will return soon enough.

The CHP Sergeant picks up the knife from the road beside the driver's door.

"Did you know he had this?" he asks me.

"Yes," I reply and I can predict what his next question will be.

"Weren't you worried he was going to stab your dog?"

"Every time."

I look around at the cops all doing their separate tasks to complete this arrest and vehicle recovery. One of them thanks Brag as he walks past our car. A CHP officer takes pictures for evidence and two others sit with the suspect who is being treated for the bite by paramedics. Another CHP officer stands in the roadway, waving traffic by us with a good-natured smile on his face. Each of them is relieved it ended this way.

These cops are the best kind of people. I'm fortunate to work with them. They're all a bit uneasy around the Werewolf and maintain a respectful distance. This separation between K-9 handler and other cops – especially with a dog as intimidating as Brag – exists because the handler has traded his normal professional relationships for a different one that is mysterious and unique. The transformation that began with me abandoning my "regular citizen" thinking and becoming a street-wise cop has continued. I'm not a street cop anymore, I'm a hybrid. So is Brag. He's adopted a few of our rules of civility and I've adopted some of his behaviors. I see humans through his eyes, smell the world through his nose, and embrace the hunting of men as if it were the most natural thing I've ever done. It's wonderfully visceral. My nature has changed and I never want to go back to what I was before.

I have a quiet de-brief with Brag, telling him what a good dog he is. He knows.

Time to wrap it up. While I'm jotting down the case number and the suspect information for my report, some movement catches my eye below the setting sun and I spot a solitary coyote on the other side of the highway, a hundred yards away. He's so lean and dusty brown he's nearly invisible and trots through the drying grass as if he weighs nothing at all. Before I can point him out to anyone else, he vanishes behind a rise.

I look into the back of the K-9 car and see Brag's amber eyes fixed on the spot where the coyote disappeared. He usually barks at other dogs but he never made a sound. Perhaps he understood that his wild cousin was hunting and didn't want to interrupt.

I turn our car around on the highway and head back toward the city. We're within a few miles of home but we might as well be a thousand leagues away. A dispatcher asks me how long it will be before we're clear to assist on another call. Not long. Brag stares out at the road in front of us, looking like nothing could ever stop him.

LAST WATCH

This is Southern California. We don't get much of that leaves-are-turning-and-the-air-is-wonderfully-crisp period that heralds the arrival of fall. October always brings crushing heat and then, mercifully, the light changes. The sun's intensity diminishes as if it were passing through a filter. Leaves do fall from trees – mainly the species brought from somewhere else – and by Halloween a coolness creeps into the evenings. It's my favorite time of the year. I don't know why, because this year it means I can no longer ignore Brag's rear leg. It's time to retire him. He'll never ask for it and never want it, so it's up to me.

When I hear about a position opening up in the detective bureau, I know it's time to make a move. If I don't transfer into the bureau, I'll have to retire Brag and work patrol. I don't want to work patrol without Brag. I'm not sure I remember how to work patrol without Brag. But if I get the detective spot, I'll be doing a new job. Also, I'll have four months to prepare for that transition. I'm not worried about me. I'm worried about Brag.

I tell Ted at training and he lets me off the hook right away. "All good things come to an end," he says. "You two have had a great run, the best I've ever seen." He's never let me or Brag off easy in training, so I know he would tell me if this decision seemed the least bit premature.

I put in for the detective position and then sit for the oral board and get the call a week later that I have the spot. For the first time, there is an end date to my partnership with Brag. Tyler is in the detective bureau and Hondo has been retired at home for a year now and doing well. When I call Tyler to ask him how to make the transition less painful, he laughs and replies, "You can't." He's right. I'm looking for an easy way to do it but there's no way to tell Brag he's not a police dog anymore without breaking his heart. But if anyone is going to do that, it should be me. He will forgive me, I'm sure of it. He's forgiven every mistake I've ever made in training and on the street. He will know my heart is breaking, too.

Luckily, I don't have to decide how these last few months are going to go. The calls for service will decide that, and they never stop. We'll keep doing what we do.

Any time there is a 9-1-1 call where the caller mentions the sound of breaking glass, it's never good. Glass is a polite, fragile barrier: it only keeps things out that want to be kept out. It's always the first to shatter when people lose control. Accident scenes are liberally sprinkled with glass; the more horrific the accident, the more glass everywhere. Whenever I hear the words "sound of breaking glass" over the radio I'm already turning that direction because it means we're about to get some work.

There's a man breaking windows at a sober living home. Brag and I are on our way, backing up two other units. Before the first cops arrive, dispatch says the suspect is now trying to stab residents with a shard of glass. Since there's no way to safely hold a piece of glass and stab someone, this is a clue to the suspect's mental state. That glass is slicing his hand and he doesn't care. It would be serious enough to know a man is running amok stabbing people, but this particular detail has me concerned about how this one will end.

Brag's looking over my shoulder from the cage behind me, trying to divine from the series of hurried turns down darkened streets what we're about to do. The primary and cover units arrive before we do and I understand they can't wait for us so when I pull up, they've already run to the rear of the sober living house where the suspect is rampaging.

I pull Brag out and attach the long-line and we're jogging across the dark front yard when three gunshots ring out from the back of the property. I charge through the side gate with

Brag to the rear house and find three cops with their guns out, facing an open door. One of them is Epstein, Brag's buddy.

An enormous, bare-chested man fills the doorway. He's twice my size and he is furious. He stares down the cops as they shout commands at him to get on the ground and then I see that he has a bullet hole in his chest. There's not a single drop of blood coming out, just a perfectly round hole where the bullet went into the engine room. But the suspect's hands and face are smeared with blood.

Brag barks and lunges on the long line but I've choked up on it so he has only a foot of slack. The suspect doesn't seem to notice the police dog.

"Is he shot?" I ask Epstein, the most banal question ever.

"Yes," he answers.

"You shot me!" the suspect bellows as if he overheard us talking and suddenly realized he'd been hit. He's no longer holding a shard of glass but there are large pieces of glass all around him. The cops order him to get on the ground and he lowers his bulk down onto the floor. I don't want to have to go in there to arrest this man but the other cops already know this so they try to coax the suspect out. He scoots toward us on his butt as I tell him to keep coming and for an instant I think he might let us arrest him. Suddenly he raises one foot and kicks the door shut in our faces. Negotiations have ended.

I turn to Epstein. "Kick it."

Epstein, no small man himself, blasts the door open with his boot and I send Brag in for the bite. Brag clamps onto the enormous man's lower leg and I pull with all I've got and Brag pulls with three-and-a-half legs and miraculously the suspect slides out the door toward us. Once the suspect is clear of the doorway I grab onto Brag's badge collar with two hands and take him off of the bite.

The suspect howls with pain from the bite. Why he is indifferent to getting shot but feels such pain from the K-9 bite is a mystery I will never solve because the suspect is loaded into an ambulance and rushed to the hospital. They will try to save his life and I haven't any idea if he will survive.

The waiting is the strange part. Epstein and the other officers are out of service for the rest of the night, and whichever one of them pulled the trigger will be out for longer. Weeks, possibly. An Officer-Involved Shooting Team comes in and gathers all the evidence and our Crime Lab will process the scene meticulously. The involved cops are immediately separated and aren't allowed to talk to each other; it's important to prevent us from affecting how we each remember the incident. Since I was on the other side of the house when the shooting occurred, my interview is brief. I still don't know if the suspect is alive or dead but I know that a bullet hole in the chest is not good. There may be a day in the future of law enforcement where these episodes are resolved in a peaceful way, but I've seen enough men in that mental state to know there's little chance of talking them down, especially when they are shot and the clock is ticking. For now, monstrous behavior is met by monstrous force. The Werewolf was necessary to bring that enormous man under control. The bullets may kill him, but they sure didn't stop him. Only Brag could do that.

I take Brag to the showgrounds to let him out onto the grass. I don't throw the ball for him to chase anymore, especially tonight after he pulled a 280-pound man through a doorway. I toss him the Kong and Brag catches it deftly and trots around me, sniffing the grass and marking in his usual spots. The calls for service are stacking up but before we clear the scene, I check the pads on Brag's feet to make sure he wasn't cut by the broken glass. Somehow, he wasn't. When we run calls later every cop wants to hear how Brag dragged an enormous, bullet-resistant suspect out of a house.

The suspect survives. There's a lot of talk about the concept of "closure" and how that's helpful and healing but I don't seek closure on our cases. I don't call the District Attorney's office and ask about the disposition of any of the suspects Brag bites. Some go to prison, some get probation. A few of them fled the country and have not been seen again.

Another hung himself before the case was adjudicated. Each chose their own fate.

I've learned to exist like Brag: in the moment. He hunts men and doesn't concern himself with their lives after they are caught. He is so pure in his thinking and his actions that the concepts of self-doubt and regret are alien to him. I envy Brag for that, especially every night at 3:37 a.m. when the ghosts come to call. Someday I hope to sleep the way a dog sleeps. My dreams will be of the vast outdoors and brilliant blue skies.

With less than three weeks left on patrol, Brag and I are winding down an eight-year-long run together. Cops grumble about our impending absence; they like having Brag on the street. I'm not always easy to work with but I suspect they might miss having me around as well, because of my association with Brag if nothing else. When I transfer into the detective bureau, I will have worked twenty-four years on patrol. I've never sat behind a desk and I'm not sure how I'm going to like it.

If Brag suspects a big change is coming, he doesn't show it. He's as enthusiastic as ever, raking his nails across the metal window screen when we arrive on a call and he sees anyone who might be a suspect. There's a superstition among cops that you have to be especially careful on the street in the last few weeks before you leave patrol, whether you are retiring or rotating into a desk job. I don't believe in any of that; one should be careful all of the time.

It's one of our last training days and Brag and I meet Ted and the other K-9 units at a shuttered processing plant outside of the city of Santa Maria. The training location is enormous: huge warehouses with gaping holes in the roofs, rusting railroad tracks crisscrossing in all directions, and open concrete pits surrounded by weeds.

Danny Muller – the K-9 trainer for Santa Maria Police Department – and I tour the abandoned complex, making note of the areas to avoid. Safety for the K-9's is paramount and we've both worked dogs so long we share a good eye for the dangers that you always find at industrial locations: jagged metal, old machinery, poisonous spills, and collapsed floors.

Muller and I pause to take in a towering, rusted structure that is too decayed to be used safely for building searches. He makes a joke about spending so much of his time in the most dilapidated places in the county. I survey the building, taking a few steps back, and when my boot finds only air behind me, I realize in the span of a millisecond that I've stepped backward into an open pit. A question flashes through my mind as I fall: *how deep is it?*

Stars explode across my vision and everything goes black.

I'm only knocked out for a split-second and I'm dangling, hanging onto a metal beam I crashed into as I fell.

My legs feel like they weigh a thousand pounds; I can't hold on.

Muller leans over the edge above me, reaching down and grabbing onto my arms. In an astonishing display of strength, he lifts me up off the beam and onto the ground beside the pit: a 200-pound deadlift from a prone position. I rise and stagger away from the edge, trying to breathe and I know he wants to hear I'm all right but all I can do is push out the words "it's broken."

There's no mistaking a broken rib and I've torn some other stuff inside there as well when I crashed into that beam but it's a hell of a lot better than landing skull-first at the bottom of a concrete pit. I'm lucky. I just don't feel lucky at this particular moment.

One of the Santa Maria PD handlers was a paramedic for years and he takes one look at me and says "We're not driving you to the hospital. If your rib pierced an organ, you'll bleed out internally before we get there." Another handler remarks that the pit wasn't deep enough to kill me so it might have been better to fall to the bottom. Cop humor – always a dark roast.

They call an ambulance despite my weak objections and Ted drives my K-9 car with Brag in it over to where I am. The other handlers strip off my gun belt and secure it in the trunk. Brag knows something is wrong: he doesn't bark at anyone. I can't see him through the dark window tint but I know he's watching. I wish I could tell him everything is okay but they shut the ambulance doors and we pull away.

People assume the worst when a cop in uniform rolls into the hospital emergency department on a stretcher: a shoot-out, or a fight with ninjas. The doctor comes into my exam room and says "so you fell into a pit" and I can't help but laugh painfully with him at the absurdity of it. I should have been more superstitious.

I feel like the painkillers aren't working, but when Ted arrives at the hospital I keep asking him where Brag is and he has to tell me several times that another handler is driving Brag and my K-9 car home. I find out later that Brag was completely beside himself the entire forty-minute drive, turning panicked circles in the car and whining because I'd been left behind. We'd never been separated like that before and he was understandably upset. I knew he was in good hands, but he didn't know where his partner had gone.

Once I'm home I shuffle out to the gate in the backyard. Brag stands on his hind legs, leaning over it as far as he can to inhale my scent and reassure himself that I'm there. A dog doesn't believe in anything until he smells it. Once I tell him I'm all right he sits down, watching quietly as I turn around and limp back into the house.

I can't lie down or get up without help. I can barely move my left arm. My last patrol shift with Brag is in two weeks. I won't rob him of his opportunity to say good-bye to all the cops he's worked with for so many years. He must have his final shift.

Two weeks later I'm in the city doctor's office and she presses her hand against my ribs and tells me to raise my arm. Normally a cop who is injured returns to work on light-duty, which means no patrol and definitely no running a police dog. I tell her I'm ready to return to full duty. She's not stupid; she knows I'm still hurt despite my attempts to keep a relaxed face. She asks when I want to go back.

"Tomorrow *night*," I tell her, as if adding a few extra hours would help convince.

"I'll clear you for light duty," she says.

No, that won't work. Time to lay it all out. "I have to go back full duty. It's my K-9 partner's last shift. We've been together for eight years and he needs to say goodbye."

She relents. Minutes later I'm holding my medical clearance paper in my hand and it flaps like a flag as I go out the door.

Friday. I come out of the garage in the afternoon and Brag is waiting at the gate and his tail wags and he grins as I put on his black leather collar with the silver police badges on either side. When I open the gate he runs past me into the garage, doing a two-step at the rear door of the K-9 car until I open it and then he hops inside, crying with excitement.

I take him to briefing and he plays tug with a few of the cops in the room and I breezily announce that I'm back and it's Brag's last shift and the last part gets caught in my throat. Brag pulls me hard back to the car and we clear on the radio like every shift before but tonight is a night of lasts.

I want to kick off our final shift with coffee but I can't decide who I should drink it with, so I go by myself and lean against the K-9 car with Brag sitting beside me.

My sergeant, Todd Johnson, calls me into the station and reminds me that Brag is a piece of equipment that belongs to the city. When I scowl at his awkward timing, he smiles and hands me an official-looking document. It states that as of tomorrow the city is selling me this piece of used equipment and will therefore have no more legal responsibility for it. The equipment is listed as "one German Shepherd dog, sable, used." The purchase price of the dog is one dollar. Sgt. Johnson has written the word "paid" beside the amount and initialed it. I sign at the bottom that I will be taking possession.

"Who paid the dollar?" I ask him.

"I held a fundraiser," he jabs. "We took it out of our curse cup."

That cup is always filled with money because when anyone in the room uses profanity, they are supposed to drop a dollar in. It's appropriate that this fund should pay for Brag to be mine forever.

The night speeds by. I cover Josh Morton – who's been on dozens of manhunts and SWAT call-outs with Brag – and another officer on a disturbance call. When the suspect we're preparing to arrest becomes agitated, Josh steps right in front of me, standing between me and the suspect. I'm irritated at his odd tactical positioning until I realize he knows I'm still hurt and doesn't want me fighting with anybody. In the end there's no fight but I'm reminded that my goal is to finish the shift with Brag, not return to the hospital.

Brag's muzzle is dusted with gray but he looks as terrifying as he ever did. His bark hits the same decibel level; my ears ring when he spies a couple of gang members glowering at us from a street corner. But I notice Brag's foot drags as he gets out on every call.

I want to leave the K-9 car with a full tank of gas for my replacement so at 2 a.m. we go to the city yards and as I'm filling up, I crawl into the back with Brag. He's lying on his side, eyes open, and licks my hand as I tell him a dozen times what a good police dog he is and how proud I am of him.

I drive back to the station and park in our spot at the rear corner of the building and begin downloading the gear that belongs to me, transferring it from the trunk into my uncool Volvo. There isn't much going home with us. Most of it will go to the new handler and K-9 but I am keeping three items that technically still belong to the city: the four-foot leather lead, Brag's badge collar, and the long-line. These have been with us since the beginning and on every call. They're too personal to pass on. I'm also going to miss my Ford Interceptor, who never quit. She's the last Crown Vic the city purchased and Ford won't be making anymore.

One by one, officers come up the driveway in their patrol cars and stop to say goodbye to Brag. A couple of them want a game of tug. Brag is happy to oblige; it keeps him occupied while I go through our equipment. Shamordola stops by and Brag seems curious about why she is so subdued. He tries to cheer her up with an enthusiastic game, not realizing it will be their last. Sham waves at us as she leaves but her smile fails to conceal her sadness. She was Brag's first, most staunch supporter on patrol. How many years ago was that? They slipped past in the chaos.

Our story is unique to us, yet it would ring familiar to all K-9 handlers and their partners, their own narratives similarly punctuated with sweat and elation. Sooner or later, every K-9 team reaches this bittersweet chapter – if they're lucky.

The equipment is sorted. It's done. Then I remember that Brag's name is written on both sides of the car so I'll have to painstakingly peel off each letter, erasing his ownership of it. Chad Hunt is the last cop to stop by. He thanks Brag quietly and watches while I peel off the decals. The ghost image of Brag's name remains. Chad and I look at each other; we spent decades on SWAT and patrol together so there's nothing either of us needs to say. He gives me a reassuring nod and gets into his car and drives off. Brag and I are alone. The only thing left for me to do is sign off on the radio.

I sit in the driver's seat and pick up the mic. The night has gone curiously quiet, so I don't need to wait for a break in radio traffic. I only need to say six words. Brag lets out a sigh behind me. It's our last moment as police dog and handler. Every time I try to key the mic, I feel like I won't be able to say it. Ten minutes pass. This is ridiculous. I can say six words, can't I?

I close my eyes and squeeze the mic as hard as I can.

"Fifty-five, K9-1 station, EOW."

End of watch. I put the mic down.

"K9-1 station," the dispatcher replies. "Thank you, Brag."

Cops chime in on the channel, thanking my partner but I can't listen anymore. I turn off the radio and let Brag out. I lock the K-9 car and walk away from it with Brag trotting beside me. I point to the open rear hatch of the Volvo. Brag hesitates, then hops in gingerly and turns around to look at me as I close it.

We have completed our mission. We never said no. We did as much as we could for as long as we could. It's our last winding drive home together. Brag rests his chin on his paws, thoughtful. He's my dog now, and only one thing can part us.

UNCLE BRAG

The alarm goes off at 0500 hours. I have no uniform to put on, no equipment to prepare. A desk waits for me. I'm nervous as hell, because I'm going to work without Brag. When my carpool pulls up, I tiptoe out, glancing back at the garage as we drive away. I wonder if Brag is at the gate, listening while I leave him behind.

I'm a detective working burglary and auto theft, which sounds glamorous. It's not. My new human partner is a salty nail named Ingram who lateraled to the SBPD from Boston. He starts his morning with a black coffee and shakes his head when I come into the office with my latte. He's a gifted detective but even his abrasive humor can't distract me from the fact that my real partner is at home. I'm worried about Brag, afraid he will give up when he realizes he can no longer do the thing he loved most. Like Beowulf did.

When I arrive home, I find Brag loitering at the gate, wondering if we're going to work, so I let him into the garage. He does a quick sniff tour of the interior – pausing where the long-line hangs on a hook – and walks slowly back out to the yard. He already suspected the K-9 car was gone. He just needed to confirm it.

"You're retired, buddy," I tell him and he gets the Kong and chews it hard a few times before dropping it at my feet. I pick it up and toss it directly to him and he trots away, dragging that rear leg and leaving a furrow in the wood chips.

I'm also missing the rush of patrol, the immediacy. Nothing in the detective bureau feels like an emergency. I don't mean to suggest that the job isn't important – it's critical. I'm just missing the *right now* urgency of hand-picked calls for service over the last eight years. It must be so much worse for Brag, who is stuck at home. He's bored, waiting for me, for anything. I don't know how to make it better, how to save him. And then a solution arrives that takes me by complete surprise.

Brag's best friend is our female Rottweiler named Millie. He roughhouses with her daily and when she doesn't come out to play one morning, it's because she gave birth to four puppies the night before. It wasn't an accident; she'd been paired with a nice male Rottweiler and we were hoping to pass on Sweet Millie dog genes to another generation.

The chunky black-and-tan caterpillars that will someday become Rottweilers inch around the wooden whelping box in the garage. When their eyes open and they start climbing out of the box, Rachel constructs a sturdy metal pen for them to spend their days outside. Filled with soft shavings and some playground equipment (two stumps and a length of pipe for a tunnel), the Puppy Pen sits in the middle of the backyard. Once the puppies are inside it and the door is secured, I let Brag out of his kennel. He circles the enclosure like a shark, sniffing the puppies as he stalks around the exterior. Inside the newly-renamed Shark Cage, the puppies cower whenever the Werewolf trots by. But within a few days they are running alongside him as he passes, and I catch him going nose-to-nose with them through the cage on several occasions. He doesn't growl, he wags his tail.

A week later the puppies rush the walls of the Shark Cage when they see Brag approaching. They climb on top of each other to try to get to him. Brag pauses outside the metal fence, his sable tail swishing side-to-side, and I know. I let the puppies out.

They swarm him, leaping up and licking his face and rolling onto their backs whenever he lowers his enormous head toward one of them. They adore this enormous monster and he lets them do whatever they want. They nip him, pull his tail, and jump on his back. He doesn't mind any of it. The Werewolf has become Uncle Brag, and he couldn't be happier. Now he doesn't wait at the gate to go to work, he waits at the gate for his puppies to come out and play.

Criminal cases come and go across my desk. The narcs and homicide detectives help keep me busy by inviting me to serve their high-risk warrants, but it's not enough. I'm just punching a clock, watching my cases roll down my screen like a factory worker at a conveyer belt.

At home the puppies grow and Brag loves them more with each day that passes. He boxes with them gently and never loses his temper. They adore him. He grows calmer, content to be their guardian and teacher and friend. When the puppies are adopted out at about eight weeks, Brag mopes around the empty backyard. Rachel plans another litter and before we know it, nine new puppies appear in the garage whelping box and this time there's no need to wait. Uncle Brag steps in immediately, sniffing his new pups and smiling at them. They stare into his enormous, toothy mouth in absolute astonishment. They've never seen anything so terrifying and wonderful.

Brag helps raise the second litter as enthusiastically as the first. Some of the older pups – adults now – come to visit and Brag remembers them, letting them jump on him and behave in a manner he would never tolerate from any other dogs.

I'm sitting at my desk at work scanning my ever-growing caseload when Rachel texts to tell me Brag is coughing weakly, drooling and standing with his legs spread. She knows he's bloating before I say it and somehow she finds the strength to lift Brag into the car and rushes him to the vet. Time is running out. I dash out of the detective bureau so fast I have to text my sergeant to tell her why I suddenly vanished. I burst into the vet's office thirty minutes later and find Brag lying on an exam table with a young vet tech cradling him and stroking his fur. Brag's eyes are glazed over but when he hears my voice he struggles to his feet and I have to calm him again. The vet says the x-rays show his stomach has flipped over – torsion – which makes this case of bloat deadlier. She's not comfortable doing the complicated surgery alone and the vet who owns the clinic, Dr. Dean, is out of town. The nearest emergency animal hospital is at least forty-five minutes away.

"If we could get his stomach to flip back over," the vet tells me, "I might be able to get some of the gas out, which would buy us time."

I ask her what I could do to help make that happen.

"Pick him up and shake him," she says.

I wrap my arms around Brag's ribcage and lift him so his back feet are dangling above the floor. He doesn't resist as I gently shake his body to try get his stomach to flip back over. His ribs are as wide around as mine and it's the first time I've held him like this and he really does feel like a werewolf more than a dog. The whole time I am begging him to stay with me.

We take more x-rays but the stomach didn't flip. I try again and Brag is in so much pain that he groans weakly as I shake him. More ex-rays; still no flip. He's doomed. The vet manages to release some gas from his bloating stomach with a thick needle but I'm going to have to load Brag up in the car and drive over the pass to the emergency hospital. He will likely not survive the trip. Suddenly the door opens and Dr. Dean hurries in; he'd heard Brag was in trouble and immediately drove back into town on his day off to perform the surgery. I'm so dumbstruck by his kindness I can only mumble an awkward thanks as he rushes Brag into surgery. I want to stay but there's no reason to do that. I drive home and sit staring at the wall where our history plays in jittery memory clips that only I can see.

Hours later my phone rings and I force myself to answer it, dreading the worst. It doesn't come; Brag survived. The surgery was a success and he came through it like a warrior. It's so Brag to survive both bloat and torsion. I can't wait to see him but I know he's sleeping so I have to wait. It's okay; as long as the Werewolf is still with me on this earth I can wait.

They tell me they'll keep him around for the weekend but by the following afternoon he is barking at a mischievous resident cat and the vet asks me to take him home. Gladly. His sutures look good and he acts like nothing happened. I have to keep him away from his beloved Rottweilers for a day or two because they'll jump on him with joy.

A cop named Greg Hons who served with Brag on the SWAT Team hears about the emergency and contacts the other members of the Santa Barbara Police Officers' Foundation. Since Brag is my dog now, I'm on the hook for the vet bills but Hons wants to recognize Brag's service by having the Foundation pay for half of the surgery. It is an act of respect that I don't see coming and one that leaves me humbled. Brag is my dog, but he still belongs to the cops who worked alongside him and admired his courage. He remains their ideal police officer.

Rachel's relationship with Brag was often tenuous. He was all business and believed there was only one person he needed to listen to: me. But as he aged and especially after he retired, those two became fast friends and he developed a real affection for her. That relationship is cemented when Rachel brings Brag a special gift: a Rottweiler puppy all his own. Her name is Isabel and she's staying with him forever. Brag becomes her favorite dog immediately, and when she plays with him, he lies down so she can attack his face properly.

This one puppy isn't enough. We foster pups of all breeds from the local animal shelter and Brag cares for them all, playing with the bouncy upstarts despite barely being able to use his back legs. I trust him with puppies the way I trusted him with my son. He would never harm a single one of them. He is content in his new role, as content as he ever was catching bad guys.

The day before Thanksgiving I find myself the only detective working in the station. I go out alone for lunch, taking shortcuts through alleys downtown and recalling the many times I crept along these same places late at night. When I get back to my desk, I look at my caseload and feel no urgency, no fire. Something is missing, and has been missing for a year: the fuel that made me want to do police work. Suddenly, it hits me – there's no anger. It's all gone. My time partnered with Brag was so intense that all the anger was burned away. I don't need to make the world right anymore. I've been a police officer for more than half of my life; I can't remember what it's like to be everyone else. It's time to find out, and my son needs me more than ever.

I leave work and rush home and go into the backyard and Brag is there, wagging his tail. I plop down onto the ground and tell him I'm done and he leans into me so I can scratch that spot on his flank and he smiles at me while I'm going on and on because he already knew.

The crusade is finished. The eleven-year-old in me puts down the fire poker forever.

PARTING

I file my retirement paperwork with human resources and no one is remotely surprised at my decision and before I know it the big day arrives. I turn in my badge and gun and walk out the back door as an ex-cop. The city thanks me for my twenty-five years of service by giving me a pen. It's not gold, just a metal ball-point pen adorned with the words "Santa Barbara Police Department." It's as impersonal as anything could ever be, and exactly what I would have expected. I will keep the pen as a reminder that material possessions don't matter. I have Brag – purchased for one dollar – and he is priceless to me.

The first thing I do as an ex-cop is sleep for eight hours that night. I wake up at 3:37 a.m. but I go back to sleep soon enough and it feels so right to sleep for that long I do it the following night. And again. I may be *ronin* – a master-less samurai – but I'm well-rested. The SWAT team holds a barbecue and presents me with a plaque displaying a SBPD badge and SWAT shoulder patch and a photo of Brag and I hunting, the black long-line taut between us. Beneath it, a quote from the epic poem "Beowulf," which Ed Olsen knew was a source of inspiration for my entire career. SWAT team members are the bravest, gentlest, most misunderstood people in police work. I will miss them most of all.

Now I am like Brag. Our services are no longer required by the city we once watched over through the long nights. Dog and man have closed that chapter, and our skills will perish with us.

The days pass peacefully. Without the psychological aerobatics of my former profession, my life takes on a monastic feel. Strieker and I go on long walks together in companionable silence. Brag's health declines; he often stands motionless in the yard – lost in some reverie – while the other dogs cavort around him. One evening I return home and discover Brag fast asleep near the back gate. Beside him, a foster pup chews contentedly on a stick. When the pup leaps to his feet and bounds to the gate to greet me, Brag doesn't awaken. I open the gate quietly, bringing the pup back into the garage while Brag slumbers. That should have been the moment Brag's life ended: snoozing in the cool of a perfect afternoon while a puppy plays happily beside him. What more fitting end for this fearsome hunter-of-men?

But that's not how it works. Death cannot come and claim the life of the Werewolf; It must be invited, and not by anyone. Death must be invited by me.

Tomorrow is the Fourth of July. I'm going to do what I've done for the last three years and drive my pickup down a dirt road about a mile from the fireworks show and park at the dead end. We'll sit in the bed of the truck and watch the show. My son can't be any closer to the fireworks because they are too loud for him. At this distance it feels like you're watching someone else's celebration; the cheers of the crowd follow the booming explosions like a whisper. Strieker usually runs in place beside the truck while the fireworks detonate, unable to contain his excitement. He enjoys things more from a safe distance.

I'm enjoying my safe distances these days as well. I did not have a Fourth of July off for twenty-five years. It was always an event marked by throngs of people and chaos and long hours. Now the day belongs to me. I have begun to associate it with barbecues and celebration. This year will be an Independence Day I will always remember, because it will be the day after I said farewell to my best friend.

Our lives are marked by the completion of simple tasks. Most of them are easily done without us having to think about them. Make the bed. Check phone. Get groceries. Then, one task gets in front of us that is just as simple but incredibly difficult. Delete the inflammatory text. Ignore the bad driver. Write that difficult email.

I have a few simple tasks to complete today. Call the vet. Open the back gate. Hold on tightly to my partner while his life ends. These tasks feel impossible, but I must do them. Brag has been suffering terribly; his breathing is labored when he sleeps at night and he can't keep his food down. He's dying.

It must be so strange for him to look at me and see essentially the same person he met eleven years ago. I'm older, with my own aches and pains, but on the outside I'm not so different. I wonder if it puzzles him how he has lived a life so unaccountably shorter than mine.

Dr. Dean, the same veterinarian who saved Brag's life two years ago, agrees to come to the house and perform this final task. I sit outside with Brag in the warm afternoon on a huge dog bed that was a gift to celebrate his retirement. He tries to lie beside me but he is so uncomfortable that he cannot be still and has to struggle to get up again and then walks in a crooked circle and comes back. I have so many things I should say to him, that I need to say to him, but watching him suffer has rendered me mute. I run my hand along his bony back and his fur feels dry and brittle, like an aged taxidermy animal on display for too many years.

I let the Rottweiler girls out to say goodbye to him but they're so excited to see him they knock him down accidentally. He doesn't get annoyed but I do and usher them back into the garage. I offer Brag the Kong ball. He doesn't want it. He is too tired.

I go inside to tell Strieker what is about to happen. He's watching a movie, mimicking the drama on the screen with his hands, a common technique he uses to calm himself. I sit on the couch next to him and tell him he needs to look at me for a moment. He looks me in the eye, knowing I have something important to say.

"You should come say goodbye to Brag," I tell him.

"Do you know why Brag is leaving?" His question sounds clinical, but it is really a plea for the truest answer I can give him.

"He's very old and very sick."

"He's not coming back?"

I'm clenching my jaw so hard I can barely speak. "No, he's going to die and that's why you should see him one more time."

There is heartbreaking resignation in his reply: "Okay."

He follows me out and stands beside the dog, still puppeting with his hands. He glances down at Brag for a few seconds, pausing his imaginary drama and says, "Goodbye, Brag."

Brag looks up at Strieker and something passes between them, a quiet kindness. My son has demonstrated to me how simple it is to accept this moment. I'm humbled by it.

"Do you want to be here when the doctor comes or do you want to be inside?" I ask him.

"I want to be inside," he says. Safe distance. He's been brave enough for one day.

He leaves Brag and I alone. An idea suddenly occurs to me and I hurry upstairs to where Brag's badge collar hangs in my office. Brag should be wearing it today. He hasn't had it on since he retired more than three years ago. I rub the two silver badges on it with the bottom of my t-shirt to make them shine again.

When I return outside and put the badge collar on Brag, he suddenly turns away from me and beelines for the gate, dragging both back legs pathetically. He thinks he's going back to work. At that moment the incredible drive and heart of this thirteen-year-old dog is made plain to me. He will happily go hunt bad guys with only two of his legs working.

Panting and trembling from the effort, he stops at the gate and looks back at me expectantly but I haven't followed him and I think at that moment he knows.

Rachel comes out of the house to tell me the vet is here and is driving around to the rear of the yard. I bring Brag back to the dog bed beneath the apple tree and Dr. Dean comes into the yard carrying his bag. Brag looks away as Dr. Dean crouches down beside Rachel and I hold on tightly while a vet tech shaves down the fur on Brag's foreleg.

"I'm going to give him a shot first to make him more comfortable," Dr. Dean says. His manner is so kind and he knows I won't be able to answer so he injects Brag immediately and Brag growls at him, baring his dulled teeth.

I stroke Brag's mane, trying to calm him.

"Let's give it a few minutes," Dr. Dean says, and I can only nod. We wait like that in silence, listening to Brag's ragged breathing.

Brag's body relaxes and he rolls slowly over onto his side. He looks like he always did when we were getting gas at the city yards, relaxed and ready to sleep. He no longer seems to mind that these people are huddled over him.

"Are you ready?" Dr. Dean asks me and I nod again.

I don't watch the deadly mixture go in; I lean further over Brag as if I were shielding him from harm instead of presiding over his last seconds of life. Brag's breathing slows and suddenly time is going too fast. I've changed my mind; I want one more day with him. One more hour. Ten more minutes. I want to tell him exactly how I feel about him and thank him for everything he taught me. But it's too late. Instead, I put my face against his ear and say "You're a good boy, Brag. I love you."

Brag's exhales quietly, and does not breathe in again. He is entirely still, his eyes black pupils frozen in amber. The Werewolf is dead.

An unbearable silence. The vet tech unzips a nylon bag to carry his body away.

"No," I tell her. "I'll carry him."

Dr. Dean pats my shoulder. He and his tech walk quietly out the gate to the truck.

Rachel strokes Brag's mane.

"He can still hear you," I tell her.

"Brag, you are a good dog," she says and we both sit there stroking him and I look up because I know his spirit is rising and I smile in case he is looking down at us one last time. I don't see anything but even if he was there, I wouldn't know it because I am crying like a child: openly and unashamed.

I take off Brag's badge collar and scoop up his lifeless body and carry him to the bed of the truck and lay him as gently as I can into it and Dr. Dean zips him into the bag and I thank them hoarsely before I turn away. I'm halfway across the yard before I realize I forgot to say the words "good bye" to my best friend.

I don't want Strieker to see me like this so I go into the garage to pull myself together. The long line hangs on a hook, and I take it down and unroll it, laying it flat in my palm. But it is slack; there is no dog at the end of it and there never will be. I coil it up the way I have a thousand times before and hang it back on the hook, where it will stay.

The world is utterly and irrevocably diminished.

Now I know how this story ends.

The fireworks blossom in their usual colors but it feels like it takes longer for the sound to reach us, as if the celebration has moved farther off. Each of us is quiet, lost in our own thoughts. Strieker does not run in place like he used to when the fireworks exploded and when the show is over, he gets back in the truck without a word. At home I pull the red, white and blue bunting off of the front porch in the dark.

It's a week before I go into the back yard again. Brag's kennel door hangs open. Inside, sable fur swirls on the concrete. I walk beneath the apple tree looking for the Kong ball but the other dogs have taken it. I am searching for some sign of Brag, any evidence that he has been there again, even though I know that is ridiculous. Then I go around the back shed and trip on that stupid rock he used to push around the yard.

In a week Dr. Dean's office calls to tell me that Brag's remains have arrived. They won't take money for it; the cremation company insists on providing the service for police and military dogs for free. Included with the cardboard box that contains Brag's ashes is a fired clay tablet with the impression of his front paw. I run my finger over the delicate cracks left by the toes and pad, remembering the raw power of Brag's limbs. Whoever it was that took a piece of wet clay and carefully pressed it against my partner's toes so I could touch them again must be one of the kindest people on earth. In block letters beside the huge paw print is one word: "BRAG."

The summer ends. The house feels empty. I go into the garage to consolidate the used K-9 equipment into one container. When I zip open one of the gear bags the smell propels me back in time with Brag and I shut my eyes, inhaling deeply. For a moment I experience the world as dogs do, immersed in odor and recalling everything at once. I'm not sure how long I stand there with these fresh memories coursing through me but when Strieker's school bus pulls up outside the spell is broken; the scents fade and I am just holding a leather muzzle and bite sleeve frayed by the teeth of a police dog. I put both into a plastic tub and snap it shut.

The trappings associated with my partner may occupy a dusty shelf now, but the hole left by his absence will never be filled. I prefer that void to remain as it is, a monument not to loss but a life victorious. I intend to live the way Brag lived, without reservation or regret. And when my own story ends, I hope it is Brag who comes to lead me away, the *clickclickclick* of his toenails on the floor and his deep sigh as he draws up next to me. I'll happily go with him through that last door, where everything that was dark vanishes in the light.

I wondered for so long; why did Brag care about the evil that men do? What made a dog so eager to risk his life every night? I understand now. He simply wanted to help, to live a life of purpose. He needed his existence on this earth to matter, as we all do. Also – perhaps most significantly – Brag did it for me, his partner. He put himself in harm's way, again and again, to protect the human being he loved most.

People often ask, "Did Brag ever save your life?" There is only one answer to that question: "Every single day."

I have a recurring dream. Brag and I are training on a sunny afternoon at some place that is a compilation of many of our old training sites, with seemingly-endless stretches of grass and trees. Dogs bark in their K-9 cars parked behind us and I can hear the banter among the handlers. I straddle Brag while Ted runs away in the bite suit cracking his whip with a grin on his face and Brag bucks in the harness and I strain to hold onto him until I release.

Brag explodes away from me, pure energy and speed. I feel my soul spring forward with the power of the animal. He never misses. He never gives up. No one will ever outrun him. There is an inexorableness to his pursuit, a finality.

He is the Werewolf, and he loves it when a man runs.

EPILOGUE

Tomorrow is the Fourth of July. There was that moment during a police call, crouched outside an open door leading into darkness, where I hesitated to let Brag go. I knew it was his job – our job – but I grew to hate that separation, and the silence that followed. The delay in releasing him may have been only a few seconds, but my heart always stayed my hand for that agonizing instant.

It's been exactly one year since Brag died. I've held onto him this whole time but now I must let him go.

I drive to Santa Barbara with him on the seat beside me. I'd planned to scatter his ashes at a dozen different places in the city where we loved to train and work and also the front of the police station. But in the end, I don't like the idea of him being portioned out so I go to the empty lot where we ended every shift, our last stop before the drive home where I dropped my gun belt into the trunk and peeled off my Kevlar vest while Brag marked his domain. I would call his name and he would come trotting out of the night to join me again. He was never far.

Now there is no K-9 car and Brag is in a cardboard box. I walk out past the edge of the lot and look out over the city where we spent so many shifts. This time I'll be going home alone.

A dog's greatest gift to us is love that does not diminish. We rarely deserve it. Brag also taught me that the thoughts of dogs, and indeed all animals, are complicated and profound. Humans need not look for animal intelligence, we need to stop overlooking it. I catch glimpses of it every day, in the politeness of honeybees that appear as I add fresh water to the backyard fountain, in a horse's dark examining eye, and when the crows present their babies to me every spring, letting the youngsters hop as close as curiosity dares. These creatures' lives are hardly different from ours: they struggle to survive, care for their offspring, and pass on their collective wisdom.

Humankind must re-learn to accept responsibility for every living thing around us. It may determine our own survival. Our canine companions are ambassadors who remind us – in the kindest way – not to rule the animal kingdom but to keep it.

And who has ever had a better friend than a dog?

It's time. I open the box and tear the plastic and upend it and Brag pours out like a swirling gray spirit, borne on the breeze away from me. I press my hand into his ashes and wipe some on my face, an act that might appear savage to any onlooker, but it's just Brag and me for this final moment. He smells like fire and dust. Scooping up the last of his chalky remains, I raise my hand as high as I can and let my friend slip through my fingers.

Good bye, Brag.

The wind rises and he is gone.

AFTERWORD

I promised Brag that I would tell his story. Fulfilling this vow proved daunting; I'd compiled a digital mountain of police reports, documents, transcripts, notes, photos, and anecdotes. Many are contained here, but much has been left out. To anyone whose acts of courage I omitted or whose favorite Brag moment I failed to share, I apologize. One never knows, when setting out, exactly where a journey will lead. Things get lost along the way. My singular hope is that Brag's courage and incandescence are brought to life again in these pages.

Some readers will have noticed that at no point in this narrative did I recount an incident of racism in police work. This is not an omission. At no time during these events did I witness a police officer act out of hatred of any other race. I wish I could say I saw no evidence of racism at all, but I was the target of it on a regular basis. In the larger picture these were mere distractions, most often an attempt to interfere with a lawful arrest. A failure in every instance.

The overwhelming majority of suspects that demanded to be bitten by Brag were white. Brag never demonstrated that he was aware of different races and I can't imagine why he would have cared. In my experience, this is true of all police work; the color of a suspect's skin is about as noteworthy as the color of his shirt.

Racism afflicts all ethnicities and occupations. I have no doubt that on many occasions law enforcement officers have behaved abominably toward people of other races. I'm glad there are policies and laws in place to examine what every law enforcement officer does every day.

This is not the last word on this sensitive topic, but it is my last word on it. I envision a better future where people no longer suffer racism, no longer perpetuate it, and no longer see it where it does not exist.

Things are different now. I don't hunt human beings any more. Some of my favorite cop pals have become police administrators, and by all accounts are good ones. I usually sleep through the night and if I do awaken at 3:37 it feels less like a haunting and more like a visit from an old nemesis who just wants to be remembered.

The violence and intensity of my former existence has drained away, leaving a different person behind. A better one, hopefully. A lonelier one, to be sure.

The cop in me may be fading, but whenever I see a police vehicle with "K-9" emblazoned on the side my heart leaps with joy because I'm near to a police dog – the purest form of law enforcer that ever existed. In that moment I feel Brag smiling.

ACKNOWLEDGEMENTS

There are many extraordinary people to thank for the existence of this book. I'll begin with two special humans who lived through this story before it was written: Rachel, who loved the Werewolf as much as I did, and my son, Strieker – the toughest dude I know.

I wish to thank Jill Vaccaro for her generosity and for trusting me to care for her magnificent puppy. Ted Bowman deserves a big bowl of thanks for enduring my stubbornness and Brag's jaws. Thank you to my (human) K9 partners Mike Claytor and Tyler Larson. Thanks to Danny McGrew, Ed Olsen, Chad Hunt, Craig Rullman, Greg Hons, Mike Lazarus, Andy Feller, Mike Epstein, Mike McGrew, Mitch Jan, Kristin Shamordola, Rayshun Drayton, Shawn Hill, Todd Johnson, Corina Terrence, Ken Kushner, the Santa Barbara Police Department SWAT Team, the San Luis County Sheriff's Department K9 Unit, the Santa Maria Police Department K9 Unit, the Santa Barbara County Sheriff's Department, the California Highway Patrol, and all the other cops – too numerous to mention – who had Brag's back on countless manhunts.

Thanks to Marlin Sheik, Danny Muller, Sonnia Sosa, Dan Lamarca, Mary Ann Sampson, Judith Wright, Neil and Karla Zuehlke, Rodney Spicer and Gold Coast K9, Dr. Alan Moelleken, Michael Brian, Jessica Maher, Jeff Meyer, Ken Licklider, Brad Smith, Dr. Kenneth Furton, the instructors at K9 HITS and CNCA, and all the other trainers and experts who generously shared their expertise. Thanks to the Officer Down Memorial Page for remembering all the heroes who didn't finish their shifts.

Thanks to Jim Corbett, Anthony Bourdain, and Helen MacDonald for leaving a trail of words for me to follow.

Thanks to my agent Emerson Davis, who refused to leave me for dead.

Thanks to Thalia Chaltas, a gifted wordsmith who saw this story in its entirety before a word was written and had already formed an opinion about it. I admit you were right.

A special thank you to Rob Raisch, Bruce McBroom, and Robin Deshayes, three dear friends who insisted I simply write down that story I just told them. This book would not exist without your unwavering belief in it.

But my deepest gratitude belongs to the Werewolf, the most courageous police officer I've ever met.

There will never be another dog like you, Brag. You changed my life forever when you let me take part in your amazing story. We heard the chimes at midnight, didn't we, my friend?

ABOUT THE AUTHOR

During his law enforcement career, David Alton Hedges served as a SWAT Team Leader, Field Training Officer, K-9 Handler, and Burglary Detective. Now a full-time writer, he lives in the Santa Ynez Valley with his family and a pack of wonderful dogs.

You can reach him at davidaltonhedges@gmail.com.

Made in the USA
Coppell, TX
01 May 2023

16281508R00216